Rick Steves

SCANDINAVIA

200 MILES

N

ARCTIC OCEAN

NORDKAPP

KIRKENES

TROMSØ

LOFOTEN ISLANDS

NARVIK

LAPLAND

BODØ

LAPPLAND (SAMI)

RUSSIA

NORWEGIAN SEA

NORWAY

TRONDHEIM

OULU

ÅLESUND

GEIRANGER-FJORD

FINLAND

SOGNE-FJORD

SWEDEN

JYVÄS-KYLÄ

SAVON-LINNA

BERGEN

DALARNA

ÅLAND ISLANDS

TURKU

HELSINKI

OSLO

ST. PETE.

STAV.

SETES-DAL

GÖTA CANAL

STOCK-HOLM

TALLINN

KRIS.

GÖTEBORG

GOTLAND

ESTONIA

RUSSIA

NORTH

DENMARK

VÄXJO

KALMAR

ÖLAND

BALTIC SEA

LATVIA

SEA

ÅRHUS

COPENHAGEN

LITHUANIA

DCH

ÆRØ

BALTIC

RUSSIA

BELARUS

GERMANY

POLAND

John Muir Publications
Santa Fe, New Mexico

Other JMP travel guidebooks by Rick Steves
Rick Steves' Europe Through the Back Door
Europe 101: History and Art for the Traveler (with Gene Openshaw)
Rick Steves' Postcards from Europe
Rick Steves' Mona Winks: Self-Guided Tours of Europe's Top Museums
    (with Gene Openshaw)
Rick Steves' Best of Europe
Rick Steves' France, Belgium & the Netherlands (with Steve Smith)
Rick Steves' Germany, Austria & Switzerland
Rick Steves' Great Britain & Ireland
Rick Steves' Italy
Rick Steves' London (with Gene Openshaw)
Rick Steves' Paris (with Steve Smith and Gene Openshaw)
Rick Steves' Rome (with Gene Openshaw)
Rick Steves' Spain & Portugal
Rick Steves' Phrase Books: German, French, Italian,
    Spanish/Portuguese, and French/Italian/German
Asia Through the Back Door (with Bob Effertz)

Thanks to my wife, Anne, for making home my favorite travel destination.
Thanks also to Thor, Hanne, Geir, Hege, and Kari-Anne, our Norwegian
family. In loving memory of Berit Kristiansen, whose house was my house
for 20 years of Norwegian travel.

John Muir Publications, P.O. Box 613, Santa Fe, NM 87504
Copyright © 2000, 1998, 1997, 1996 by Rick Steves
Cover copyright © 2000 by John Muir Publications. All rights reserved.

Printed in the United States of America
First printing January 2000

For the latest on Rick's lectures, guidebooks, tours, and public
television series, contact Europe Through the Back Door, Box 2009,
Edmonds, WA 98020, tel. 425/771-8303, fax 425/771-0833,
www.ricksteves.com, or e-mail: rick@ricksteves.com.

ISSN 1084-7206
ISBN 1-56261-501-7

Europe Through the Back Door Editor Risa Laib
John Muir Publications Editors Laurel Gladden Gillespie,
    Krista Lyons-Gould, Chris Hayhurst
Research Assistance Dave Fox, Ian Watson
Production & Typesetting Kathleen Sparkes, White Hart Design
Design Linda Braun
Cover Design Janine Lehmann
Maps David C. Hoerlein
Printer Banta Company
Cover Photo Stave church, Oslo, Norway; Leo de Wys Inc./Fridmar
    Damm

Distributed to the book trade by
Publishers Group West
Berkeley, California

*Although the authors and publisher have made every effort to provide
accurate, up-to-date information, they accept no responsibility for loss,
injury, bad herring, or inconvenience sustained by any person using this book.*

CONTENTS

The Best Destinations in Scandinavia

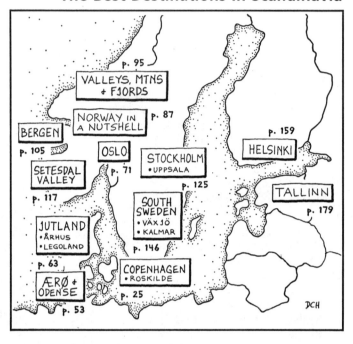

INTRODUCTION

This book breaks Scandinavia into its top big-city, small-town, and rural destinations. It gives you all the information and opinions necessary to wring the maximum value out of your limited time and money in each of these destinations. If you plan a month or less in Scandinavia and have a normal appetite for information, this lean and mean little book is all you need.

Experiencing the culture, people, and natural wonders of Scandinavia economically and hassle free has been my goal for over 25 years of traveling, tour guiding, and travel writing. With this book, I pass on to you the lessons I've learned, updated for 2000.

Rick Steves' Scandinavia is your smiling Swede, your Nordic navigator, a tour guide in your pocket. This book is balanced to include a comfortable mix of exciting capital cities and cozy small towns. It covers the predictable biggies and mixes in a healthy dose of Back Door intimacy. Along with seeing Tivoli Gardens, Hans Christian Andersen's house, and *The Little Mermaid*, you'll take a bike tour of a sleepy remote Danish isle, dock at a time-passed fjord village, and wander among eerie, prehistoric monoliths in Sweden. To save time, maximize diversity, and avoid tourist burnout, I've been very selective. We won't cruise both the Geirangerfjord and Sognefjord, just the better of the two—Sognefjord.

The best is, of course, only my opinion. But after more than two busy decades of travel writing, lecturing, and tour guiding, I've developed a sixth sense of what tickles the traveler's fancy.

This Information Is Accurate and Up-to-Date

This book is updated every year. Most publishers of guidebooks that cover a country from top to bottom can afford an update only every two or three years (and even then, it's often by letter). Since this book is selective, covering only the places I think make the top month or so, I'm able to get it updated each year. Even with an annual update, things change. But if you're traveling with the current edition of this book, I guarantee you're using the most up-to-date information available. If you're packing an old book, you'll learn the seriousness of your mistake... in Scandinavia. Your trip costs about $10 per waking hour. Your time is valuable. This guidebook saves lots of time.

Planning Your Trip

This book is organized by destinations. Each of these destinations is a mini-vacation on its own, filled with exciting sights and homey, affordable places to stay. In each chapter, you'll find:

Planning Your Time, a suggested schedule with thoughts on how best to use your limited time.

Orientation, including tourist information, city transportation, and an easy-to-read map that's designed to make the text clear and your arrival as smooth as possible.

Sights with ratings: ▲▲▲—Don't miss; ▲▲—Try hard to see; ▲—Worthwhile if you can make it; no rating—Worth knowing about.

Sleeping and Eating, with addresses and phone numbers of my favorite budget hotels and restaurants.

Transportation Connections to nearby destinations by train and route tips for drivers.

The **Appendix** is a traveler's tool kit, with telephone tips, a climate chart, and public transportation routes.

Browse through this book, choose your favorite destinations, and link them up. Then have a great trip! You'll travel like a temporary local, getting the absolute most out of every mile, minute, and kroner. You won't waste time on mediocre sights because, unlike other guidebooks, I cover only the best. Since your major financial pitfall is lousy expensive hotels, I've worked hard to assemble the best accommodations values for each stop. And as you travel the route I know and love, I'm happy you'll be meeting some of my favorite Scandinavian people.

Trip Costs

Five components make up the cost of your trip: airfare, surface transportation, room and board, sightseeing/entertainment, and shopping/miscellaneous.

Airfare: Don't try to sort through the mess. Get and use a good travel agent. A basic round-trip United States–Copenhagen flight should cost $800 to $1,000, depending on where you fly from and when. Always consider saving time and money in Europe by flying "open jaws" (for instance, flying into Copenhagen and out of Bergen).

Surface Transportation: For a three-week whirlwind trip of all my recommended destinations, allow $500 per person for public transportation (first-class 21-day Scanrail pass and extra boat rides; only $400 if you go second class), or $600 per person (based on two people sharing car and gas) for a three-week car rental, tolls, gas, and insurance. Car rental is usually cheapest if arranged from the United States.

Room and Board: You can eat and sleep well in Scandinavia for $70 a day for room and board. A $70-a-day budget allows $10 for lunch, $15 for dinner, and $45 for lodging (based on two people splitting the cost of a $90 double room that includes breakfast). That's basic and alcohol free but doable. Students and tightwads do it on $40 ($15–20 a bed, $20 for meals and snacks). But budget sleeping and eating requires the skills and information covered in this book (and in greater detail in my book *Rick Steves' Europe Through the Back Door*).

Sightseeing/Entertainment: In big cities, figure $5 to $8 per major sight, $2 for minor ones, and $25 for splurge experiences (e.g., tours or folk concerts). The major cities have cards giving you a 24-hour free run of the public transit system and entrance to all the sights for about $20. An overall average of $15 per day works for most people. Don't skimp here. After all, this category directly powers most of the experiences all the other expenses are designed to make possible.

Shopping/Miscellaneous: While Scandinavia is expensive, transportation passes, groceries, alternative accommodations, admissions, and enjoying nature are affordable (about what you'd pay in England or Italy). When things are expensive, remind yourself you're not getting less for your travel dollar. Up here, there simply aren't any lousy or cheap alternatives to classy, cozy, sleek Scandinavia. Electronic eyes flush youth-hostel toilets and breakfasts are all-you-can-eat.

Shopping can brutalize your budget in Scandinavia. Good budget travelers find that this category has little to do with assembling a trip full of lifelong and wonderful memories.

If you take full advantage of this book, you'll save a shipload of money and days of headaches. Read it carefully from start to finish. Many of the skills and tricks used in Copenhagen work in Oslo and Stockholm as well.

Exchange Rates

I've priced things in local currencies throughout the book. While each of the Scandinavian countries' kroner (crowns) have different values, they are close.

$1 equals about . . .
7 Danish kroner, 7.5 Norwegian kroner, 8 Swedish kroner, 5 Finnish markka, 14 Estonian kroons

---

In Scandinavia, kroner are decimalized: 100 øre = 1 krone. Kroner are not accepted abroad (except at foreign exchange services and banks).

Standard abbreviations are: Danish krone, DKK; Swedish krone, SEK; and Norwegian krone, NOK. I'll keep it simple. For all three countries, I'll use the krone abbreviation, "kr," and "7 kr = $1" as the exchange rate. To translate local Scandinavian prices into U.S. dollars, divide by seven (80 kr = about $11). One krone is worth approximately 15 cents.

Finland's markka (FIM or mk) is worth 20 cents. To convert to U.S. dollars, divide Finnish prices by five (40 mk = about $8).

Tallinn's kroon (kr) is worth about seven cents. To convert prices, divide by 14 (or sloppily but easily divide by 10).

Prices, Times, and Discounts

I've done all I can to insure that the hours, prices, telephone numbers, and addresses in this book are accurate and up-to-date, but I know you'll understand that this, like any other guidebook, starts to yellow even before it's printed.

In Scandinavia—and in this book—you'll be using the 24-hour clock. After 12:00 noon, keep going—13:00, 14:00, etc. For anything over 12, subtract 12 and add p.m. (14:00 is 2:00 p.m.)

This book lists peak-season hours for sightseeing attractions (July and August). Off-season, roughly October through April, expect shorter hours and fewer activities. Confirm your sightseeing plans locally, especially when traveling between October and May.

I have not listed special age discounts in this book. But in keeping with its social orientation, Scandinavia is Europe's most generous corner when it comes to youth, student, senior, and family discounts. If you are any of the above, always mention it. Students should travel with the ISIC (International Student Identity Card, normally available at university foreign study offices in North America). Spouses often pay half price when doing things as a couple. Children usually pay half price or less (for example, in hostels).

When to Go

Summer is by far the best time to go. Scandinavia bustles and glistens under the July and August sun. Scandinavian schools get out around June 20, most local industries take July off, and the British and central Europeans tend to visit Scandinavia in August. You'll notice crowds during these times, but it's never as crowded as southern Europe.

"Shoulder season" travel (in late May, early June, and September) lacks the vitality of summer but offers decent weather and minimal crowds (though big cities can be very crowded in early June). Things quiet down when the local kids go back to school (around August 20).

Winter has no tourist crowds for good reason. It's a bad time to explore Scandinavia. Many sights and accommodations are closed or open on a limited schedule. Business travelers drive hotel prices way up. Winter weather can be cold and dreary, and nighttime will draw the shades on your sightseeing well before dinner.

Sightseeing Priorities

Depending on the length of your trip, here are my recommended priorities:

3 days:	Copenhagen, Stockholm (connected by night train)
5 days, add:	Oslo
7 days, add:	"Norway in a Nutshell" fjord trip, Bergen
10 days, add:	14-hour cruise to Helsinki, and slow down

14 days, add: Ærø, Odense, Roskilde, Frederiksborg
17 days, add: Jutland, Kalmar
21 days, add: Lillehammer, Jotunheimen, Växjö, Setesdal
24 days, add: Tallinn (Estonia)

Red Tape

Traveling throughout this region requires only a passport—no shots and no visas. Border crossings between Norway, Sweden, Denmark, Finland, and Estonia are a wave-through. When you change countries, however, you do change money, postage stamps, and more. Local sales taxes on souvenirs and gifts purchased are refunded when you leave Scandinavia. When purchasing expensive items, ask the local merchant for tax-refund instructions.

Banking

Bring plastic (ATM, credit, or debit cards) along with some traveler's checks in dollars. ATMs are everywhere and offer a good exchange rate. To get a cash advance from a bank machine, you'll need a four-digit PIN (numbers only, no letters) with your bankcard. Before you go, verify with your bank that your card will work, then use it whenever possible.

Visa and MasterCard are more commonly accepted than American Express. Just like at home, credit or debit cards work easily at larger hotels, restaurants, and shops, but smaller businesses prefer payment in hard kroner.

Banking in Scandinavia is straightforward and exchange rates are nearly standard. Buy and sell rates are within about two percent of each other. The banks make their money off a stiff 20-to-40-kr-per-check fee. Bring traveler's checks in large denominations. If you have only small-denomination checks, shop around.

In Norway, some banks charge 1 or 2 percent rather than per check. In many cases, small cash exchanges are cheaper outside of banks, at places that offer worse rates but smaller (or no) fees such as exchange desks on international boats and the handy FOREX windows at the Copenhagen and Stockholm train stations. American Express offices in each capital change AmExCo checks (and sometimes other brands as well) for no extra fee. Even with their worse-than-banks' exchange rates, AmExCo can save you money if you're changing less than $1,000. Post offices (with longer hours, nearly the same rates, and smaller fees) can be a good place to change money.

You should use a money belt. Thieves target tourists. A money belt (call 425/771-8303 for our free newsletter/catalog) provides peace of mind. You can carry lots of cash safely in a money belt.

Don't be petty about changing money. The greatest avoidable money-changing expense is wasting time every few days returning to a bank. Change a week's worth of money, get big bills, stuff them in your money belt, and travel!

Whirlwind Three-Week Tour

Travel Smart

Upon arrival in a new town, lay the groundwork for a smooth departure. Reread this book as you travel and visit local tourist information offices. Buy a phone card and use it for reservations, reconfirmations, and double-checking hours. Enjoy the friendliness of the local people. Ask questions. Most locals are eager to point you in their idea of the right direction. Wear your money belt, learn the local currency, and develop a simple formula to quickly estimate rough prices in dollars. Keep a notepad in your pocket for organizing your thoughts, and practice the virtue of simplicity. Those who expect to travel smart, do.

Plan ahead for banking, laundry, post office visits, and picnics. Mix intense and relaxed periods. Every trip (and every traveler) needs at least a few slack days. Pace yourself. Assume you will return.

Scandinavia's Best Three-Week Trip

Day	Plan	Sleep in
1	Arrive in Copenhagen	Copenhagen
2	Copenhagen	Copenhagen
3	Copenhagen	Copenhagen
4	North Zealand, into Sweden	Växjö
5	Växjö, Kalmar, Glass Country	Kalmar
6	Kalmar to Stockholm	Stockholm
7	Stockholm	Stockholm
8	Stockholm	boat
9	Helsinki	boat
10	Uppsala to Oslo	Oslo
11	Oslo	Oslo
12	Oslo	Oslo
13	Lillehammer, Gudbrandsdalen	Jotunheimen: Sogndal
14	Jotunheimen Country	Sogndal: Aurland
15	Sognefjord, Norway in Nutshell	Bergen
16	Bergen	Bergen
17	Long drive south, Setesdal	boat
18	Jutland, Århus, Legoland	Århus/Billund
19	Jutland to Ærø	Ærøskøbing
20	Ærø	Ærøskøbing
21	Odense, Roskilde	Copenhagen

While this itinerary is designed to be done by car, it can be done by train and bus. Scandinavia in 21 days by train is most efficient with a little reworking: I'd go overnight whenever possible on any train ride six or more hours long. Streamline by doing North Zealand, Odense, and Ærø as a three-day side trip from Copenhagen, skipping the Växjö–Stockholm train (there is no Copenhagen–Kalmar overnight train). The Bergen/Setesdal/Århus/Copenhagen leg is possible on public transit, but Setesdal (between Bergen and Kristiansand) is not worth the trouble if you don't have the freedom a car gives you.

If you really want to see Legos and the Bogman, do Jutland from Copenhagen. A flight home from Bergen is wonderfully efficient. Otherwise, it's about 20 hours by train from Bergen to Copenhagen via Oslo. British Midland has $139 flights from Bergen to London (800/788-0555 in U.S.A.).

Tourist Information

Any town with much tourism has a well-organized, English-speaking tourist information office (which I'll abbreviate as "TI" in this book). The TI should be your first stop in a new city. Prepare. Have a list of questions and a proposed sightseeing plan to confirm. If you're arriving late, telephone ahead (and try to get a map for your next destination from a TI in the town you're leaving). Important: Each big city publishes a *"This Week In..."* guide (to Copenhagen, Stockholm, Oslo, Bergen, and Helsinki). These are free, found all over town, and packed with all the tedious details about each city (24-hour pharmacy, embassies, tram fares, restaurants, sights with hours/admissions/phone numbers), plus a great calendar of events and a map of the town center.

While the TIs offer room-finding services, this is a good deal only if you're in search of summer and weekend deals on business hotels. The TIs can help you with small pensions and private homes, but you'll save both yourself and your host money by going direct with the listings in this book.

The **Scandinavian National Tourist Office in the United States** is a wealth of information (P.O. Box 4649, Grand Central Station, New York, NY 10163, tel. 212/885-9700, fax 212/885-9710, www.goscandinavia.com). Before your trip, get their free general information booklet on all the Scandinavian countries and request any specific information you may want (city maps, calendars of events, and lists of festivals).

Roger Greenwald's Scandinavia Links has the best collection of online resources I've seen: www.chass.utoronto.ca/~roger/scand .html. You'll find lots more information on my Web site at www .ricksteves.com.

Recommended Guidebooks

Especially if you'll be traveling beyond my recommended destinations, you may want some supplemental information. When you consider the improvements they'll make in your $3,000 vacation, $30 for extra maps and books is money well spent. Especially for several people traveling by car, the weight and expense are negligible. One simple budget tip can easily save the price of an extra guidebook.

Lonely Planet's *Scandinavian & Baltic Europe* is thorough, well researched, and packed with good maps and hotel recommendations for low- to moderate-budget travelers (not updated annually). The hip *Rough Guide's Scandinavia* is thick, but also not updated annually. *Let's Go: Europe*, which is updated every year, has skimpy chapters on Scandinavia. Due to the relatively small market, there just aren't many guidebooks out on Scandinavia. Of all my European destination guidebooks, this one fills the biggest void.

For Estonia, consider Bradt's *Guide to Estonia* (published by Globe Pequot Press).

Rick Steves' Books and Videos

Rick Steves' *Europe Through the Back Door 2000* (John Muir Publications) gives you budget travel skills for minimizing jet lag, packing light, planning your itinerary, traveling by car or train, finding budget beds without reservations, changing money, avoiding rip-offs, outsmarting thieves, hurdling the language barrier, staying healthy, taking great photographs, using your bidet, and much more. The book also includes chapters on 34 of my favorite "Back Doors," three of which are in Scandinavia.

Rick Steves' Country Guides are a series of seven guidebooks covering the Best of Europe; Britain and Ireland; France, Belgium, and the Netherlands; Germany, Austria, and Switzerland; Italy; and Spain and Portugal, just as this one covers Scandinavia.

Rick Steves' City Guides feature London, Paris, and, new for 2000, Rome. These easy-to-read, annually updated guides offer thorough coverage of the best of these grand cities. Enjoy self-guided, illustrated tours of top sights, with a focus on great art.

Europe 101: History and Art for the Traveler (cowritten with Gene Openshaw, John Muir Publications, 1996) gives you the interesting story of Europe's people, history, and art. Written for smart people who were asleep during their history and art classes before they knew they were going to Europe, *101* helps resurrect the rubble. (Like most European histories, it has little to say about Scandinavia, but it will broaden your knowledge of Europe and give depth to your sightseeing.)

Rick Steves' Mona Winks: Self-Guided Tours of Europe's Top Museums (cowritten with Gene Openshaw, John Muir Publications, 1998) gives you one- to three-hour self-guided tours through Europe's 20 most exhausting and important museums (but nothing on Scandinavia).

While I've designed a series of four phrase books, there is virtually no language barrier in Scandinavia, so I wouldn't bother with a phrase book for traveling here.

My television series, *Travels in Europe with Rick Steves*, will air 13 new shows throughout the U.S.A. this year. Of the 52 earlier shows, three feature Scandinavia (Copenhagen/Ærø, Stockholm/Helsinki, and Oslo/Fjords/Bergen). All of the earlier episodes, which cover Europe from top to bottom, air on most public television stations and the Travel Channel. They are also available as home videos (two or three shows per tape). Our Scandinavia video, with all three shows, is a particularly good value. (For specifics on these tapes along with my two-hour video slide-show lecture on Scandinavia, call 425/771-8303 for our free newsletter/catalog.)

Maps

The maps in this book, drawn by Dave Hoerlein, are concise and simple. Dave, who is well-traveled in Scandinavia, has designed the maps to help you locate recommended places and the tourist offices, where you'll find more in-depth maps of the necessary cities or regions (cheap or free).

Excellent city and regional maps are available from local TIs and are usually free. Train travelers can also use a simple rail map (such as the one that comes with your train pass). But drivers shouldn't skimp on maps—get one good overall road map for Scandinavia (either the Michelin "Scandinavia" or the Kummerly and Frey "Southern Scandinavia" 1:1,000,000 edition). The only detailed map worth considering is the "Southern Norway-North" (Sør Norge-nord, 1:325,000) by Cappelens Kart ($12 in Scandinavian bookstores). Study the key carefully to get the most sightseeing value out of your map.

Transportation

Getting to Scandinavia

Copenhagen is the most direct and least expensive Scandinavian capital to fly into from the United States. It is also Europe's gateway to Scandinavia from points south. There are often cheaper flights from the United States into Frankfurt and Amsterdam than into Copenhagen, but it's a long, rather dull, one-day drive (with a two-hour, $60-per-car-and-passenger ferry crossing at Puttgarten, Germany). By train, the trip is effortless—overnight from Amsterdam, Paris, or Frankfurt. The $120 trip is free with your Eurailpass (not with the Scanrail pass or Europass).

In Scandinavia: By Car or Train?

While a car gives you the ultimate in mobility and freedom, enables you to search for hotels more easily, and carries your bags for you, the train zips you effortlessly from city to city, usually dropping you in the center and near the tourist office. Cars are great in the countryside but an expensive headache in places like Oslo, Copenhagen, and Bergen. Three or four people travel cheaper by car. With a few exceptions, trains cover my recommended destinations wonderfully. Pick up train schedules from stations as you go. To study ahead on the Web, check http://bahn .hafas.de/english.html.

Trains

The Scanrail pass is one of the great Nordic bargains. It's sold in the United States (see following chart) or, at higher prices, in Scandinavia at any major train station. The Scanrail pass gives you free or discounted use of many boats (such as Stockholm to Finland—50 percent off) and covers virtually all trains in the region (though you'll need reservations for long rides and express trains and there's a supplement for Norway's Myrdal-to-Flåm

Cost of Public Transportation

2000 SCANRAIL PASS

	1st cl adult	1st cl 60+	1st cl under 26	2nd cl adult	2nd cl 60+	2nd cl under 26
Any 5 out of 2 months	$270	$241	$203	$200	$178	$150
Any 10 days out of 2 months	420	374	315	310	276	233
21 consecutive days	486	432	365	360	321	270

Trolls 4-11 half price. Most of these passes are available in Scandinavia at higher prices.

2000 NORWAY RAILPASS

	1st cl	2nd cl	60+ 1st cl*	60+ 2nd cl*
3 days in a month	$181	$139	$144	$111
4 days in a month	224	172	179	139
5 days in a month	250	192	200	154

Few Norwegian trains offer 1st class, so save money and get a 2nd class pass. Kids 4-15 half price, under 4 free. *The Norway "Senior" pass offers 20% discount for those 60 and over.

2000 SWEDEN RAILPASS

	1st class	2nd class
3 days within a 7 day period	$211	$156
4 days within a 7 day period	$239	$177
5 days within a 14 day period	$268	$198

Two kids under age 15 can ride along for free.

2000 FINNRAIL PASS

	1st class	2nd class
3 days in a month	$186	$124
5 days in a month	$250	$166

Children 6-16 half price, under 6 free.

Note: For a railpass order form, or for Rick's complete Railpass Guide, visit www.ricksteves.com or call us at 425/771-8303. To order Scanrail & Drive passes, call DER at 800/549-3737 or Rail Europe at 800/438-7245.

Scandinavia: Point-to-point 1-way 2nd-class rail fares in $US. Add up fares for your itinerary to see whether a railpass will save you money.

ride). The pass goes easy on the upgrade to first class. Even though Scandinavian second class is like southern European first class, for $4 to $14 a day extra, you might consider first class.

A Eurailpass, which costs much more than a comparable Scanrail pass, is a good value only for those coming to Scandinavia from central Europe. A three-week first-class Eurailpass costs $718 (or $610 apiece if you travel with a companion).

Scandinavia: Main Train Lines

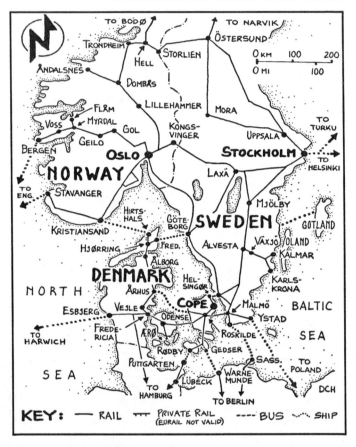

A Scanrail 'n' Drive pass offers a flexible and economical way to mix rail and car rental, and is handy if you plan to explore Sweden's Glass Country or the Norwegian mountains and fjords.

Consider the efficiency of night travel. A *couchette* (a bed in a compartment with two triple bunks) costs $25 beyond your first- or second-class ticket or pass. A "sleeper," giving you the privacy of a double or triple compartment, costs about $80 per bed.

For a free 40-page railpass guide analyzing the railpass and point-to-point ticket deals available both in the U.S.A. and in Europe, call my office at 425/771-8303 or download it at www.ricksteves.com.

Standard European Road Signs

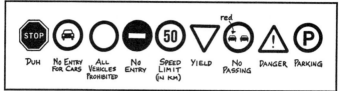

| STOP | No Entry For Cars | All Vehicles Prohibited | No Entry | Speed Limit (in km) | Yield | No Passing | Danger | Parking |

Car Rental

Car rental is usually cheapest when arranged (well in advance) in the United States through your travel agent, rather than in Scandinavia. You'll want a weekly rate with unlimited mileage. If you're traveling for more than three weeks, ask about leasing a car. Each major rental agency has an office in the Copenhagen airport. Comparison shop directly or through your travel agent. Consider Rafco, a small Danish company near the Copenhagen airport that rents nearly new Seat (Volkswagen) cars at almost troublemaking prices. The manager, Ken, promises my readers a 10 percent discount over his already affordable rates for cars, minibuses, and small motor homes (great for families). For a brochure, contact Rafco, Englandsvej 380, DK-2770 Kastrup, Denmark, tel. 45/32 51 15 00, fax 45/32 51 10 89, www.rafco.dk, e-mail: rafco@vip.cybercity.dk.

Driving

Except for the dangers posed by the scenic distractions and moose crossings, Scandinavia is a great place to drive. Your American license is accepted. Gas is expensive—over $4 per gallon (gas in Denmark is cheaper than in its northern neighbors)—but roads are good (though nerve-wrackingly skinny in western Norway); traffic is generally sparse; drivers are sober and civil; signs and road maps are excellent; local road etiquette is similar to that in the United States; and seat belts are required. Use your headlights day and night; it's required in most of Scandinavia. Bikes whiz by close and quiet, so be on guard.

There are plenty of good facilities, gas stations, and scenic rest stops. Snow is a serious problem off-season in the mountains. Parking is a headache only in major cities, where expensive garages are safe and plentiful. Denmark uses a parking windshield-clock disk (free at TIs, post offices, and newsstands; set it when you arrive and be back before your posted time limit is up). Even in the Nordic countries, thieves break into cars. Park carefully, use the trunk, and show no valuables. Never drink and drive. Even one drink can get a driver into serious trouble.

As you navigate, you'll find town signs followed by the letters N, S, Ø, V, or C. These stand for north, south, east, west, and center, respectively, and understanding them will save you lots of wrong exits. Due to recent changes, many maps have the wrong road numbers. It's safest to navigate by town names.

Telephones, Mail, and E-mail

Smart travelers use the telephone every day—for making hotel reservations, calling tourist information offices, and phoning home. Get a telephone card. Each country sells a phone card (usually in denominations of about $5 and $10) good for use only in that country. You can buy phone cards at post offices, news-stands, and tobacco shops.

Dialing Direct: Norway and Denmark do not use area codes. Just dial local numbers direct from anywhere in the country. Sweden and Finland do have area codes. When making calls within Sweden or Finland, include the entire area code (which starts with a zero).

Calling internationally, you'll need to:

1. Dial the international access code of the country you're calling from.

2. Dial the country code of the country you're calling.

3. If the country you're calling uses area codes, dial the area code, omitting the initial zero. If the country does not use area codes, skip this step.

4. Dial the local number.

To call one of my recommended B&Bs in Copenhagen from anywhere in Denmark, just dial its local number directly (32 95 96 22). To call the Copenhagen B&B from the United States, dial 011 (the United States' international access code), 45 (Denmark's country code), then 32 95 96 22.

To call Stockholm's hostel-in-a-ship from anywhere in Sweden, dial 08 (Stockholm's area code) and the local number, 679-5015. To call the Stockholm hostel from the United States, dial 011 (our international access code), 46 (Sweden's country code), 8 (Stockholm's area code without the initial zero), then 679-5015. To call my office from Sweden, dial 00 (Sweden's international access code), 1 (the United States' country code), then 425/771-8303. European time is six/nine hours ahead of the east/west coast of the United States. For a listing of international access codes and country codes, see the Appendix.

Hotel-room phones are a terrible rip-off for calls to the United States. Never call home from your hotel room unless your hotel allows toll-free access to your USA Direct Service (many don't).

USA Direct Services: Since direct-dial rates have dropped, calling cards (AT&T, MCI, and Sprint) are no longer the good value they used to be. Still, some travelers like the comfort of having an English-speaking operator do the dialing for them. Each card company has a toll-free number in each European country that puts you in touch with an English-speaking operator. The operator will take your card number and the number you want to call, put you through, and bill your home phone number for the call ($4 service charge, $2.50 for the first minute, and $1.50 per additional minute). Hanging up when you hear an answering machine is a $6.50 mistake. First use a coin or a Scandinavian phone card to call home for five seconds—long enough to say "call me," or to make sure an answering machine is off so you can call back, using your USA Direct number, to connect with a person. For a list of calling-card operators, see the Appendix. Avoid using USA Direct for calls between European countries; it's much cheaper to call direct using coins or a Scandinavian phone card.

Mail: If you must have mail stops, consider using a few reserved hotels along your route or use American Express Mail Services. Most American Express offices will hold mail for one month. (They mail out a free listing of addresses.) This service is free to anyone using an AmEx card or AmEx traveler's checks (even just one). Allow 10 days for U.S.-to-Scandinavia mail delivery. Federal Express makes two-day deliveries—for a price. Phoning is so easy that I've dispensed with mail stops altogether.

E-mail: E-mail is gradually gaining acceptance among hoteliers. I've listed e-mail addresses where possible. Cyber cafés are becoming popular in the bigger cities, giving you reasonably inexpensive and easy Internet access.

Sleeping

Accommodations expenses will make or break your budget. Vagabonds sleep happily everywhere for $15 per night. An overall average of $60 per night per double is possible using this book's listings. Unless noted, the accommodations I've listed will hold a room with a phone call until 16:00 with no deposit, and the proprietors speak English. I like small, central, clean, traditional, friendly places that aren't listed in other guidebooks. Most places listed meet five of these six virtues.

In the interest of smart use of your time, I favor hotels and restaurants handy to your sightseeing activities and public transportation. Rather than list hotels scattered throughout a city, I choose a convenient, colorful neighborhood and recommend its best accommodations values, from $15 bunk beds to $140 doubles.

Tourist information offices' room-finding services, if you have no place in mind, can be worth the 30-kr fee. Be very clear about what you want. (Say "cheap," and mention that you have sheets or a sleeping bag, and whether you will take a twin or double, if you require a shower, and so on.) They know the hotel quirks and private-room scene better than anybody. Official price listings are often misleading, since they omit cheaper oddball rooms and special clearance deals.

Sleep Code

To give maximum information in a minimum of space, I use this code to describe accommodations listed in this book. When there is a range of prices in one category, the price will fluctuate with the season, size of room, or length of stay. Prices listed are for the room, not per person.

S = Single room or price for one person using a double.
D = Double or twin room. Double beds are very often two twins pushed together.
T = Triple (often a double bed with a single bed moved in).
Q = Four-adult room (extra child's bed is usually less).
b = Private bathroom with toilet and shower or tub. (Rooms without a "b" have access to a shower and toilet down the hall.)
t = Private toilet only (the shower is down the hall).
s = Private shower only (the toilet is down the hall).
CC = Accepts credit cards (Visa, MasterCard, American Express). If CC isn't mentioned, assume you'll need to pay cash.

According to this code, a couple staying at a "Db-550 kr, CC:V" hotel would pay a total of 550 kr (about $80) for a double room with a private bathroom. The hotel will accept Visa or hard kroner in payment.

To sleep cheap, bring your own sheet or sleeping bag and offer to provide it in low-priced establishments. This can save $10 per person per night, especially in rural areas. Families can get a price break; normally a child can sleep very cheaply in mom and dad's room. To get the most sleep for your dollar, pull the dark shades (and even consider bringing your own night shades) to keep out the very early morning sun.

Hotels

Hotels are expensive ($80–150 doubles) with some exceptions. Business-class hotels dump prices to attract tourists with "summer" and "weekend" rates (Fri, Sat, and sometimes Sun). The much-advertised hotel discount cards or clubs offer nothing more than these rates, which are available to everyone anyway. To sleep in a fancy hotel, it's cheapest to arrive without a reservation and let the local tourist office book you a room. Hotels are expensive, but when a classy, modern $200 place has a $100 summer special that includes two $10 buffet breakfasts, the dumpy $60 hotel room without breakfast becomes less exciting.

There are actually several tiers of rates, including tourist office, weekend, summer, summer weekend, and walk-in. "Walk-ins" at the end of a quiet day can often get a room even below the summer rate. Many modern hotels have "combi" rooms (singles with a sofa that makes into a perfectly good double), which are cheaper than a full double. Also, many places have low-grade older rooms, considered unacceptable for the general public and often used by workers on weekdays outside of summer. If you're on a budget, ask for cheaper rooms with no windows or no water. And if a hotel is not full, any day can become a summer day.

Hostels

Scandinavian hostels, Europe's finest, are open to travelers of all ages. They offer classy facilities, members' kitchens, cheap hot meals (often breakfast buffets), plenty of doubles (for a few extra kroner), and great people experiences. Receptionists speak English and will hold a room if you promise to arrive by 18:00. Many close in the off-season. Buy a membership card before you leave home. Those without cards are admitted for a $5-per-night guest membership fee. Bring bedsheets from home or plan on renting them for about $5 per stay. You'll find lots of Volvos in hostel parking lots, as Scandinavians know hostels provide the best (and usually only) $15 beds in town. Hosteling is ideal for the two-bunk family (four-bed rooms, kitchens, washing machines, discount family memberships). Pick up each country's free hostel directory at any hostel or TI.

Making Reservations

During most of the year (except, for instance, in the capitals during conventions—early June is packed in Oslo and Stockholm), you can do this entire trip easily without reservations. Still, given the high stakes, erratic accommodations values, and the quality of the gems I've found for this book, I'd highly recommend calling ahead for rooms at least a day or two in advance as you travel. If tourist crowds are down, you might make a habit of calling between 9:00 and 10:00 on the day you plan to arrive, when the hotel knows who'll be checking out and just which rooms will be available. If you know your itinerary in advance, consider making telephone reservations before leaving home. I've taken great pains to list telephone numbers with long-distance instructions (see "Telephones," above, and the Appendix). Use the telephone and the convenient telephone cards.

Most hotels listed are accustomed to English-only speakers. A hotel receptionist will trust you and hold a room until 16:00 without a deposit, though some will ask for a credit-card number. Honor (or cancel by phone) your reservations. Long distance is cheap and easy from public phone booths. Don't let these people down—I promised you'd call and cancel if for some reason you won't show up. Don't needlessly confirm rooms through the tourist office, because they'll take a commission.

If you know which dates you need and want a particular place, reserve a room before you leave home. To reserve from home, call, e-mail, fax, or write the hotel. Phone and fax costs are reasonable, e-mail is a breeze, and simple English is fine. To fax, use the form in the Appendix (online at www.ricksteves.com/reservation). If you're writing, add the zip code and confirm the need and method for a deposit. In Europe, dates appear as day/month/year, so a two-night stay in August would be "2 nights, 16/8/00 to 18/8/00" (European hotel jargon uses your day of departure). You'll often receive a letter back from the hotel requesting one night's deposit. A credit card will usually be accepted as a deposit, though you may need to send a signed traveler's check or a bank draft in the local currency. If you provide your credit-card number as the deposit, you can pay with your card or with cash when you arrive; if you don't show up, you'll be billed for one night. Reconfirm your reservations a day in advance for safety.

Private Rooms

Throughout Scandinavia, people rent out rooms in their homes to travelers for around $40 per double. While some put out a *"Værelse," "Rom," "Rum,"* or *"Hus Rum"* sign, most operate solely through the local TI (which occasionally keeps these B&Bs a secret until all hotel rooms are taken). You'll get your own key to a lived-in, clean, and comfortable (but usually simple) private room with free access to the family shower and WC. Booking direct saves both you and your host the cut the TI takes. (The TIs are very protective of their lists. If you enjoy a big-city private home that would like to be listed in this book, I'd love to hear from you.) Many private rooms come with no sinks in the room and showers a series of steep stairs away.

Camping

Scandinavian campgrounds are practical, comfortable, and cheap (about $5–7 per person with camping card, available on the spot). The national tourist office has a fine brochure/map listing all their campgrounds. This is the middle-class Scandinavian family way to travel: safe, great social fun, and no reservation problems.

Huts

Most campgrounds provide huts (*hytter*) for wannabe campers with no gear. Huts normally sleep four to six in bunk beds, come with blankets and a kitchenette, and charge one fee (around $40, plus extra if you need sheets). Since locals typically move in for a week or two, many campground huts are booked for summer long in advance. If you're driving late with no place to stay, find a campground and try to grab a hut.

Eating

The smartest budget travelers do as most Scandinavians do—avoid restaurants. Prepared food is heavily taxed, and the local cuisine isn't worth trip bankruptcy. Especially outside Denmark, the price of alcohol is sobering. Of course, you'll want to take an occasional splurge into each culture's high cuisine, but the "high" refers mostly to the price tag. Why not think of eating on the road as eating at home without your kitchen? Get creative with cold food and picnics. I eat well on a budget in Scandinavia using the following tips.

Breakfast

Hotel breakfasts are a huge and filling buffet, about an $8 to $10 option. This includes cereal or porridge, *let* (low fat) or *sød* (whole) milk, various kinds of drinkable yogurt (pour the yogurt in the bowl and sprinkle the cereal over it), bread, crackers, cheese (the brown stuff is goat's cheese—your trip will go better when you develop a taste for it), cold cuts, jam, fruit, juice, and coffee or tea. Coffee addicts can buy a thermos and get it filled in most hotels and hostels for $3 or $4.

If you skip your hotel's breakfast, you can visit a bakery to get a sandwich and cup of coffee. Bakeries have wonderful inexpensive pastries. The only cheap breakfast is one you make yourself. Many simple accommodations provide kitchenettes or at least hot pads and coffee pots.

Lunch

Scandinavians, not big on lunch, often just grab a sandwich (*smørrebrød*) and a cup of coffee at their work desk. Follow suit with a quick picnic or a light meal at a sandwich shop.

Especially in Denmark, you'll find *smørrebrød* shops turning sandwiches into an art form. These open-faced delights taste as good as they look. My favorite is the one piled high with *rejer* (shrimp). The roast beef is good, too. The shop will wrap them up for a perfect picnic in a nearby park.

Picnics

Scandinavia has colorful markets and economical supermarkets. Picnic-friendly minimarkets at gas and train stations are open late. Samples of picnic treats: Wasa cracker bread (*Sport* is my favorite; *Ideal flatbrød* is ideal for munchies), packaged meat and cheese, goat cheese (*geitost*; *ekte* means pure and stronger), yogurt (drink it

out of the carton), freshly cooked fish in markets, fresh fruit and
vegetables, lingonberries, mustard and sandwich spreads (shrimp,
caviar) in squeeze tubes, boxes of juice, milk, *pytt i panna* (Swedish
hash), and rye bread. Grocery stores sell a cheap, light breakfast:
a handy yogurt with cereal and a spoon. If you're lazy, most
places offer cheap ready-made sandwiches. If you're bored, some
groceries and most delis have hot chicken, salads by the portion,
fresh and cheap liver pâté, and other ways to picnic without sandwiches.

Dinner

The large meal of the Nordic day is an early dinner. Alternate
between cheap, forgettable, but filling cafeteria or fast-food dinners ($12) and atmospheric, carefully chosen restaurants popular
with locals ($20). Look for the *dagens rett*, an affordable one-plate
daily special. One main course and two salads or soups fill up two
travelers without emptying their pocketbooks. The cheap eateries
close early. In Scandinavia, a normal, practical, fill-the-tank dinner
is usually eaten around 18:00. Anyone eating out later is "dining,"
will linger longer, and can expect to pay much more. A $15 Scan-
dinavian meal is not that much more than a $10 American meal,
since tax and tip are included in the menu price.

In most Scandinavian restaurants, you can ask for more potatoes or vegetables, so a restaurant entrée is basically an all-you-
can-eat deal. First servings are often small, so take advantage of
this. Fast-food joints, pizzerias, Chinese food, and salad bars are
inexpensive. Booze will break you. A small beer costs $5 in Oslo.
Drink water (served free with an understanding smile at most
restaurants). Waitresses and waiters are well paid, and tips are normally included, although it's polite to round up the bill.

Most Scandinavian nations have one inedible dish that is
cherished with a perverse but patriotic sentimentality. These
dishes, which often originated with a famine, now remind the
young of their ancestors' suffering. Norway's penitential food,
lutefisk (dried cod marinated for days in lye and water), is used for
Christmas and jokes.

Smørgåsbord

At least once in your trip, seek out a Scandinavian feast, the
smørgåsbord (known in Denmark and Norway as the *store koldt
bord*). This all-you-can-eat buffet allows you to sample the culinary
delights of the Nordic lands.

Here's how it works: Resist the urge to pile everything on
your plate at once, as many Americans do, "Royal Fork" style.
Instead, watch the locals. Take your time and dine in stages. Your
first course is fish. Start with *gravad laks* (smoked salmon) or *sild*
(pickled herring) on a slice of dense rye bread called *rugbrød*. Some

folks enjoy caviar on the side. Wash it down with an ice-cold shot of aquavit (caraway-flavored liquor) or beer. *Skol!* means Cheers!

Then get a new plate and move on to the main course of fish, chicken, or another meat, often accompanied by potatoes. *Leverpostej* (liver pâté) is a specialty and is worth a try, even if you aren't a liver lover. Seafood is usually wonderful.

Next comes the cheese and fruit course with white *franskbrød* bread. Try creamy Havarti and Blue Castello, a soft, mild blue cheese. Sometimes you'll see Norwegian *geitost*, a brown goat cheese with the texture of caramel and a slightly sweet taste. For dessert there are often cakes or cookies with coffee.

You'll find these buffets open for lunch and dinner (lunch is usually cheaper). Some good places for a Nordic buffet: the main train station in Copenhagen, on the boat between Stockholm and Helsinki, and in Bergen at the Hotel Norge. Many hotels offer a scaled-down version for breakfast, surprising Yanks with herring and *geitost* next to the Corn Flakes.

The Language Barrier

In Scandinavia, English is all you need. Especially among the young, English is the foreign language of choice.

A few words you'll see a lot: *gamla* (old), *lille* (small), *stor* (big), *takk* (thanks), *slot* (palace), *fart* (trip), *centrum* (center), *gate* (street), *øl* (beer), *forbudt* (not allowed), and *udsalg* or *salg* (sale).

Each country has its own language. Except for Finnish, they are similar to English but with a few letters we don't have (Æ, Ø, Å). These letters barely affect pronunciation, but do affect alphabetizing. If you can't find, say, Århus in a map index, look after "Z."

One Region, Different Countries

Scandinavia is western Europe's least populated, most literate, most prosperous, most demographically homogenous, least churchgoing, most highly taxed, and most socialistic corner.

While Finland and Iceland are odd ducks, Denmark, Norway, and Sweden are similar. They have closely related languages (so close that they can laugh at each other's TV comedies). While the state religion is Lutheran, only a small percentage actually attend church other than at Easter or Christmas.

Each country is a constitutional monarchy with a royal family who knows how to stay out of the tabloids and work with the parliaments. Scandinavia is the home of cradle-to-grave security and, consequently, is the most highly taxed corner of Europe. Blessed with a pristine nature, the Scandinavians are environmentalists (except for the Norwegian appetite for whaling). The region is also a leader in progressive lifestyles. More than half the couples in Denmark are "married" only because they've lived together for so long and have children.

Denmark, packing 5 million fun-loving Danes into a flat land the size of Switzerland, is the most densely populated country in Scandinavia. Sweden, the size of California, has 8.5 million people; and 4.2 million Norwegians stretch out in skinny Norway. Oslo is as far from the north tip of Norway as it is from Rome.

Stranger in a Strange Land
We travel all the way to Scandinavia to enjoy differences—to become temporary locals. One of the beauties of travel is the opportunity to see that there are logical, civil, and even better alternatives to "truths" we always considered God-given and self-evident. While the materialistic culture of the United States is sneaking into these countries, simplicity has yet to become subversive. Scandinavians are into "sustainable affluence." They have experimented aggressively in the area of social welfare—with mixed results. Travel in Scandinavia can rattle a Republican. Fit in, don't look for things American on the other side of the Atlantic, and you're sure to enjoy a full dose of Scandinavian hospitality.

Back Door Manners
While updating this book, I've heard over and over again that my readers are considerate and fun to have as guests. Thank you for traveling as temporary locals who are sensitive to the culture. It's fun to follow you in my travels.

Tours of Scandinavia
Travel agents will tell you about all the normal tours of Scandinavia, but they won't tell you about ours. At Europe Through the Back Door, we organize and lead tours covering the highlights of this book. These depart each year in summer, are limited to 26 people per group, and are led by a great guide. For details, call us at 425/771-8303.

Send Me a Postcard, Drop Me a Line
If you enjoy a successful trip with the help of this book and would like to share your discoveries, please fill out the survey at the end of this book and send it to me at Europe Through the Back Door, Box 2009, Edmonds, WA 98020. I personally read and value all feedback. Thanks in advance—it helps a lot.

For our latest travel information, tap into our Web site: www.ricksteves.com. To check on any updates for this book, visit www.ricksteves.com/update. My e-mail address is rick@ricksteves .com. Anyone can request a free issue of our newsletter.

Judging from the happy postcards I receive from travelers, it's safe to assume you'll enjoy a great, affordable vacation—with the finesse of an independent, experienced traveler. Thanks, and happy travels!

BACK DOOR TRAVEL PHILOSOPHY
As Taught in *Rick Steves' Europe Through the Back Door*

Travel is intensified living—maximum thrills per minute and one of the last great sources of legal adventure. Travel is freedom. It's recess, and we need it.

Experiencing the real Europe requires catching it by surprise, going casual… "Through the Back Door."

Affording travel is a matter of priorities. (Make do with the old car.) You can travel—simply, safely, and comfortably—anywhere in Europe for $70 a day plus transportation costs. In many ways, spending more money only builds a thicker wall between you and what you came to see. Europe is a cultural carnival and, time after time, you'll find that its best acts are free and the best seats are the cheap ones.

A tight budget forces you to travel close to the ground, meeting and communicating with the people, not relying on service with a purchased smile. Never sacrifice sleep, nutrition, safety, or cleanliness in the name of budget. Simply enjoy the local-style alternatives to expensive hotels and restaurants.

Extroverts have more fun. If your trip is low on magic moments, kick yourself and make things happen. If you don't enjoy a place, maybe you don't know enough about it. Seek the truth. Recognize tourist traps. Give a culture the benefit of your open mind. See things as different but not better or worse. Any culture has much to share.

Of course, travel, like the world, is a series of hills and valleys. Be fanatically positive and militantly optimistic. If something's not to your liking, change your liking. Travel is addicting. It can make you a happier American, as well as a citizen of the world. Our Earth is home to nearly 6 billion equally important people. It's humbling to travel and find that people don't envy Americans. They like us but, with all due respect, they wouldn't trade passports.

Globetrotting destroys ethnocentricity. It helps you understand and appreciate different cultures. Travel changes people. It broadens perspectives and teaches new ways to measure quality of life. Many travelers toss aside their hometown blinders. Their prized souvenirs are the strands of different cultures they decide to knit into their own character. The world is a cultural yarn shop. And Back Door travelers are weaving the ultimate tapestry. Come on, join in!

DENMARK

COPENHAGEN

Copenhagen (København) is Scandinavia's largest city. With over a million people, it's home to more than a quarter of all Danes. A busy day cruising the canals, wandering through the palace, taking a historic walking tour, and strolling the Strøget (Europe's greatest pedestrian shopping mall) will get you oriented, and you'll feel right at home. Copenhagen is Scandinavia's cheapest and most fun-loving capital, so live it up.

Planning Your Time

A first visit deserves two days.

Day 1: If staying in Christianshavn, start the day browsing through the neighborhood, called Copenhagen's "Little Amsterdam." Catch the 10:30 city walking tour. After a Riz-Raz lunch, visit the Use It information center and catch the relaxing canal boat tour out to *The Little Mermaid*. Spend the rest of the afternoon tracing Denmark's cultural roots in the National Museum and/or touring the Ny Carlsberg Glyptotek art gallery; spend the evening strolling or biking Strøget (follow "Heart and Soul" walk described below) or Christianshavn.

Day 2: At 10:00 explore the subterranean Christiansborg Castle ruins under today's palace. At 11:00 take the 50-minute guided tour of Denmark's royal Christiansborg Palace. The afternoon is free, with many options, including a *smørrebrød* lunch, tour of the Rosenborg Castle/crown jewels, brewery tour, or Nazi Resistance museum (free tour often at 14:00). Evening at Tivoli Gardens before catching a night train out.

With a third day, side trip out to Roskilde and Frederiksborg. Remember the efficiency of sleeping in and out by train. Most flights from the States arrive in the morning. After you arrive, head for Stockholm and Oslo (both are connected to Copenhagen by overnight trains). Kamikaze sightseers see Copenhagen as a Scandinavian bottleneck. They sleep in and out heading north and in and out heading south, with two days and no nights in Copenhagen. Considering the joy of Oslo and Stockholm, this isn't that crazy if you have limited time. You can check your bag at the station and take a 10-kr shower in the Interail Center.

You can set yourself up in my best rooms for your entire Scandinavian tour with a quick trip to a pay phone. This is probably a wise thing to do.

Orientation

Nearly all of your sightseeing is in Copenhagen's compact old town. By doing things by bike or on foot you'll stumble into some surprisingly cozy corners, charming bits of Copenhagen that many miss. Study the map. The medieval walls are now roads that define the center: Vestervoldgade (literally, "western wall street"), Nørrevoldgade, and Østervoldgade. The fourth side is the harbor and the island of Slotsholmen where København ("merchants' harbor") was born in 1167. The next of the city's islands is Amager, where you'll find the local "Little Amsterdam" district of Christianshavn. What was Copenhagen's moat is now a string of pleasant lakes and parks, including Tivoli Gardens. To the north is the old "new town," where the Amalienborg Palace is surrounded by streets on a grid plan, and *The Little Mermaid* poses relentlessly, waiting for her sailor to return and the tourists to leave.

The core of the town, as far as most visitors are concerned, is the axis formed by the train station, Tivoli Gardens, the Rådhus (city hall) square, and the Strøget pedestrian street. It's a great walking town, bubbling with street life and colorful pedestrian zones. But be sure to get off the Strøget.

The character in Copenhagen's history who matters most is Christian IV, who ruled from 1588 to 1648. He was Denmark's Renaissance king, the royal Danish party animal whose personal energy kindled a golden age when Copenhagen prospered and many of the city's grandest buildings were built. Locals love to tell great stories of everyone's favorite king.

Tourist Information

The tourist office is now run by a for-profit consortium called "Wonderful Copenhagen." This colors the advice and information it provides. Still, it's worth a quick stop for the top-notch freebies it provides, such as a city map and *Copenhagen This Week* (a free, handy, and misnamed monthly guide to the city, worth reading for its good maps, museum hours with telephone numbers, sightseeing tour ideas, shopping suggestions, and calendar of events, including free English tours and concerts). The TI is across from the train station, near the corner of Vesterbrogade and Bernstorffsgade, next to the Tivoli entrance (daily May–Aug 9:00–20:00, Sept–Apr Mon–Fri 9:00–16:30, Sat 9:00–13:30, closed Sun, tel. 33 11 13 25, www.ctw.dk, www.dt.dk). Corporate dictates prohibit the TI from freely offering other brochures (such as walking-tour schedules and brochures on any sights of special interest), but ask and you shall receive. Thinking ahead, get information and ferry schedules for your entire trip in Denmark (Frederiksborg Castle, Louisiana Museum, Kronborg Castle, Roskilde, Odense, Ærø, Århus, and Legoland). The TI's room-finding service charges you and the hotel a fee and cannot give hard opinions. Do not use it. Get on the phone and call direct—everyone speaks English.

Use It is a better information service, though it's a 10-minute walk from the train station. This "branch" of Huset, a hip, city government–sponsored, student-run cluster of cafés, theaters, and galleries, caters to Copenhagen's young but welcomes travelers of any age. It's a friendly, driven-to-help, energetic, no-nonsense source of budget travel information, offering a free budget room-finding service, free Internet access (slow with long lines), a backpacker's breakfast for 25 kr, a jazz bar, a ride-finding board, a pen-pals-wanted scrapbook, free condoms, and free luggage lockers. Their free *Playtime* publication is full of Back Door–style travel articles on Copenhagen and the Danish culture, special budget tips, and events. They have brochures on just about everything, including self-guided tours for bikers, walkers, and those riding scenic bus #6. They have a list of private rooms (225–300-kr doubles without breakfast). To get to Use It from the station, head down Strøget then turn right on Rådhustræde for three blocks to #13 (daily mid-Jun–mid-Sept 9:00–19:00; otherwise Mon–Wed 10:00–15:00, Thu 10:00–18:00, Fri 10:00–14:00, closed Sat–Sun; tel. 33 15 65 18, fax 33 15 75 18). After hours, their computer touch screen lists the cheapest rooms available in town.

The **Copenhagen Card** covers the public transportation system and admissions to nearly all the sights in greater Copenhagen, which stretches from Helsingør to Roskilde. It includes virtually all the city sights, Tivoli, and the bus from the airport. It's available at any tourist office (including the airport's) and the train stations: 24 hours, 155 kr; 48 hours, 255 kr; 72 hours, 320 kr (www.woco.dk). It's hard to break even, unless you're planning to side trip on the included (and otherwise expensive) rail service. It comes with a handy book explaining the 60 included sights, such as: Christiansborg Palace (normally 40 kr), Christiansborg Castle ruins (20 kr), National Museum (40 kr, free Wed), Ny Carlsberg Glyptotek (30 kr, free Wed and Sat), Rosenborg Castle (45 kr), Tivoli (45 kr), Frederiksborg Castle (45 kr), and Roskilde Viking Ships (50 kr). It also includes round-trip train rides to Roskilde (70 kr) and Frederiksborg Castle (70 kr).

Arrival in Copenhagen

By Train: The main train station is called Hovedbanegården (HOETH-ban-gorn; learn that word—you'll need to recognize it). It's a temple of travel and a hive of travel-related activity, offering lockers (25–35 kr/day), a garderobe (40 kr/day per rucksack), a post office, a grocery store (daily 8:00–24:00), 24-hour thievery, and bike rentals. The Interail Center, a service the station provides for mostly young travelers (but anyone with a Eurailpass, Scanrail, student BIGE or Transalpino ticket, or Interail pass is welcome), is a pleasant lounge with 10-kr showers, free (if risky) luggage storage, city maps, snacks, information, and other young travelers (Jun–mid-Sept 6:30–22:00). If you just need the map and *Playtime*, a visit here is quicker than going to the TI.

Most travelers arrive in Copenhagen after an overnight train ride. Look for a cash machine when you get off the train. If you need to change traveler's checks, the station has two long-hours exchange desks. Den Danske Bank is fair—charging the standard 40-kr minimum or 20-kr-per-check fee for traveler's checks (daily 8:00–20:00). FOREX, which has a worse rate but charges only 10 kr per traveler's check with no minimum, is better for small exchanges (daily 8:00–21:00). On a $100 exchange, I saved 23 kr at FOREX. (The American Express office—a 20-minute walk away, off Strøget—may be even better; see "Helpful Hints," below.) While you're in the station, reserve your overnight train seat or *couchette* out (at Rejse-bureau). International rides and all IC trains require reservations (usually 20 kr). Bus #8 (in front of the station on the station side of Bernstorffsgade) goes to Christianshavn B&Bs. Note the time the bus departs, then stop by the TI (across the street on the left) and pick up a free Copenhagen city map that shows bus routes.

By Plane: Copenhagen's International Airport is a traveler's dream, with a tourist office, bank (standard rates), post office, telephone center, shopping mall, grocery store, and bakery. You can use U.S. dollars at the airport and get change back in kroner. (Phone service for all airline offices is split between two switch-boards: SAS services, tel. 32 32 31 25; and Copenhagen Air Service, tel. 32 47 47 47. SAS ticket hotline, tel. 32 32 68 00.) Need to kill a night at the airport? Try the fetal rest cabins, called *hvilekabiner* (Sb-325 kr, Db-480 kr for 8 hours, prices vary for 4- to 16-hour periods, reception open 6:00–22:00, easy telephone reservations, CC:VMA, sauna and showers also available, tel. 32 31 32 31, fax 32 31 31 09).

Getting Downtown from the Airport: Taxis are fast and easy, accept credit cards, and, at about 150 kr to the town center, are a good deal for foursomes. Both the new Air Rail train (17 kr, 3/hrly, 10 min) and new metro services (17 kr, 3/hrly, 12 min) link the airport with the train station. City bus #250s gets you downtown

(City Hall Square, TI) in 30 minutes for 17 kr (12/hrly, across the street and to the right as you exit the airport). If you're going from the airport to Christianshavn, ride #9 just past Christianshavn Torv to the last stop before Knippels Bridge.

Helpful Hints

Ferries: Book any ferries you plan to use in Scandinavia now. Any travel agent can book the boat rides you plan to take later on your trip, such as the Denmark–Norway ferry (ask for special discounts on this crossing) or the Stockholm–Helsinki–Stockholm cruise; Silja Line's office is at Nyhavn 43a (Mon–Thu 9:00–16:30, Fri 9:00–16:00, tel. 33 14 40 80). Drivers heading to Sweden by ferry before July 2000 should call for a reservation (two competing lines: 33 15 15 15 and 49 26 01 55); reservations are free and easy and assure that you won't be stuck in a long line. As of July 2000, the new Øresund bridge opens, linking Denmark and Sweden (toll-210kr), making the ferry obsolete.

Jazz Festival: The Copenhagen Jazz Festival—10 days starting the first Friday in July (Jul 7–16 in 2000)—puts the town in a rollicking slide-trombone mood. The Danes are Europe's jazz enthusiasts and, more than most music festivals, this one fills the town with happiness. The TI prints up an extensive listing of each year's festival events (as well as a listing of other festivals).

Telephones: Use the telephone liberally. Everyone speaks English, and *This Week* and this book list phone numbers for everything you'll be doing. All telephone numbers in Denmark are eight digits, and there are no area codes. Calls anywhere in Denmark are cheap; calls to Norway and Sweden cost 6 kr per minute from a booth (half that from a private home). Coin-op booths are often broken. Get a phone card (from newsstands, starting at 20 kr).

American Express: Amex recently moved to Nyman & Schultz (Mon–Fri 9:00–17:00, Sat 9:00–12:00, May–Aug till 14:00 on Sat, Nørregade 7a, 3rd floor, tel. 33 12 23 01).

Pharmacy: Steno Apotek is across from the train station (open 24 hours daily, on Vesterbrogade).

Getting around Copenhagen

By Bus and Subway: Take advantage of the fine bus (tel. 36 45 45 45) and subway system called S-tog (Eurail valid on S-tog, tel. 33 14 17 01). A joint fare system covers greater Copenhagen. You pay 11 kr as you board for an hour's travel within two zones, or buy a blue two-zone *klippekort* from the driver (75 kr for 10 one-hour "rides"). A 24-hour pass costs 70 kr. Don't worry much about "zones." Assume you'll be within the middle two zones. Board at the front, tell the driver where you're going, and he'll sell you the appropriate ticket. Drivers are patient, have change, and speak English. City maps list bus and subway routes. Locals are friendly and helpful. Copenhagen is a bit torn up as it puts together a slick new subway system to celebrate the year 2000.

By Bus Tour: "The Official Copenhagen Sightseeing Tour" runs continuously in a one-hour hop-on hop-off loop each day from 9:00 to 18:00. The trip connects all the major sights: Tivoli, Royal Palace, National Museum, *The Little Mermaid*, Rosenborg Castle, Nyhavn, and more. Catch the bus on the left side of city hall behind the *Lur Blowers* statue, or at many other stops throughout the city (100 kr for 1-day pass, free for kids under 12, tel. 38 28 01 88).

Budget do-it-yourselfers simply ride city bus #6: from the Carlsberg Brewery, it stops at Tivoli, city hall, National Museum, Royal Palace, Nyhavn, Amalienborg Castle, Kastellet, and *The Little Mermaid* (11 kr for 1 stop-and-go hour). The entire tour is described in a free Use It brochure.

By Taxi: Taxis are plentiful and easy to call or flag down (22-kr drop charge, then 9 kr per km). For a short ride, four people can travel cheaper by taxi than by bus (e.g., 50 kr from train station to Christianshavn B&Bs). Taxis accept all major credit cards. Calling 35 35 35 35 will get you a taxi within minutes.

Free Bikes! Copenhagen's radical "city bike" program is great for sightseers (though bikes can be hard to find at times). Two thousand clunky but practical little bikes are scattered around the old-town center (basically the terrain covered in the Copenhagen map in this chapter). Simply locate one of the 150 racks, unlock a bike by popping a 20-kr coin into the handlebar, and pedal away. When you're done, park the bike at any other rack, pop in the lock, and you get your deposit coin back (if you can't find a rack, leave the bike on the street anywhere and a bum will take it back and pocket your coin). These simple bikes come with "theft-proof" parts (unusable on regular bikes) and—they claim—computer tracer chips embedded in them so bike patrols can retrieve strays. These are constructed with prison labor and funded by advertisements painted on the wheels and by a progressive electorate. Try this once and you'll find Copenhagen suddenly a lot smaller and easier.

For a serious bike tour, rent a more comfortable bike at Central Station's Cykelcenter (50 kr/day, Mon–Fri 8:00–18:00, Sat 9:00–13:00, summer Sun 10:00–13:00, closed Sun off-season, tel. 33 33 86 13). In the summer, City Safari offers guided bike tours (prices and routes vary, depart from train station Mon–Fri at 16:00, tel. 33 23 94 90, www.citysafari.dk, or ask at Use It).

Do-It-Yourself Orientation Walk: "Strøget and Copenhagen's Heart and Soul"

Start from **Rådhuspladsen** (City Hall Square), the bustling heart of Copenhagen, dominated by the city hall spire. This used to be the fortified west end of town. The king cleverly quelled a French

Copenhagen

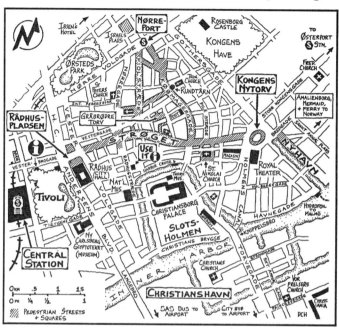

Revolution–type thirst for democracy by giving his people Europe's first great public amusement park. **Tivoli** was built just outside the city walls in 1843. When the train lines came, the station was placed just beyond Tivoli. The **golden girls** high up on the building on the square opposite the Strøget's entrance tell the weather: on a bike (fair) or with an umbrella. These two have been called the only women in Copenhagen you can trust. Here in the traffic hub of this huge city you'll notice...not many cars. Denmark's 200 percent tax on car purchases makes the bus or bike a sweeter option.

Old Hans Christian Andersen sits to the right of the city hall, almost begging to be in another photo (as he did in real life). On a pedestal left of the city hall, note the *Lur Blowers* sculpture. The *lur* is a horn that was used 3,500 years ago. The ancient originals (which still play) are displayed in the National Museum.

The American trio of Burger King, 7-Eleven, and McDonald's marks the start of the otherwise charming **Strøget**. Copenhagen's 25-year-old experimental, tremendously successful, and most-copied pedestrian shopping mall is a string of lively (and individually named) streets and lovely squares that bunny-hop through the old town from the city hall to Nyhavn, which is a 15-minute stroll (or "*strøget*") away.

As you wander down this street, remember that the commercial focus of a historic street like Strøget drives up the land value, which generally tears down the old buildings. While Strøget has become quite hamburgerized, charm lurks in adjacent areas and many historic bits and pieces of old Copenhagen are just off this commercial cancan.

After one block you can side trip two blocks left up Larsbjørnsstræde into Copenhagen's colorful **university district**. Formerly the old brothel area, today this is Soho chic.

Back on Strøget, the first segment, Frederiksberggade, ends at **Gammel Torv and Nytorv** (Old Square and New Square). This was the old town center. The Oriental-looking kiosk was one of the city's first community telephone centers before phones were privately owned. The squirting woman and boy on the very old fountain was so offensive to people from the Victorian age that the pedestal was added, raising it—they hoped—out of view. The brick church at the start of Amager Torv is the oldest building you'll see here.

Side trip two blocks north of Amager Torv to the leafy and caffeine-stained **Gråbrødretorv** (Grey Brothers' Square). At the next big intersection, Købmagergade—an equally lively but less-touristy pedestrian street—is worth exploring.

The final stretch of Strøget leads past **Pistolstræde** (a cute street of shops in restored 18th-century buildings leading off Strøget to the right from Østergade), McDonald's (good view from top floor), and major department stores (Illum and Magasin—see "Shopping," below) to a big square called Kongens Nytorv, where you'll find the Royal Theater.

Nyhavn, a recently gentrified sailors' quarter, is just opposite Kongens Nytorv. This formerly sleazy harbor is an interesting mix of tattoo parlors, taverns, and trendy (mostly expensive) cafés lining a canal filled with glamorous old sailboats of all sizes. Any historic sloop is welcome to moor here in Copenhagen's ever-changing boat museum. Hans Christian Andersen lived and wrote his first stories here.

Continuing north along the harborside (from end of Nyhavn canal, turn left), you'll pass a huge ship that sails to Oslo every evening (for information, see "Transportation Connections," near end of chapter). Follow the water to the modern fountain of Amaliehave Park.

The **Amalienborg Palace and Square** (a block inland, behind the fountain) is a good example of orderly Baroque planning. Queen Margrethe II and her family live in the palace to your immediate left as you enter the square from the harbor side. Her son and heir to the throne, Frederik, recently moved into the

palace directly opposite his mother's. While the guards change
with royal fanfare at noon only when the queen is in residence,
they shower every morning.

Leave the square on Amaliegade, heading north to Kastellet
(Citadel) Park and a small museum about Denmark's World War II
resistance efforts. A short stroll past the Gefion fountain (showing
the mythological story of the goddess who was given one night to
carve a chunk out of Sweden to make into Denmark's main island,
Zealand—which you're on) and a church built of flint brings you to
the overrated, overfondled, and overphotographed symbol of
Copenhagen, *Den Lille Havfrue—The Little Mermaid.*

You can get back downtown on foot, by taxi, or on bus #1, #6,
or #9 from Store Kongensgade on the other side of Kastellet Park
(a special bus may run from the mermaid in summer).

Tours of Copenhagen

▲**Walking Tours**—Once upon a time, American Richard Karpen
visited Copenhagen and fell in love with the city (and one of its women). He gives daily two-hour walking tours of his adopted hometown covering its people, history, and contemporary scene. He
offers four entertaining tours: three city walks—each about 1.5
miles with breaks, covering different parts of the city center—and a
Rosenborg Castle tour (city tours leave TI daily at 10:30 Mon–Sat
May–Sept, 50 kr, kids under 12 free; Rosenborg Castle tour leaves
TI at 13:30 Mon and Thu, 100 kr, 50 kr with Copenhagen Card,
prices include castle admission; pick up schedule at TI or call
Richard at tel. 32 97 14 40). All of Richard's tours, while different,
complement each other and are of equal "introduction" value.

▲▲**Harbor Cruise and Canal Tours**—Two companies offer
basically the same live, three-language, 50-minute tours through
the city canals (daily 10:00–17:00, later in Jul, 2/hrly, Apr–late
Oct; dress warmly—boats are open-top). Both boats leave from
near Christiansborg Palace, cruise around the palace and Christianshavn area, and then proceed into the wide-open harbor. It's a
pleasant way to see the mermaid and take a load off those weary
feet. The low-overhead 20-kr Netto-Bådene Tour boats (tel. 38 87
21 33) leave from Nyhavn. The competition, Canal Tours Copenhagen, does a 42-kr harbor tour with a hop-on-and-hop-off version. It leaves from Gammel Strand near Christiansborg Palace
and Nyhavn (tel. 33 13 31 05). Don't be confused. If you don't
plan to get off the boat, go with Netto. There's no reason to pay
double. Tour boats also start at Nyhavn.

Sights—Copenhagen

▲**Copenhagen's City Hall (Rådhus)**—This city landmark,
between the station/Tivoli/TI and Strøget pedestrian mall, offers
private tours and trips up its 350-foot-high tower. It's draped,

inside and out, in Danish symbolism. Bishop Absalon (the city's founder) stands over the door. The polar bears climbing on the rooftop symbolize the giant Danish protectorate of Greenland. The city hall is free and open to the public (Mon–Fri 10:00–15:00). Tours are given in English and get you into otherwise-closed rooms (30 kr, 45 min, Mon–Fri at 15:00, Sat at 10:00). Tourists romp up the tower's 300 steps for the best aerial view of Copenhagen (20 kr, Mon–Fri 10:00, 12:00, and 14:00, Sat 12:00; off-season Mon–Sat 12:00, tel. 33 66 25 82).

▲**Christiansborg Palace**—This modern *slot*, or palace, built on the ruins of the original 12th-century castle, houses the parliament, supreme court, prime minister's headquarters, and royal reception rooms. Guided 40-minute English tours of the queen's reception rooms let you slip-slide on protect-the-floor slippers through 22 rooms and gain a good feel for Danish history, royalty, and politics in this 100-year-old, still-functioning palace (40 kr, Jun–Aug daily 11:00, 13:00, and 15:00; May and Sept daily 11:00 and 15:00; off-season Tue, Thu, Sat, and Sun 11:00 and 15:00, tel. 33 92 64 92). For a rundown on contemporary government, you can also tour the parliament building. From the equestrian statue in front, go through the wooden door, past the entrance to the Christiansborg Castle ruins, into the courtyard, and up the stairs on the right.

▲**Christiansborg Castle ruins**—An exhibit in the scant remains of the first castle built by Bishop Absalon—the 12th-century founder of Copenhagen—lies under the palace (20 kr, daily 9:30–15:30, closed off-season Mon, Wed, and Sat, good 1-kr guide). Early birds note that this sight opens 30 minutes before other nearby sights.

▲▲▲**National Museum**—Focus on the excellent and curiously enjoyable Danish collection, which traces this civilization from its ancient beginnings. Exhibits are laid out chronologically and are described in English. Pick up the museum map and consider the 10-kr miniguide that highlights the top stops. Find room 1 opposite the new entrance and begin your walk by following the numbers through the "prehistory" section on the ground floor—oak coffins with still-clothed and armed skeletons from 1300 B.C., ancient and still-playable *lur* horns, the 200-year old Gunderstrup Cauldron of art-textbook fame, lots of Viking stuff, and a bitchin' collection of well-translated rune stones. Then go upstairs, find room 101, and carry on—fascinating dirt on the Reformation, everyday town life in the 16th and 17th centuries, and, in room 126, a unique "cylinder perspective" of the royal family (from 1656) and two peep shows. The next floor takes you into modern times (40 kr, Tue–Sun 10:00–17:00, free Wed, closed Mon; mandatory bag check, 10-kr locker deposit, refunded with returned key; enter at Ny Vestergade 10, tel. 33 13 44 11). Occasional free English tours are offered in the summer—call ahead.

▲**Ny Carlsberg Glyptotek**—Scandinavia's top art gallery, with especially intoxicating Egyptian, Greek, and Etruscan collections; the best of Danish Golden Age (early 19th century) painting; and a heady, if small, exhibit of 19th-century French paintings (in the new "French Wing," including Géricault, Delacroix, Manet, Impressionists, Gauguin before and after Tahiti) is an impressive example of what beer money can do. Linger with marble gods under the palm leaves and glass dome of the very soothing winter garden. Designers, figuring Danes would be more interested in a lush garden than classical art, used this wonderful space as leafy bait to cleverly introduce locals to a few Greek and Roman statues. (It works for tourists, too.) One of the original Rodin *Thinker*s (wondering how to scale the Tivoli fence?) can be seen for free in the museum's backyard. This collection is artfully displayed and thoughtfully described—good even after a visit to Rome (30 kr, Mon–Sat 10:00–16:00, free Wed and Sun; mandatory bag check, 10-kr locker deposit, refunded with returned key; 2-kr English brochure/guide, classy cafeteria under palms, behind Tivoli, Dantes Plads 7, tel. 33 41 81 41).

▲▲**Rosenborg Castle**—This finely furnished Renaissance-style castle houses the Danish crown jewels and 500 years of royal knick-knacks. It's musty with history (including some great Christian IV lore…like the shrapnel he pulled from his eye after a naval battle and made into earrings for his girlfriend) and would be fascinating if anything was explained in English. Consider purchasing the guide. The castle is surrounded by the royal gardens, a rare plant collection, and, on sunny days, a minefield of sunbathing Danish beauties and picnickers (45 kr, daily May–Sept 10:00–16:00, Oct 11:00–15:00, Nov–Apr 11:00–14:00; there's no electricity inside, so visit at a bright time; Richard Karpen—see "Walking Tours," above—does 2 Rosenborg tours a week; S-train: Nørreport, tel. 33 15 32 86). When the royal family is in residence, there is a daily changing-of-the-guard miniparade from Rosenborg Castle (at 11:30) to Amalienborg Castle (at 12:00). The King's Rosegarden (across the canal from the palace) is a royal place for a picnic (for cheap open-face sandwiches to go, walk a couple of blocks to Lorraine's at the corner of Borgergade and Dronningenstværgade). The fine statue of Hans Christian Andersen in the park, actually erected in his lifetime (and approved by H.C.A.), is meant to symbolize how his stories had a message even for adults.

▲**Denmark's Resistance Museum (Frihedsmuseet)**—The fascinating story of a heroic Nazi resistance struggle (1940–1945) is well explained in English (free, May–mid-Sept Tue–Sun 10:00–16:00, closed Mon; off-season Tue–Sun 11:00–15:00; between the Queen's Palace and *The Little Mermaid*, bus #1, #6, or #9, tel. 33 13 77 14). If prioritizing, the Resistance Museum in Oslo is more interesting.

▲**Our Savior's (Vor Frelsers) Church**—The church's bright Baroque interior is worth a look (free, daily Mar–Nov 9:00–16:30, Dec–Feb 10:00–14:00, closed during church functions, bus #8, tel. 31 57 27 98). The unique spiral spire that you'll admire from afar can be climbed for a great city view and a good aerial view of the Christiania commune below. It's 311 feet high, claims to have 400 steps, and costs 20 kr.

Lille Mølle—This tiny intimate museum shows off a 1916 house in Christianshavn (open Tue–Sun afternoons, closed Mon; mandatory guided tours at 13:00, 14:00, 15:00, 16:00; just off south end of Torvgade, tel. 33 47 38 38). A fine café serves light lunches and dinners in its terrace garden. On Saturday and Sunday, enjoy their huge brunch (95 kr, 10:00–14:00).

Carlsberg Brewery Tour—Denmark's beloved source of legal intoxicants, Carlsberg provides free one-hour brewery tours followed by 30-minute "tasting sessions" (Mon–Fri 11:00 and 14:00, bus #6 to Ny Carlsberg Vej 140, tel. 33 27 12 74).

Museum of Erotica—This museum's focus: the love life of *Homo sapiens*. Better than the Amsterdam equivalents, it offers a chance to visit a porno shop and call it a museum. It took some digging, but they've documented a history of sex from Pompeii to present day. Visitors get a peep into the world of 19th-century Copenhagen prostitutes and a chance to read up on the sex lives of Martin Luther, Queen Elizabeth, Charlie Chaplin, and Casanova. After reviewing a lifetime of *Playboy* centerfolds, visitors sit down for the arguably artistic experience of watching the "electric *tabernakel*," a dozen silently slamming screens of porn seething to the gentle accompaniment of music (worth the 59-kr entry fee only if fascinated by sex, daily May–Sept 10:00–23:00, Oct–Apr 11:00–20:00, a block north of Strøget at Købmagergade 24, tel. 33 12 03 11). For the real thing—unsanitized but free—wander Copenhagen's dreary little red-light district along Istedgade behind the train station.

Hovedbanegården—The great Copenhagen train station is a fascinating mesh of Scandinanity and transportation efficiency. Even if you're not a train traveler, check it out (fuller description under "Orientation," above).

Nightlife—For the latest on Copenhagen's hopping jazz scene, inquire at the TI or pick up the "alternative" *Playtime* magazine at Use It.

Tivoli

The world's grand old amusement park—which just turned 156 years old—is 20 acres, 110,000 lanterns, and countless ice-cream cones of fun. You pay one admission price and find yourself lost in a Hans Christian Andersen wonderland of rides, restaurants, games, marching bands, roulette wheels, and funny mirrors. Tivoli is wonderfully Danish. It doesn't try to be Disney (45 kr,

Apr–mid-Sept Sun–Thu 10:00–24:00, Fri–Sat 10:00–01:00, also open for Christmas Market mid-Nov–Dec daily 11:00–21:00, with ice skating on Tivoli Lake, tel. 33 15 10 01, www.tivoli.dk). Rides range in price from 10 to 50 kr (205 kr for all-day pass). All children's amusements are in full swing by 11:30; the rest of the amusements open by 13:30.

Entertainment in Tivoli: Upon arrival, go directly to the Tivoli Service Center (through main entry, on left) to pick up a map and events schedule. Take a moment to sit down and plan your entertainment for the evening (events on the half hour 18:30–23:00; 19:30 concert in concert hall can be free or cost up to 500 kr, depending on performer). Free concerts, mime, ballet, acrobats, puppets, and other shows pop up all over the park, and a well-organized visitor can enjoy an exciting evening of entertainment without spending a single krone (though occasionally the schedule is a bit sparse). The children's theater, Valmuen, plays excellent traditional fairy tales (daily except Mon, 12:00, 13:00, and 14:00). If the Tivoli Symphony is playing, it's worth paying for. Friday evenings feature a 22:00 rock or pop show. On Wednesday and Saturday at 23:45, fireworks light up the sky. If you're taking an overnight train out of Copenhagen, Tivoli (across from the station) is the place to spend your last Copenhagen hours.

Eating at Tivoli: Generally, you'll pay amusement-park prices for amusement park–quality food inside. **Søcafeen,** by the lake, allows picnics if you buy a drink. The *pølse* (sausage) stands are cheap. **Færgekroen** is a good lakeside place for a beer or some typical Danish food. The Croatian restaurant, **Hercegovina,** is a decent value (119-kr lunch buffet includes glass of beer or wine; 199-kr dinner buffet includes half a bottle of wine). For a cake and coffee, consider the **Viften** café. **Georg,** to the left of the Concert Hall, has tasty 40-kr sandwiches and 100-kr dinners (dinner includes glass of wine).

Christiania

In 1971 the original 700 Christianians established squatters' rights in an abandoned military barracks just a 10-minute walk from the Danish parliament building. A generation later this "free city"—an ultra-human mishmash of 1,000 idealists, anarchists, hippies, dope fiends, nonmaterialists, and people who dream only of being a Danish bicycle seat—not only survives, it thrives. This is a communal cornucopia of dogs, dirt, soft drugs, and dazed people—or haven of peace, freedom, and no taboos, depending on your perspective. Locals will remind judgmental Americans that a society must make the choice: allow for alternative lifestyles... or build more prisons.

For 25 years Christiania was a political hot potato... no one in the Danish establishment wanted it—or had the nerve to mash it. Now that Christiania is no longer a teenager, it's making an effort to connect better with the rest of society. The community is paying its utilities and even offering daily walking tours (see below).

Passing under the city gate you'll find yourself on "Pusher Street"... the main drag. This is a line of stalls selling hash, pot, pipes, and souvenirs leading to the market square and a food circus beyond. Make a point of getting past this "touristy" side of Christiania. You'll find a fascinating ramshackle world of moats and earthen ramparts, alternative housing, unappetizing falafel stands, carpenter shops, hippie villas, children's playgrounds, and peaceful lanes. Be careful to distinguish between real Christianians and Christiania's uninvited guests—motley lowlife vagabonds from other countries who hang out here in the summer, skid row–type Greenlanders, and gawking tourists.

Soft Drugs: While hard drugs are out, hash and pot are sold openly (huge joints for 20 kr, senior discounts) and smoked happily. While locals will assure you you're safe within Christiania, they'll remind you that it's risky to take pot out—Denmark is required by Uncle Sam to make a token effort to snare tourists leaving the "free city" with pot. Beefy marijuana plants stand on proud pedestals at the market square. Beyond that an open-air food circus (or the canal-view perch above it, on the earthen ramparts) creates just the right ambience to lose track of time. Graffiti on the wall declares "a mind is a wonderful thing to waste."

Nitty-Gritty: Christiania is open all the time and visitors are welcome (follow the beer bottles and guitars down Prinsessegade behind Vor Frelsers' spiral church spire in Christianshavn). Photography is absolutely forbidden on Pusher Street (if you value your camera, don't even sneak a photo). Otherwise, you are welcome to snap photos, but ask residents before you photograph them. Guided tours leave from the front entrance of Christiania at 15:00 (daily Jun–Aug, 25 kr, in English and Danish, tel. 32 95 65 07 to confirm). Morgenstedet is a cheap and good vegetarian place (left after Pusher Street). Spiseloppen is the classy good-enough-for-Republicans restaurant (see "Eating," below).

More Sights—Copenhagen

Thorvaldsen's Museum features the early 18th–century work of Denmark's greatest sculptor (20 kr, Tue–Sun 10:00–17:00, closed Mon, next to Christiansborg Palace). The noontime **changing of the guard** at the Amalienborg Palace is boring—all they change is places. **Nyhavn**, with its fine old ships, tattoo shops (pop into Tattoo Ole at #17—fun photos, very traditional), and jazz clubs, is a wonderful place to hang out. The **Round Tower**, built in 1642 by Christian IV, connects a church, library, and observatory (the oldest functioning observatory in Europe) with a ramp that spirals up to a fine view of Copenhagen (15 kr; Jun–Aug Mon–Sat 10:00–20:00, Sun 12:00–20:00; Sept–May Mon–Sat 10:00–17:00,

Sun 12:00–17:00; nothing to see but the ramp and the view, just off Strøget on Købmagergade).

Copenhagen's **Open Air Folk Museum (Frilandsmuseet)** is a park filled with traditional Danish architecture and folk culture (40 kr, Mar–Sept Tue–Sun 10:00–17:00, closed Mon, shorter hours off-season, outside of town in the suburb of Lyngby, tel. 33 13 44 11). From Copenhagen, hop on the S-train to Sorgenfri; then either take a 20-minute walk to the museum (as you exit the station, turn right and walk about a kilometer to next traffic light, turn left and go 2 blocks to museum) or catch bus #184 from the north end of Nørreport station (this bus takes a circuitous route through several towns before stopping at museum).

Danes gather at Copenhagen's other great amusement park, **Bakken** (free, daily late Mar–Aug 12:00–24:00, 30 minutes by S-train to Klampenborg, then walk through the woods, tel. 39 63 35 44).

If you don't have time to get to the idyllic island of **Ærø** (see Central Denmark chapter), consider a trip to the tiny fishing village of **Dragør** (30 minutes on bus #30 or #33 from Copenhagen's City Hall Square).

Shopping

Copenhagen's colorful flea market is small but feisty and surprisingly cheap (summer Sat 8:00–14:00 at Israels Plads). An antique market enlivens Nybrogade (near the palace) every Friday and Saturday. For other street markets, ask at the TI.

Shops are open Monday through Friday from 10:00 to 19:00 and Saturday from 9:00 to 16:00. For a street's worth of shops selling "Scantiques," wander down Ravnsborggade from Nørrebrogade. At UFF on Kultorvet you can buy nearly new clothes for peanuts and support charity at the same time.

The city's top department stores (Illum at Østergade 52, tel. 33 14 40 02, and Magasin at Kongens Nytorv 13, tel. 33 11 44 33) offer a good, if expensive, look at today's Denmark. Both are on Strøget and have fine cafeterias on their top floors. The department stores and the Politiken Bookstore on the Rådhus Square have a good selection of maps and English travel guides.

If you buy more than 300 kr ($50) worth of stuff from a shop displaying the Danish Tax-Free Shopping emblem, you can get back 80 percent of the 25 percent VAT (MOMS in Danish). If you have your purchase mailed, the tax can be deducted from your bill. Call 32 52 55 66 (Mon–Fri 7:00–22:00), see the shopping-oriented *Copenhagen This Week*, or ask a merchant for specifics.

Sleeping in Copenhagen
(7 kr = about $1)
Sleep Code: **S** = Single, **D** = Double/Twin, **T** = Triple, **Q** = Quad, **b** = bathroom, **CC** = Credit Card (Visa, MasterCard, Amex).

Copenhagen Hotels

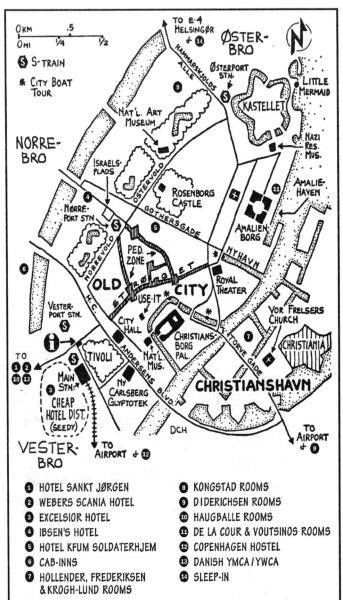

1. HOTEL SANKT JØRGEN
2. WEBERS SCANIA HOTEL
3. EXCELSIOR HOTEL
4. IBSEN'S HOTEL
5. HOTEL KFUM SOLDATERHJEM
6. CAB-INNS
7. HOLLENDER, FREDERIKSEN & KROGH-LUND ROOMS
8. KONGSTAD ROOMS
9. DIDERICHSEN ROOMS
10. HAUGBALLE ROOMS
11. DE LA COUR & VOUTSINOS ROOMS
12. COPENHAGEN HOSTEL
13. DANISH YMCA / YWCA
14. SLEEP-IN

Breakfast is often included at hotels and rarely included with private rooms and hostels.

I've listed the best budget hotels in the center, cheaper rooms in private homes an easy bus ride or 15-minute walk from the station, and even cheaper dormitory options.

Ibsen's Hotel is a cheery and central budget hotel, run by three women who treat you like you're paying top dollar (Sb-845–945 kr, Db-1,050–1,250 kr, 3rd person-200 kr, CC:VMA, Vendersgade 23, DK-1363 Copenhagen, bus #5, #7E, #16, or #40 from the station, or S-train: Nørreport, tel. 33 13 19 13, fax 33 13 19 16, e-mail: hotel@ibsenshotel.dk).

Hotel Sankt Jørgen has big, friendly-feeling rooms with plain old wooden furnishings. Brigitte and Susan offer a warm welcome and a great value, though the rooms are musty from smokers (S-450 kr, D-550 kr, 3rd person-150 kr, 5-bed family rooms, 10 percent less in winter, breakfast served in your room, elevator, a 12-minute walk from station or catch bus #13 to first stop after lake, Julius Thomsensgade 22, DK-1632 Copenhagen V, tel. 35 37 15 11, fax 35 37 11 97).

Webers Scania Hotel is my best fine hotel by the train station. Just a five-minute walk down Vesterbrogade from the station, it offers breakfast in a peaceful garden courtyard (if sunny); a classy, modern but inviting interior; and generous weekend/summer rates (late Jun–Jul and Fri–Sun all year: Sb-875 kr, Db-1,150 kr, 1,250 kr, and 1,350 kr depending on size/grade of room; high season: Sb from 1,195 kr, Db-from 1,395 kr; CC:VMA, sauna/exercise room, Vesterbrogade 11B, DK-1620 Copenhagen, tel. 31 31 14 32, fax 31 31 14 41, e-mail: webers@webers-hotel.dk).

Excelsior Hotel is a big, mod, normal, tour-group hotel a block behind the station, in a sleazy but safe area just half a block off the decent, bustling Vesterbrogade (Sb-995 kr, Db-1,195 kr, CC:VMA, Colbjørnsensgade 4, DK-1652 Copenhagen, tel. 33 24 50 85, fax 33 24 50 87).

Hotel KFUM Soldaterhjem, originally for soldiers, rents eight singles and three doubles on the 5th floor, with no elevators (S-315 kr, S plus hideabed-425 kr, D-480 kr, no breakfast, Gothersgade 115, Copenhagen K, tel. 33 15 40 44). The reception is on the first floor up (Mon–Fri 8:30–23:00, Sat–Sun 15:00–23:00) and is next to a budget cafeteria.

Cab-Inn is a radical innovation: 86 identical, mostly collapsible, tiny but comfy, cruise ship–type staterooms, all bright, molded, and shiny with TV, coffeepot, shower, and toilet. Each room has a single bed that expands into a twin with one or two fold-down bunks on the walls. The staff will hardly give you the time of day, but it's tough to argue with this efficiency (S-470 kr, D-640 kr, T-810 kr, Q-980 kr, includes breakfast, easy parking-30 kr, CC:VMA). There are two virtually identical Cab-Inns in the same neighborhood: **Cab-Inn Copenhagen** has a nicer locale (Danasvej 32-34, 1910 Frederiksberg C, 5 minutes on bus #29 to center, tel. 33 21 04 00, fax 33 21 74 09). **Cab-Inn Scandinavia** has a bigger building with a bigger cafeteria. Some rooms come with a real double bed for 100 kr extra (Vodroffsvej 55, tel. 35 36 11 11, fax 35 36 11 14). E-mail either at cabinn@inet.uni-c.dk.

Sleeping in Rooms in Private Homes
Following are a few leads for Copenhagen's best accommodations values. Most are in the lively Christianshavn neighborhood. While each TI has its own list of B&Bs, by booking direct you'll save yourself and your host the tourist-office fee. Always call ahead—they book in advance. Most are run by single professional women supplementing their income. All speak English and afford a fine peek into Danish domestic life. Rooms generally have no sink. Don't count on breakfast.

Private Homes in Christianshavn
This area—my Copenhagen home—is a never-a-dull-moment hodgepodge of the chic, artistic, hippie, and hobo, with beer-drinking Greenlanders littering streets in the shadow of fancy government ministries. Colorful with lots of shops, cafés, and canals, it's an easy 10-minute walk to the center and has good bus connections to the airport and downtown.

Annette and Rudy Hollender enjoy sharing their 300-year-old home with my readers. Even with a long and skinny staircase, sinkless rooms, and three rooms sharing one toilet/shower, it's a comfortable and cheery place to call home (S-250 kr, D-350 kr, T-400 kr, Wildersgade 19, 1408 Copenhagen K, closed Nov–Apr, tel. 32 95 96 22, fax 32 57 24 86). Take bus #9 from the airport, bus #8 from the station, or bus #2 from the city hall. From downtown, push the button immediately after crossing Knippels Bridge, and turn right off Torvegade down Wildersgade.

Morten Frederiksen, a laid-back, ponytailed sort of guy, rents five spacious rooms and two four-bed suites in a mod-funky-pleasant old house. The furniture is old-time rustic but elegant. The posters are Mapplethorpe. It's a clean, comfy, good look at today's hip Danish lifestyle in a great location right on Christians-havn's main drag (S-200 kr, D-300 kr, T-400 kr, Q-500 kr, no breakfast, 2 minutes from Annette's, Torvegade 36, tel. 32 95 32 73, cellular 20 41 92 73).

Britta Krogh-Lund rents two spacious doubles in an old Christianshavn house (S-250 kr, D-350 kr, T-400 kr, kitchen for self-serve breakfast only, Amagergade 1, C-1423 Copenhagen K, tel. 32 95 55 85).

South of Christianshavn, **Gitte Kongstad** rents two apart-ments, each taking up an entire spacious floor in her flat. You'll have a kitchenette, little garden, and your own bike (D-350 kr, family deals, no breakfast, bus #9 or #19 from airport, bus #12 or #13 from station, a 10-minute ride past Christianshavn to Badensgade 2, 2300 Copenhagen, tel. & fax 32 97 71 97, e-mail: g.kongstad@post.tele.dk). While it's not central, you'll feel at home here and the bike ride into town is a snap.

More Private Rooms

Puk (pook) **De La Cour** rents two rooms in her mod, bright, and easygoing house near Amalienborg Palace. It's in a stately embassy neighborhood—no stress but a bit bland and up lots of stairs. You can look out your window to see the queen's palace (and the guards changing). It's a 10-minute walk north of Nyhavn and Strøget (D-350 kr with no breakfast but tea, coffee, and a kitchen/family room available, Amaliegade 34, 4th floor, tel. 33 12 04 68). Puk's friend **Line** (lee-nuh) **Voutsinos** offers a similar deal May through September only (D-400 kr, extra bed-100 kr, enough room for four people, good for family with two kids; each room comes with a double bed, tea and coffee in the morning, long-term parking—5 kr/hr or 50 kr/day on street, Amaliegade 34, third floor, tel. & fax 33 14 71 42).

Annette Haugballe rents three modern, pleasant rooms in the quiet, green, residential Frederiksberg area (summer only, D-325 kr, no breakfast, easy parking, Hoffmeyersvej 33, 2000 Frederiksberg, on bus line #1 from station or City Hall Square, and near Peter Bangsvej S subway station, tel. 38 74 87 87).

Gørli and Viggo Hannibel, Annette's parents, have two rooms in the same neighborhood (D/Db-325 kr, from train station take bus #1 to P. G. Rammsalle plus 3-minute walk, or S-tog to Peder Bangsvej station plus 7-minute walk, Folketsalle 17, 2000 F Copenhagen, tel. 31 86 13 10).

Solveig Diderichsen rents three rooms in her comfortable, high-ceilinged, ground-floor apartment home. It's located in a quiet embassy neighborhood next to a colorful residential area with fun shops and eateries behind Østre Anlæg park. Unfortunately, Solveig can be rude, distracted, and unreliable. (S-300 kr, D-350 kr, extra bed-125 kr, no breakfast, direct train from the airport or 3 stops on the subway from train station to Østerport station, then a 3-minute walk to Upsalagade 26, 2100 Copenhagen Ø, tel. 35 43 39 58, fax 35 43 22 70, cellular 40 11 39 58). If her place is full she can find you a room in a B&B nearby. An avid sledder, Solveig shares her home with her sled dog, Maya.

Sleeping in Hostels

Copenhagen energetically accommodates the young vagabond on a shoestring. The Use It office is your best source of information. Each of these places charges about 100 kr per person for a bed and breakfast. Some don't allow sleeping bags, and if you don't have your own hostel bedsheet you'll normally have to rent one for around 30 kr. IYHF hostels normally sell noncardholders a "guest pass" for 25 kr.

The modern **Copenhagen Hostel** (IYHF) is huge, with 60 220-kr doubles and five-bed dorms at 85 kr per bed (sheets extra, no curfew, excellent facilities, cheap meals, self-serve laundry). Unfortunately, it's on the edge of town (bus #10 from the station to Mozartplads, then #37; or, daytime only, ride bus #46 direct from the station; no breakfast; Vejlands Alle 200, 2300 Copenhagen S, tel. 32 52 29 08, fax 32 52 27 08).

The **Danish YMCA/YWCA**, open only in July and August, is a 10-minute walk from the train station or a short ride on bus #3, #6, or #16 (dorm bed-75 kr, 4- to 10-bed rooms, breakfast-25 kr, Valdemarsgade 15, tel. 33 31 15 74).

The **Sleep-In** is popular with the desperate or adventurous (80 kr with sheets, Jul–Aug, 4-bed cubicles in a huge 452-bed coed room, no curfew or breakfast, pretty wild, lockers, always has room and free condoms, Blegdamsvej 132, bus #1 or #6 to "Triangle" stop and look for sign, tel. 35 26 50 59).

Eating in Copenhagen

Copenhagen's many good restaurants are well listed by category in *Copenhagen This Week*. Since restaurant prices include a 25 percent tax, your budget may require alternatives. These survival ideas for the hungry budget traveler in Copenhagen will save lots of money.

Picnics

Irma (in arcade on Vesterbrogade next to Tivoli) and **Brugsen** are the two largest supermarket chains. **Netto** is a cut-rate outfit with the cheapest prices. The little grocery store in the central station is expensive but handy (daily 8:00–24:00).

Viktualiehandler (small delis) and bakeries, found on nearly every corner, sell fresh bread, tasty pastries (a *wienerbrød* is what we call a "Danish"), juice, milk, cheese, and yogurt (drinkable, in tall liter boxes). Liver paste (*leverpostej*) is cheap and a little better than it sounds.

Smørrebrød

While virgins no longer roll around carts filled with delicate sandwiches, Denmark's 300-year-old tradition of open-face sandwiches survives. Open-face sandwiches cost a fortune in restaurants, but the many *smørrebrød* take-out shops sell them for 8 kr to 30 kr. Drop into one of these no-name, family-run budget savers, and get several elegant OFSs to go. The tradition calls for three sandwich courses: herring first, then meat, then cheese. It makes for a classy—and cheap—picnic. Downtown you'll find these handy local alternatives to Yankee fast-food chains: **Centrum** (open long hours, Vesterbrogade 6C, across from station), **Tria Cafe** (Mon–Fri 8:00–14:00, closed Sat–Sun, Gothersgade 12, near Kongens Nytorv), **Domhusets Smørrebrød** (Mon–Fri 7:00–14:30, Kattesundet 18), and one in Nyhavn, on the corner of Holbergsgade and Peder Skrams Gade.

The Pølse

The famous Danish hot dog, sold in *pølsevogn* (sausage wagons) throughout the city, is one of the few typically Danish institutions to resist the onslaught of our global fast-food culture. "Hot dog" is a Danish word for wienie—study the photo menu for variations. These are fast, cheap, tasty, easy to order, and almost worthless nutritionally. Even so, the local "dead man's finger" is the dog kids love to bite.

By hanging around a *pølsevogn* you can study this institution. Denmark's "cold feet café" is a form of social care: only people who have difficulty finding jobs, such as the handicapped, are licensed to run these wiener-mobiles. As they gain seniority they are promoted to work at more central locations. Danes like to gather here for munchies and *pølsesnak* ("sausage talk"), the local slang for empty chatter.

Inexpensive Restaurants

Riz-Raz, around the corner from Use It at Kompagnistræde 20, serves a healthy all-you-can-eat 49-kr Mediterranean/vegetarian buffet lunch (daily 11:30–17:00) and an even bigger 59-kr dinner buffet (until 24:00, tel. 33 15 05 75). The dinner has to be the best deal in town. And they're happy to serve free water with your meal. Department stores serving cheery, reasonable meals in their cafeterias include **Illum**, an elegant top-floor circus of reasonable food under a glass dome (Østergade 52), **Magasin** (Kongens Nytorv 13), and **Dælls Varehus** (Nørregade 12).

Det Lille Apotek, the "little pharmacy," is a reasonable, candlelit place that has been popular with locals for 200 years (sandwich lunches, bigger dinners, just off Strøget, between Frue Church and Round Tower at St. Kannikestræde 15, tel. 33 12 56 06). Their specialty is "Stone Beef," a big slab of tender, raw steak plopped down in front of you on a scalding-hot lava stone. Flip it over a few times and it's cooked within minutes.

At **El Porron**, you'll find good Spanish tapas (Vendersgade 10, 1 block from Ibsen's Hotel). **Nemsis**, across the street from Ibsen's Hotel, has cheap, tasty sandwiches and a friendly staff.

Bryggeriet is a lively brew pub that serves meals light (50–100 kr) or hearty (115–160 kr). They also have an impressive salad bar and brew a tasty beer of the month on the premises (kitchen open Mon–Sat 11:30–14:00, 17:30–22:00,

Sun 17:30–22:00, located around the corner from the train station and TI at Vesterbrogade 3, tel. 33 12 33 13).

To explore your way through a world of traditional Danish
food, try a Danish *koldt bord* (an all-you-can-eat buffet). The
central station's **Bistro Restaurant** is handy but touristy (145-kr
dinner, served daily 11:30–22:00, tel. 33 14 12 32).

Eating in Christianshavn

This neighborhood is so cool, it's worth combining an evening
wander with dinner even if you don't live here. **Café Wilder**
serves creative and hearty dinner salads by candlelight to a trendy
local clientele (corner of Wildersgade and Skt. Annæ Gade, a
block off Torvegade). To avoid having to choose just one of their
interesting salads, try their three-salad plate (61 kr with bread).
They also feature a budget dinner plate for around 85 kr and are
happy to serve free water. Across the street, **Luna Café** is also
good and serves a slower-paced meal. Choose one of three good
dinner salads and bread for 45 kr.

Ravelin Restaurant, on a tiny island on the big road just south
of Christianshavn, serves good and traditional Danish-style food at
reasonable prices to happy local crowds. Either dine indoors or on
the lovely lakeside terrace (*smørrebrød* lunches 40–100 kr, dinners
100–170 kr, Torvegade 79, tel. 32 96 20 45). A block away, at the
little windmill (Lille Mølle), **Bastionen & Løven** serves Scandinavian nouveau cuisine on a Renoir terrace or in its Rembrandt
interior (55-kr lunch specials, 130–160-kr dinners, 265 kr for 3-
course menu, menu is small but fresh, Voldgade 50, walk to the end
of Torvegade and follow the ramparts up to the restaurant, at south
end of Christianshavn, tel. 32 95 09 40).

Lagkagehuset, with a big selection of pastries and excellent
fresh-baked bread and focaccia, is a great place for breakfast
(coffee and pastries for 15 kr, Torvegade 45).

In Christiania, the wonderfully classy **Spiseloppen** (meaning
"the flea eats") serves great 100-kr vegetarian meals and 140-kr
meaty ones by candlelight. Christiania is the free city/squatter
town, located three blocks behind the spiral spire of Vor Frelser's
church (restaurant open Tue–Sun 17:00–22:00, closed Mon, on
the top floor of an old brick warehouse, turn right just inside
Christiania's gate, reservations often necessary on weekends,
tel. 31 57 95 58).

Base Camp offers an unusual eating/drinking/partying
experience in an old military barracks that has been converted
into three sprawling restaurants with enough seating for you and
800 travel companions. Dance under an enormous disco ball inside,
or head outside to where the food is served raw. Grill it at your
table and play beach volleyball in the sand. Were it not for the
off-the-beaten-path location, Base Camp would be filled with

the American-Aussie-Brit frat party crowd. But it's tucked away, 10 minutes on foot from Christiania, making it a great place to mingle with young, festive Danes. From Christianshavn, follow Prinsessegade past Christiania. You'll cross a canal at Trangravsvej. Continue till you see the big "BASE CAMP" sign in camouflage stencil on the right-hand side of the road (disco usually Fri-Sat, occasionally closes for private parties, call ahead for evening's events, tel. 70 23 23 28).

Morten, who runs a local B&B, recommends: **Long Feng** (good, cheap Chinese, south end of Torvegade) and **Skipperkroen** (cheap traditional Danish, east end of Strandgade). Right on the community square you'll find a huge grocery store, fruit stands under the Greenlanders monument, and a delightful bakery (facing the square at Torvegade 45).

Transportation Connections—Copenhagen

By train to: Hillerød/Frederiksborg (6/hrly, 30 min), **Louisiana Museum** (Helsingør train to Humlebæk, 3/hrly, 30 min), **Roskilde** (1–3/hrly, 30 min), **Odense** (2/hrly, 2 hrs), **Helsingør** (ferry to Sweden, 40/day, 50 min), **Stockholm** (5/day, 8 hrs), **Oslo** (4/day, 9 hrs), **Växjö** (via Alvesta, 10/day, 5 hrs), **Kalmar** (10/day, via Alvesta and Växjö, 7 hrs), **Berlin** (via Hamburg, 4/day, 9 hrs), **Amsterdam** (2/day, 11 hrs), **Frankfurt/Rhine** (4/day, 8 hrs). Through June 2000 all Norway- and Sweden-bound trains go right onto the Helsingør–Helsingborg ferry. (You get 20 minutes to romp on the deck, eat the wind, grab a bite, and change money.) The crossing is included in any train ticket. As of July 2000, trains will take the slick new Øresund bridge linking Denmark with Sweden. Convenient overnight trains from Copenhagen run directly to Stockholm, Oslo, Amsterdam, and Frankfurt. National train info tel. 70 13 14 15. International train info tel. 70 13 14 16. Cheaper bus trips are listed at Use It.

A quickie cruise from Copenhagen to Oslo: A luxurious cruise ship leaves daily from Copenhagen (departs 17:00, returns 2 days later by 9:15; 16 hours sailing each way and 7 hours in Norway's capital). Special packages give you a bed in a double cabin, a fine dinner, and two *smørgåsbord* breakfasts for around $175 in summer ($210 for single, Fri–Sat cost more). Call DFDS Scandinavian Seaways (tel. 33 42 30 00). It's easy to make a reservation in the United States (tel. 800/5DF-DS55).

NEAR COPENHAGEN: ROSKILDE, FREDERIKSBORG CASTLE, LOUISIANA, KRONBORG CASTLE

Copenhagen's the star, but there are several worthwhile sights nearby, and the public transportation system makes side tripping a joy. Visit Roskilde's great Viking ships and royal cathedral. Tour

Frederiksborg, Denmark's most spectacular castle, and slide along the cutting edge at Louisiana—a superb art museum with a coastal setting as striking as its art. At Helsingør, do the dungeons of Kronborg Castle before heading on to Sweden.

Planning Your Time
Roskilde's Viking ships and the Frederiksborg Castle are the area's essential sights. Each (an easy 30-minute commute from Copenhagen followed by a 15-minute walk) can be done in half a day. You'll find fewer tour-bus crowds in the afternoon. While you're in Roskilde, pay your respects to the tombs of the Danish royalty. By car, you can see these sights on your way in or out of Copenhagen. By train, do day trips from Copenhagen—then sleep to and from Copenhagen to heavyweight sights 8 or 10 hours away. Consider getting a Copenhagen Card (see "Orientation," above), which covers your transportation and admission to all major sights.

Roskilde
Denmark's roots, both Viking and royal, are on display in Roskilde, a pleasant town 20 miles west of Copenhagen. Five hundred years ago, Roskilde was Denmark's leading city. Today, the town that introduced Christianity to Denmark in A.D. 980 is most famous for hosting northern Europe's biggest annual rock/jazz/folk festival (four days in early July). Wednesday and Saturday are flower/produce market days. Its TI is helpful (three blocks from cathedral, follow signs to "*turistbureau*," tel. 46 35 27 00). Roskilde is an easy side trip from Copenhagen by train (1–3/hrly, 30 min).

Sights—Roskilde
▲▲**Roskilde Cathedral**—Roskilde's imposing 12th-century, twin-spired cathedral houses the tombs of 38 Danish kings and queens. It's a stately, modern-looking old church with great marble work, paintings (notice the impressive 3-D painting with Christian IV looking like a pirate, in the room behind the small pipe organ), wood carvings in and around the altar, and a silly little glockenspiel that plays high above the entrance at the top of every hour (10 kr, good 20-kr guidebook, Apr–Sept Mon–Sat 9:00–16:45, Sun 12:30–16:45; off-season Tue–Fri 10:00–15:45, Sat 11:30–15:45, Sun 12:30–15:45, closed Mon, tel. 46 35 16 24). It's a pleasant walk through a park down to the harbor and Viking ships. Just around the corner from the cathedral, the Raadhuskælderen restaurant offers excellent 70-kr lunch entrées in a 14th-century wine cellar.
▲▲▲**Viking Ship Museum (Vikingeskibshallen)**—Roskilde's award-winning museum displays five different Viking ships—one is like the boat Leif Erikson sailed to America 1,000 years ago; another is like those depicted in the Bayeux Tapestry. The

Sights near Copenhagen

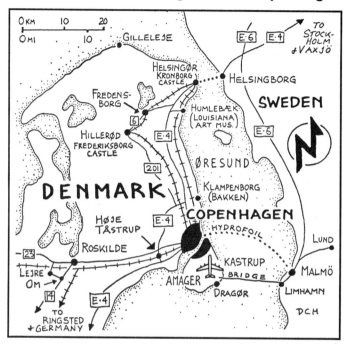

descriptions are excellent—and in English. It's the kind of museum where you want to read everything. As you enter, buy the 15-kr guide booklet and request the 15-minute English movie introduction. These ships were deliberately sunk 1,000 years ago to block a nearby harbor and were only recently excavated, preserved, and pieced together. The ships aren't as intact as those in Oslo, but the museum does a better job of explaining shipbuilding. The museum cafeteria serves a traditional *smørrebrød*—great after a hard day of pillage, plunder, or sightseeing (40 kr entry, daily May–Sept 9:00–17:00, Oct–Apr 10:00–16:00, from station catch bus #216, #258, or #605, tel. 46 30 02 00).

Frederiksborg Castle and Hillerød

The traffic-free center of the Danishly cute town of Hillerød is worth a wander (just outside the gates of the mighty Frederiksborg Castle, past the TI). The Hillerød TI can book rooms in private homes for 125 kr per person plus a 30-kr booking fee (tel. 48 24 26 26).

▲▲**Frederiksborg Castle**—This grandest castle in Scandinavia is often called the Danish Versailles. Frederiksborg (built 1602–1620) is the castle of Christian IV, Denmark's great builder king. You can almost hear the crackle of royal hoofs as you walk over the moat through the stately cobbled courtyard, past the Dutch Renaissance brick facade and into the lavish interior. Much of the castle was reconstructed in 1860, with the normal Victorian flair. The English guidebook is unnecessary, since many rooms have a handy English information sheet and there are often tours on which to freeload. Listen for hymns on the old carillon at the top of each hour. The many historic paintings are a fascinating scrapbook of Danish history. Savor the courtyard. Picnic in the moat park or enjoy the elegant Slotsherrens Kro cafeteria at the moat's edge (45 kr, daily Apr–Oct 10:00–17:00, Nov–Mar 10:00–16:00; easy parking). From Copenhagen, take the S-train to Hillerød (6/hrly, 30 min) and enjoy a pleasant 15-minute walk, or catch bus #701 or #702 (free with S-tog ticket) from the train station (tel. 48 26 04 39).

Louisiana

This is Scandinavia's most raved-about modern art museum. Located in the town of Humlebæk, beautifully situated on the coast 20 miles north of Copenhagen, Louisiana is a holistic place that masterfully mixes its art, architecture, and landscape. Wander from famous Chagalls and Picassos to more obscure art. Poets spend days here nourishing their creative souls with new angles, ideas, and perspectives. The views over one of the busiest passages in the nautical world are nearly as inspiring as the art. The cafeteria (indoor/outdoor) is reasonable and welcomes picnickers who buy a drink (55-kr admission or included in a special round-trip tour's ticket—ask at Copenhagen's TI, daily 10:00–17:00, Wed until 22:00, tel. 49 19 07 19).

Take the train from Copenhagen toward Helsingør and get off at Humlebæk (3/hrly, 30 min). Then it's a free bus (#388) connection or a 10-minute walk through the woods. If you're coming from Frederiksborg Castle, catch a train at Hillerød station toward Helsingør. Change trains at Snekkersten or Helsingør and go south to reach Humlebæk.

Kronborg Castle and Helsingør

Often confused with its Swedish sister, Helsingborg, just two miles across the channel, Helsingør is a small, pleasant Danish town with a medieval center, Kronborg Castle, and lots of Swedes who come over for lower-priced alcohol. There's a fine beachfront hostel, **Vandrerhjem Villa Moltke** (dorm bed-85 kr, S-180 kr, Sb-300 kr, D-200 kr, Db-325 kr, T-275 kr, Tb-350 kr, larger rooms available, a mile north of the castle, tel. 49 21 16 40, www.danhostels.dk). I've met people who prefer small towns and small prices touring

Copenhagen with this hostel as their base (2 50-min trains/hrly to Copenhagen). Helsingør TI: tel. 49 21 13 33.

▲▲**Kronborg Castle**—Helsingør's Kronborg Castle (also called Elsinore) is famous for its questionable (but profitable) ties to Shakespeare. Most of the "Hamlet" castle you'll see today, darling of every big bus tour and travelogue, was built long after Hamlet died, and Shakespeare never saw the place. But there was a castle here in Hamlet's day, and a troupe of English actors worked here in Shakespeare's time (Shakespeare may have known them or even been one of them). "To see or not to see?" It's most impressive from the outside.

If you're heading to Sweden, Kalmar Castle (see the South Sweden chapter) is a better medieval castle. But you're here, and if you like castles, see Kronborg.

The royal apartments include English explanations (30 kr, daily May–Sept 10:30–17:00, Apr and Oct 11:00–16:00, Nov and Mar 11:00–15:00; closed Mon off-season, tel. 49 21 30 78 or 49 21 80 88). Don't miss the 20-minute dungeon tours that leave on the half hour. In the basement, notice the statue of Holger Danske, a mythical Viking hero revered by Danish children. The story goes that this Danish superman will awaken if the nation is ever in danger and will restore peace and security to the land.

The free grounds between the walls and sea are great for picnics, with a pleasant view of the strait between Denmark and Sweden. If you're rushed, the view from the ferry (or bridge, as of July 2000) will suffice.

Route Tips for Drivers

Copenhagen to Hillerød (45 min) **to Helsingør** (30 minutes) **to Växjö, Sweden** (3.5 hours including ferry): Just follow the town-name signs. Leave Copenhagen, following signs for E-4 and Helsingør. The freeway is great. "Hillerød" signs lead to the Frederiksborg Castle (not to be confused with the nearby Fredensborg *slot* (palace) in the pleasant town of Hillerød. Follow signs to Hillerød C (for "center") then "*slot*" (for "castle"). While the E-4 freeway is the fastest, the "Strandvejen" coastal road (152) is pleasant, passing some of Denmark's finest mansions (including that of Danish writer Karen Blixen—a.k.a. Isak Dinesen of *Out of Africa* fame—in Rungstedlund, which is now a museum: 30 kr, daily May–Sept 10:00–17:00, off-season shorter hours and closed Mon–Tue, tel. 45 57 10 57).

If you're traveling during the second half of 2000, drive directly onto the new 16-kilometer Øresund bridge linking Denmark with Sweden (opens in July, toll-210 kr).

If you're traveling before July 2000, take the ferry to Sweden (follow the signs to Helsingborg, Sweden; freeway leads to dock). Boats leave every 20 minutes. Buy your ticket as you roll on board

(230 kr one-way for car, driver, and up to 5 passengers; round-trip gives you the return at less than half price). Reservations are free and smart (tel. 33 15 15 15 and press 1 when you hear the Danish voicemail message, or call 49 26 01 55 and wait out the obnoxious tune, or book online at www.scandlines.dk). If you arrive before your time, you can probably drive onto any ferry. The 30-minute Helsingør–Helsingborg ferry ride gives you just enough time to enjoy the view of the Kronborg "Hamlet" castle, be impressed by the narrowness of this very strategic channel, and change money. The ferry exchange desk's rate is decent, and its 5-kr-per-check fee beats Sweden's standard 40-kr minimum fee for traveler's checks.

In Helsingborg, follow signs for E-4 and Stockholm. The road's good, traffic's light, and towns are all clearly signposted. You can change money at the post office in the pleasant town of Markaryd's (just off the road, open late). At Ljungby, road 25 takes you to Växjö and Kalmar. Entering Växjö, skip the first Växjö exit and follow the freeway into "Centrum," where it ends. It takes about six hours to drive from Copenhagen to Kalmar.

CENTRAL DENMARK: ÆRØ AND ODENSE

The sleepy isle of Ærø is the cuddle after the climax. It's the perfect time-passed world in which to wind down, enjoy the seagulls, and take a day off. Get Ærø-dynamic and pedal a rented bike into the essence of Denmark. Stop for lunch in a traditional *kro* (country inn). Settle into a cobbled world of sailors, who, after someone connected a steam engine to a propeller, decided that maybe building ships in bottles was more their style.

On your way to (or from) Ærø, drop by the bustling city of Odense, home of Hans Christian Andersen and a fine open-air folk museum.

Planning Your Time
Odense is a transportation hub, the center of the island of Funen. It is an easy stop, worth half a day on the way to or from Ærø. More out of the way, Ærø is a well-worthwhile headache to get to. Once there, you'll want two nights and a day to properly enjoy it.

ISLAND OF ÆRØ
This small (22-by-6-mile) island on the south edge of Denmark is salty and sleepy as can be. A typical tombstone reads: "Here lies Christian Hansen at anchor with his wife. He'll not weigh until he stands before God." It's the kind of island where baskets of strawberries sit in front of houses—for sale on the honor system. Since it's about 10 miles across the water from Germany, you'll see plenty of smug Germans who return regularly to this peaceful retreat.

Ærøskøbing
Ærøskøbing is Ærø's town in a bottle. The government, recognizing the value of this amazingly preserved little town, prohibits

Central Denmark

modern building anywhere in the center. It's the only town in Denmark protected in this way. Drop into the 1680s, when Ærøskøbing was the wealthy home port of more than 100 windjammers. The many Danes who come here for the tranquillity—washing up the cobbled main drag in waves with the landing of each boat—call it the fairy-tale town. The Danish word for "cozy" is *hyggelig* (hew-glee), and that describes Ærøskøbing well.

Ærøskøbing is just a pleasant place to wander. Stubby little porthole-type houses lean on each other like drunk, sleeping sailors, with their birth dates displayed in proud decorative rebar. Wander under flickering old-time lampposts. The harbor now caters to holiday yachts, and on midnight low tides you can almost hear the crabs playing cards. Snoop around town. It's OK. Notice the many "snooping mirrors" on the houses. Antique locals are following your every move.

The town economy, once rich with the windjammer trade, hit the rocks in the 20th century. Outside of tourism, there are few jobs. Kids 15 to 18 years old go to a boarding school in Svend-

Ærøskøbing

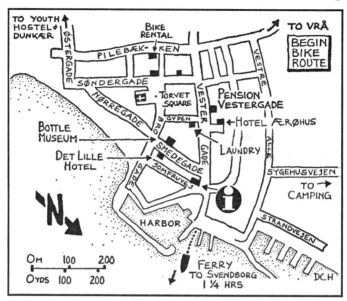

borg; many don't return. It's an interesting discussion: Do the island folk pickle their culture in tourism or forget about the cuteness and get modern?

Orientation

The town of Ærøskøbing is tiny. Everything is just a few cobbles from the ferry landing.

Tourist Information: The TI is straight ahead as you get off the ferry (Mon–Fri 9:00–17:00, shorter hours Sat, Sun, and off-season, tel. 62 52 13 00, fax 62 52 14 36, www.aeroe.dk). They can find you a 300-kr double, including breakfast, in a private home (no booking fee). They also have information on boat rentals.

Ferries: If you're driving, plan ahead. When you arrive in Ærø, reserve a spot on the ferry for your departure (call during office hours, Mon–Fri 8:00–16:00, less on weekends, tel. 62 52 40 00, fax 62 52 20 88, e-mail: info@aeroe/ferry.dk).

Sights—Ærøskøbing

▲"Bottle Peter" Museum—This fascinating house has 750 different bottled ships. Old Peter Jacobsen, who made his first bottle at 16 and his last at 85, bragged that he drank the contents of each bottle, except those containing milk. He died in 1960 (most likely buried in a glass bottle), leaving a lifetime of tedious little creations for visitors to squint and marvel at (25 kr, daily May–Sept 10:00–15:00, off-season Tue–Thu 13:00–15:00, on Smedegade).

▲**Hammerich House**—These 12 funky rooms in three houses are filled with 200- to 300-year-old junk (15 kr, daily Jun–Aug 11:00–15:00, closed off-season). The third sight in town, the Ærø Museum, is nowhere near as interesting as the Hammerich House.

▲▲**Ærøskøbing Evening Walk**—With the sun low, the shadows long, and the colors rich, join the locals in an evening stroll. Start at the harbor. Facing the ferry landing, head right past the smoked-fish joint. Wander out the breakwater to see what the yachters are barbecuing and to see the historic wooden boats coming in. The dreamy-looking island immediately across the way is a natural preserve and a resting spot for birds making their huge journey from north to south. In the winter, when the water freezes, locals love to slip and slide over for a visit. Continue down the peaceful Molestyen Lane—peaceful beach on the left, a row of much-loved houses and gardens on your right. (If you continue on the trail along the water you'll come to a place where fishermen pull out their boats and tidy up their nets.) From the end of Molestyen, cut back into town along Nørregade. Peek into living rooms. Catch snatches of Danish life. Ponder the beauty of a society with such a keenly developed sense of civic responsibility that fishing permits commit you "to catch only what you need." At Brogade you can detour left to the town square (Torvet) or continue straight back to Vestergade.

▲▲**Beach Bungalow Sunset Stroll**—For the actual sunset, stroll in the other direction. Facing the ferry dock, go left, following the harbor. Upon leaving the town you'll pass a children's playground and see a row of tiny, Monopoly-like huts past the wavy wheat field. This is the Vestre Strandvej, facing the sunset. And these tiny huts are little beach escapes. Each is different and many are filled with locals enjoying themselves Danish style. It's a fine walk out to the end of Urehoved, as this spit of land is called.

The Ærø Island Bike Ride (or Car Tour)

While serious biking maps take you on more involved routes, this 18-mile trip shows you the best of this windmill-covered island's charms. While the highest point on the island is only 180 feet, the wind can be strong, and the hills seem long. This ride is good exercise. If your hotel can't loan you a bike (ask), rent one from the Energi Station (40 kr for three-speeds, 20 kr for worthwhile "*cykel* map"; Mon–Fri 8:00–17:00, Sat 9:00–13:00, Sun 10:00–13:00; go through the door at Søndergade end of Torvet, past garden to next road, Pilebækken 7, tel. 62 52 11 10). The hostel and the campground also rent bikes (longer hours). On Ærø there are no deposits and few locks.

Ærøskøbing

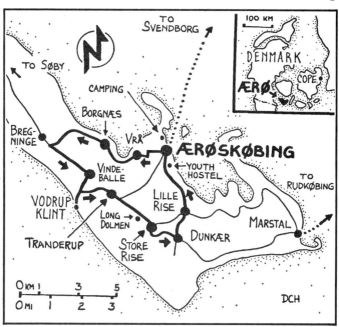

Ready to go? May the wind be always at your back. Leave
Ærøskøbing to the west on the road to Vrå (Vråvejen). You'll see
the first of many U-shaped farms, typical of Denmark. The three
sides block the wind and are used for storing cows, hay, and people. *Gaard* (farm) shows up on many local names. Until the old
generation's gone, you'll see only sturdy old women behind the
wheelbarrows. Bike along the coast in the protection of the dike
that made the once-salty swampland to your left farmable. At the
T-junction take a right turn to Borgnæs. You'll see a sleek modern
windmill, and soon, a pleasant cluster of mostly modern summer
cottages called Borgnæs. (At this point, you can take a shortcut by
turning left directly to Vindeballe.)

Keep to the right, following the sign (behind bushes) toward
"Ø. Bregninge," pass another Vindeballe turnoff, go along a
secluded beach, and then climb uphill over the island's 180-foot
summit to Bregninge. Unless you're tired of thatched and half-
timbered cottages, turn right and roll through Denmark's "second
longest village" to the church. Peek inside. (Public WC in churchyard.) Then roll back through Bregninge past many more U-

shaped *gaards*, heading about a mile down the main road towards Vindeballe, taking the Vodrup turnoff to the right. (The Vindeballe Kro is a traditional inn serving fine food.)

A straight road leads you downhill (with a jog to the right) to a rugged bluff called Vodrup Klint. If I were a pagan, I'd worship here—the sea, the wind, the chilling view. Notice how the land slipped in long chunks to make terraces stepping down to the sea. Hike down to the foamy beach. While the wind can drag a kite-flier at the top, the beach can be ideal for sunbathing.

Then it's on to Tranderup. You'll roll past the old farm full of cows, a lovely pond, and left past a row of wind-bent stumps. (Care to guess the direction of the prevailing wind?) Follow the sign to Tranderup, stay parallel to the big road through town, pass a lovely farm (that does bed and breakfast) and a potato stand, and, finally, arrive at the main road. Turn right. At the Ærøskøbing turnoff, just before the tiny little white house, turn left to the big stone (commemorating the return of the island to Denmark from Germany in 1750). Seattle-ites should be sure to visit Claus Clausen's rock (in the picnic area), a memorial to an extremely obscure Washington state pioneer.

Return to the big road, pass the little white house, and head toward Store Rise, the next church spire in the distance. Just after the Stokkeby turnoff, follow the rough tree-lined path on your right to the Langdysse (Long Dolmen) Tingstedet, just behind the church spire. Here you'll see a 5,000-year-old early Neolithic burial place. Ærø had more than 100 of these prehistoric tombs, but few survive.

Carry on down the lane to the Store Rise church. Inside, notice the little ships hanging in the nave, the fine altarpiece, and Martin Luther keeping his Protestant hand on the rudder in the stern. Can you find anyone buried in the graveyard whose name doesn't end in "sen"? Continue down the main road with the impressive—and hopeful—forest of modern windmills on your right, until you get to Dunkær.

For the home stretch, take the small road, signed "Lille Rise," past the topless windmill. Except for the Lille Rise, it's all down-hill from here, as you coast past great sea views and the hostel back home to Ærøskøbing.

Still rolling? Bike past the campground along the Urehoved *strand* (beach) to poke into the coziest little beach houses you'll never see back in the "big is beautiful" U.S.A. This is Europe, where the concept of sustainability is neither new nor subversive.

Sleeping in Ærøskøbing
(7 kr = about $1)
Sleep Code: **S** = Single, **D** = Double/Twin, **T** = Triple, **Q** = Quad, **b** = bathroom, **CC** = Credit Card (Visa, MasterCard, Amex). The TI books B&Bs for no charge.

Pension Vestergade is a pleasantly quirky old place (built for a sea captain's daughter in 1784) located right on the main street in the town center. Susanna Greve and her daughters Henrietta and Celia speak the queen's English and take good care of their guests, with six big homey rooms (S-300 kr, D-440 kr, includes breakfast, Vestergade 44, 5970 Ærøskøbing, tel. & fax 62 52 22 98). This is your ideal home on Ærø. Picnic in the backyard. Call well in advance for a place here.

Det Lille Hotel, a former 19th-century captain's home, is as warm, tidy, and modern as a sailboat. It's one street off the harbor next to the cutest house in town (S-340 kr, D-480 kr, extra bed-145 kr, includes huge breakfast, CC:VM, Smedegade 33, 5970 Ærøskøbing, tel. & fax 62 52 23 00, www.det-lille-hotel.dk, run by Heidi).

Hotel Ærøhus is big and sprawling, the closest thing to a grand hotel in this capital of quaint (33 rooms, D-460 kr, Db-680 kr, fancy Db with terrace-760 kr, 15 percent less Sept–May, CC:VMA, on Vestergade, two blocks up from ferry, tel. 62 52 10 03, fax 62 52 21 23, e-mail: mail@aeroehus.dk).

Mrs. Petersen rents a couple rooms in her clean, comfortable, and modern home in a quiet residential area along the edge of town (D-340 kr, includes breakfast, Sygehusvejen 4, just 3 blocks from the ferry landing, tel. 62 52 23 09).

If you have a car, you may want to try one of the many B&Bs in the countryside. Julie and Aksel Hansen's **Graasten B&B** is a kid-friendly dairy farm 300 meters from the sea (D-280 kr, breakfast-40 kr, fridge and coffee maker for guests, camping available Jul–Aug at 20 kr per person per night, showers for campers-10 kr, Østermarksvej 20, 7 km from Ærøskøbing toward Marstal, tel. 62 52 24 25, fax 62 52 13 49, e-mail: aeroe-graasten@forum.dk, English spoken).

Ærøskøbing Youth Hostel is a glorious place, equipped with a fine living room, members' kitchen, and family rooms with two or four beds (90 kr each, D-220 kr, T-290 kr, breakfast-40 kr, sheets-35 kr, Smedevejen 15, 500 yards out of town, tel. 62 52 10 44, fax 62 52 16 44). The place is packed in July and closed November through March.

The three-star **campground**, on a fine beach, offers a lodge with fireplace, campsites (46 kr per person), and cottages (4 people-770–1,155 kr, 6 people-1,750 kr, May–Sept; facing the water, follow waterfront to the left, a short walk from center, tel. 62 52 18 54).

Eating in Ærøskøbing

Ærøskøbing has only a handful of eateries and each has a different character: starting at the ferry dock you'll find a grocery store and **Lille Claus Café** (a Danish Denny's without the class, young crowd, cheap). Facing the harbor a wonderful little snack joint

serves traditional Danish herring along with burgers and salads.
Heading up Vestergade, past the pink and popular **Vaffel-
bageriet** (homemade waffles and ice cream), you'll find another
burger joint and the classy **Greta's Restaurant** (fine cooking, a
bit pricey). At the top of Vestergade, **Restaurant Pilebækken**
serves what is probably the best reasonable daily special (120 kr,
55 Vestergade, tel. 62 52 19 91). **Det Lille Hotel** serves a good
118-kr *dagens rett* in a pleasant dining room or garden (next to
photogenic "littlest house" and across from the ship-in-a-bottle
museum). **MUMM**'s candlelit ambience is occasionally blown out
by the German yachting crowd, but the food is fine—if expensive
(Søndergade 12). There's a **pizzeria** on the main square (Torvet).
The **bakery** (top of Vestergade) serves homemade bread, cheese,
tins of liver paste, and liter boxes of drinkable yogurt. The liveli-
est bar in town is the **Arrebo Pub** near the ferry landing at the
bottom of Vestergade.

Transportation Connections—Ærøskøbing

Ærøskøbing is accessible by ferry from **Svendborg**. It's a pleasant
70-minute crossing (255-kr round-trip per car and driver, 113-kr
round-trip per person; you can leave the island via any of the three
different Ærø ferry crossings; you'll save a little money with
round-trip tickets).

   Svendborg–Ærø ferry: Departures are from Svendborg
Monday through Saturday at 7:45, 10:45, 13:45, 16:45, 19:45, and
22:30; no early departures on Saturday. All Sunday departures are
30 minutes earlier, except there's no early departure on Sunday
morning and the last boat from Svendborg to Ærøskøbing is still
at 22:30. Departures from Ærøskøbing are daily at 6:20, 9:15,
12:15, 15:15, 18:15, 21:10; no early departure on weekend mornings. While walk-ons always make it on board, cars need reservations (tel. 62 52 40 00). A ferry/bus combo ticket gives you the
whole island with stopovers.

   Trains connecting with Svendborg–Ærø ferry: A train is
scheduled to arrive in Svendborg within 15 minutes of each boat
crossing. From the train station it's a four-block walk to the ferry
dock. Head downhill to the harbor and look right for the "Ærø"
sign. A train leaves for Copenhagen (via Odense) within 15 minutes of each ferry arrival in Svendborg. The Copenhagen-to-
Svendborg trip takes about 2.5 hours (with a 30-minute wait for a
connection in Odense).

ODENSE

Founded in 988 and named after Odin (the Nordic Zeus), Odense
is the hometown of storyteller Hans Christian Andersen. He once
said, "Perhaps Odense will one day become famous because of me."
Today Odense (OH-then-za) is one of Denmark's most visited

towns. Denmark's third-largest city, with 183,000 people, is big and industrial. But its old center retains some of the fairy-tale charm it had in the days of H.C.A.

Tourist Information: The TI, in the town hall right downtown, runs a "Meet the Danes" program (Mon–Sat 9:00–19:00, Sun 11:00–19:00; off-season Mon–Fri 9:30–16:30, Sat 10:00–13:00, closed Sun, tel. 66 12 75 20). For a quick visit, all you need is the free map/guide from the Hans Christian Andersen Hus. (Note: The Danes call him "Hoe See," for "H. C." Andersen.)

Sights—Odense
▲**Den Fynske Landsby Open-Air Museum**—This sleepy gathering of 26 old buildings preserves the 18th-century culture of this region. There are no explanations in the buildings, because the many school groups who visit play guessing games. Pick up the 15-kr guidebook. (30-kr admission, daily mid-Jun–mid-Aug 9:30–19:00; Apr–mid-Jun and mid-Aug–Oct 10:00–17:00, tel. 66 13 13 72.) From mid-July to mid-August, there are H. C. Andersen musicals (in Danish) in the theater daily at 16:00. The 50-kr ticket for the musical includes admission 90 minutes early (not before 14:30) to see the museum.

▲▲**Hans Christian Andersen Hus**—This museum is packed with mementos from the writer's life, his letters and books, and hordes of children and tourists. It's fun if you like his tales (30 kr, daily in summer 9:00–19:00, less off-season, Hans Jensens Stræde 37, tel. 66 13 13 72 and ask to be connected to the H. C. Andersen Museum). You'll find good descriptions in English, so the guidebook is unnecessary (but pick up the free city guide). The garden fairy-tale parade, with pleasing vignettes, thrills kids daily (late Jun–Jul) in the museum garden at 11:00, 13:00, and 15:00. Across the street is a shop full of mobiles and Danish arts and crafts. Just around the corner is Flensted Uromagerens Hus (mobile-maker's house).

▲**Møntergarden Urban History Museum**—Very close to the H. C. A. Hus, this fun little museum (15 kr, daily 10:00–16:00) offers Odense history, early photos, a great coin collection, and the cheapest coffee in Denmark.

Sleeping in Odense
(7 kr = about $1)
Radisson H.C.A. Hotel offers a deal from mid-June to August 29 (Sb or Db-675 kr, with breakfast, regular price Sb-1,055, Db-1,255 kr, CC:VMA, tel. 66 14 78 00, fax 66 14 78 90). **Jytte** (u-ter) **Gamdrup** rents two rooms in her 17th-century home a few doors down from the H. C. A. Museum (D-280–300kr, breakfast-135kr, Ramsherred 17, 5000 Odense C, tel. 66 13 89 36).

Transportation Connections—Odense

By train to: Copenhagen (hrly, 90 min), **Århus** (hrly, 2 hrs),
Svendborg (hrly, 1 hr, to Ærø ferry), **Roskilde** (hrly, 1 hr).

Route Tips for Drivers

Århus or Billund to Ærø: The freeway takes you over a suspension bridge on the island of Fyn. At Odense take Highway 9 south to Svendborg. Figure about two hours to drive from Billund to Svendborg.

Leave your car in Svendborg (at the easy long-term parking lot two blocks from the ferry dock) and sail for Ærø. It's an easy 70-minute crossing (255-kr round-trip per car and driver, 113-kr round-trip per person). There are only six boats a day (see "Transportation Connections"—Ærø, above; cars need reservations; call 62 52 40 00). A ferry/bus combo ticket gives you the whole island with stopovers.

Ærø to Copenhagen via Odense: Catch the 6:20 ferry to Svendborg (tel. 62 52 40 00). Reservations for walk-ons are never necessary. On weekends, there are no early trips. By 7:40 you'll be driving north on Highway 9; follow signs first to Fåborg, past the Egeskov Castle to Odense. For the folk museum, leave Route 9 just south of town at Højby, turning left toward Dalum and the Odense Campground (on Odensevej). Look for "Den Fynske Landsby" signs (near the train tracks, south edge of town). If you're going directly to H. C. Andersen Hus, follow the signs.

Continuing toward Copenhagen, you'll take the world's longest suspension bridge (12 miles long, opened to traffic in 1998). This bridge will save you an hour (over the ferry) but cost drivers the same (210 kr, tel. 58 35 01 00, exhibition center in Halsskov). Follow signs to København (Copenhagen). At Ringsted, signs take you to Roskilde. Aim toward twin church spires and follow signs to Vikingskibene—Viking ships.

Copenhagen is 30 minutes from Roskilde. If you're heading to the airport, stay on the freeway to the end, following signs to København C, then to Dragør/Kastrup Airport.

JUTLAND: LEGOLAND AND ÅRHUS

Jutland, the part of Denmark that juts up from Germany, is a land of sand dunes, Lego toys, moated manor houses, and fortified old towns. Make a pilgrimage to the most famous land in all of Jutland: the pint-sized kid's paradise, Legoland. In Århus, the lively capital of Jutland, wander the pedestrian street of this busy port, tour its boggy prehistory, and visit centuries-old Danish town life in its open-air museum.

Planning Your Time

Jutland (Jylland in Danish) is worth two days on a three-week trip through Scandinavia. On a quick trip, drivers coming from Norway might take the overnight boat from Kristiansand to Hirtshals. By noon you'll be in Århus. Den Gamle By (Old Town museum) is worth an afternoon. Spend the next morning at Legoland, on the way to Funen and Ærø. Speedier travelers could make Århus an afternoon stop only and drive to Legoland that evening (which is free if you enter late).

LEGOLAND

Legoland is Scandinavia's top kids' sight. If you have a child (or think you might be one), it's a fun stop. This huge park is a happy combination of rides, restaurants, trees, smiles, and 33 million Lego bricks creatively arranged into such wonders as Mt. Rushmore, the Parthenon, "Mad" King Ludwig's castle, and the Statue of Liberty. It's a Lego world here, as everything is cleverly related to this very popular toy. Surprisingly, the restaurants don't serve Legolamb.

The indoor "museum" features the history of the company, high-tech Lego creations, a great doll collection, and a toy museum full of mechanical wonders from the early 1900s, many ready to jump into action as soon as you push the button. There's a Lego playroom for hands-on fun—and a campground across the street if your kids refuse to move on (140-kr entry, 130 kr for kids ages 3–13, 95 kr for kids over 60; gets you on all the rides; open daily Apr–Oct 10:00–20:00; until 21:00 in summer; closed off-season, tel. 75 33 13 33). Legoland doesn't charge in the evening (free after 19:00 in Jul and late Aug, otherwise after 18:00). Activities close an hour before the park, but it's basically the same place after dinner as during the day—with fewer tour groups.

Legoland is located in the unremarkable town of Billund. The TI in Legoland (tel. 76 50 00 55) can arrange rooms for about 350 kr for a double. (See "Sleeping," below.)

Sights—Near Legoland

Jelling—I know you've always wanted to see the hometown of the ancient Danish kings Gorm the Old and Harald Bluetooth. Here's your chance. Jelling is a small village (12 miles from Legoland, just off the highway near Vejle) with a small church that has Denmark's oldest frescoes and two old runic stones in its courtyard—often called "Denmark's birth certificate."

▲**Ribe**—A Viking port 1,000 years ago, Ribe is the oldest, and possibly loveliest, town in Denmark. It's an entertaining mix of cobbled lanes and leaning old houses, with a fine church (10 kr, modern paintings under Romanesque arches). Drop by the TI for its handy walking-tour brochure, or better yet, catch a guided town walk (40 kr, Jul–mid-Aug Mon–Fri at 11:30, Torvet 3, tel. 75 42 15 00) or the free Night Watchman tour (May–Sept at 22:00, extra tour at 20:00 Jun–Aug). A smoky, low-ceilinged, atmospheric inn, the Weis' Stue, rents a few rooms and serves good meals across the street from the church (tel. 75 42 07 00).

Sleeping near Legoland, in Billund
(7 kr = about $1)

Sleep Code: **S** = Single, **D** = Double/Twin, **T** = Triple, **Q** = Quad, **b** = bathroom, **CC** = Credit Card (Visa, MasterCard, Amex). Prices include breakfast unless otherwise noted.

Legoland Hotel adjoins Legoland (1,315 kr for room big enough for two adults and two kids, includes discounted admission to park, CC:VMA, tel. 75 33 12 44, fax 75 35 38 10). **Hotel Svanen** is nearby in Billund (Sb-700 kr, Db-750 kr, Qb-920 kr, extra bed-150 kr, CC:VMA, Nordmarksvej 8, tel. 75 33 28 33, fax 75 35 35 15).

Private rooms are the key to a budget visit here. **Erik and Mary Sort** have four doubles and a great setup in a forest just outside of town. Their guests enjoy a huge living room, a kitchen, lots of Lego toys, and a kid-friendly yard (D-300 kr, discounts for kids; leave Billund on Grindsted Road, turn right on Stilbjergvej after

Jutland: Legoland and Århus

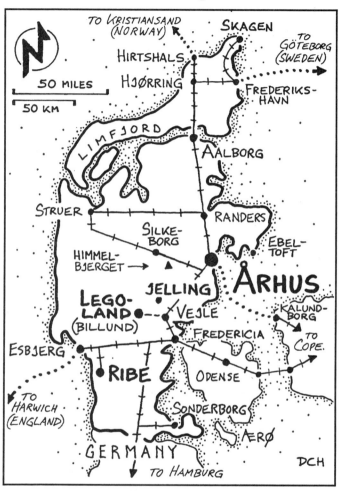

Shell station, about a half mile down the road on the right at Stilbjergvej 4, tel. 75 33 23 27).

Billund Youth Hostel is brand new and has 100-kr dorm beds in 10-bed rooms (D-380 kr, sheets-45 kr, one-night membership 25 kr, no breakfast, Ellehammers Alle 2, 7190 Billund, bus #912 or #44 from Vejle train station stops nearby, tel. 75 33 27 77, fax 75 33 28 77).

ÅRHUS

Denmark's second-largest city (and self-proclaimed as the "World's Smallest Big City"), Århus (OAR-hoos) has a population of 280,000 and is Jutland's capital and cultural hub. Its Viking founders, ever conscious of aesthetics, chose a lovely wooded setting where the river hits the sea. Today Århus bustles with a lively port and an important university. It's well worth a stop.

Tourist Information: Visit the town hall TI to get the helpful Århus brochure and map (mid-Jun–mid-Sept Mon–Fri 9:30–18:00, Sat 9:30–17:00, Sun 9:30–13:00, shorter hours and closed Sun off-season, tel. 86 12 16 00, fax 86 12 95 90). They run a fine introductory bus tour (daily in summer at 10:00, 2.5 hours, 45 kr, includes 24 hours unlimited city bus travel). Consider the Århus Passet (88 kr/day, 110 kr/2 day), which covers all sights, the introductory bus tour, and transportation.

Getting around Århus: City buses easily connect the center and train station with the open-air and prehistory museums.

Sights—Århus

▲▲▲**Den Gamle By**—The Old Town open-air folk museum puts Århus on the touristic map. Seventy half-timbered houses and crafts shops are wonderfully furnished just as they were back in Hans Christian Andersen's day. The Mayor's House (from 1597) is the nucleus and reason enough to visit. Unlike other Scandinavian open-air museums that focus on rural folk life, Den Gamle By re-creates old Danish town life (55 kr, daily Jun–Aug 9:00–18:00; Apr–May and Sept–Oct 10:00–17:00; shorter hours off-season; some English descriptions inside; take bus #3, #14, or #25, or walk 15 minutes from train station to Viborgvej 2, tel. 86 12 31 88). Ask about walking tours in English (2/day in summer) and pick up the schedule of tours. After hours, the buildings are locked but the peaceful park is open. A fine botanical garden is next door.

▲**Forhistorisk Museum Moesgård**—This prehistory museum at Moesgård, just south of Århus, is famous for its incredibly well-preserved Grauballe Man. This 2,000-year-old "bog man" looks like a fellow half his age. You'll see his skin, nails, hair, and even the slit in his throat given him at the sacrificial banquet. The museum has fine Stone, Bronze, Iron, and Viking Age exhibits (35 kr, daily 10:00–17:00; off-season 10:00–16:00 and closed Mon, Moesgård Alle 20, take bus #6 from Århus station to last stop, tel. 89 42 11 00). Behind the museum, a prehistoric open-air museum ("trackway," good 10-kr guide booklet) stretches two miles down to a fine beach from which, in the summer, bus #19 takes you back downtown. The museum cafeteria sells picnics to go.

Århus Cathedral—This late Gothic church (from 1479) is Denmark's biggest—over 300 feet long and tall (Mon–Sat 9:30–16:00, off-season 10:00–15:00).

Århus

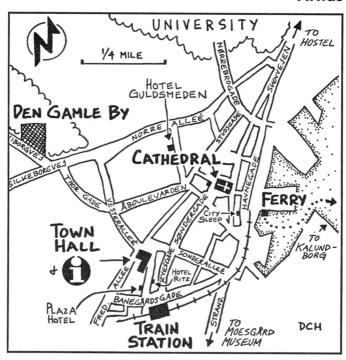

Other Århus Attractions—Århus has a great pedestrian street that lasts at least two ice-cream cones from the cathedral to the train station (Søndergade/Clements Torv). There's lots more to see and do in Århus, including an art museum (Århus Kunstmuseum, 30 kr, Tue–Sun 10:00–17:00, closed Mon, buses #1 and #6 from train station, tel. 86 13 52 55), a small Viking museum (free, Mon–Wed and Fri 9:30–16:00, Thu 9:30–18:00, closed Sat–Sun, in a bank basement across from cathedral), and a "Tivoli" amusement park.

Sleeping in Århus
(7 kr = about $1)
Sleep Code: **S** = Single, **D** = Double/Twin, **T** = Triple, **Q** = Quad, **b** = bathroom, **CC** = Credit Card (Visa, MasterCard, Amex). All accommodations are centrally located near the train station and TI. The TI can set you up in a private home for 150 kr per person in a double room, and they also have summer deals on ritzy hotels (Db-700 kr).

Hotel Guldsmeden is a brand-new, sparkling clean hotel with 15 rooms, fluffy comforters, and a young and friendly staff. The steep staircase is worth the climb (Sb-595 kr, Db-695 kr, suites available, includes breakfast buffet, 10-minute walk from station at Guldsmedgade 40, tel. 86 13 45 50, fax 86 13 76 76).

Plaza Hotel is 100 meters from the station and a good value (Sb-560–790 kr, Db-890–960 kr depending on big/small/old/new, extra bed-160 kr, includes breakfast, CC:VMA, sauna, Banegards-pladsen 14, tel. 87 32 01 00, fax 87 32 01 99, www.plaza-hotel-aarhus.dk).

Hotel Ritz, across the street from the Plaza Hotel, has similar-quality rooms (Sb-595–750 kr, Db 795–920 kr, includes large breakfast buffet, tel. 86 13 44 44, fax 86 13 45 87, www.hotelritz.dk).

The basic City Sleep In is open 24 hours a day year-round (dorm beds-85 kr, D-240 kr, Db-280 kr, sheets-30 kr, breakfast-30 kr, Havnegade 20, tel. 86 19 20 55, fax 86 19 18 11, www.citysleep-in.dk).

The hostel, with 80-kr beds and plenty of two- and four-bed rooms, is near the water two miles out of town (Marienlundsvej 10, bus #1 to the end, follow signs, tel. 86 16 72 98, fax 86 10 55 60).

Eating in Århus

Det Grønne Hjørne, at the corner of Frederiksgade and Østegade, offers an ethnic all-you-can-eat buffet (59 kr before 16:00, 79 kr after). Restaurant Italia is reasonable (35-kr lunches, 99-kr steak and lobster dinners, corner of Mindebrogade and Åboulevarden). Munkestuen has good meals (lunch-60 kr, dinner-80–120 kr, Klostertorvet 5, tel. 86 12 95 67). At Dee Dee's Sandwiches & Salads, nothing costs more than 40 kr (just across from train station). Try the brunch at cozy Café Jorden (11:00–16:00, Badstuegade 3, tel. 86 19 72 22). The area around Klostertorvet/Klostergade offers great cafés and people watching. The park in front of Musikhuset concert hall is good for picnics.

Transportation Connections—Århus

By train to: Hirtshals (hrly, 2.5 hrs), Odense (hrly, 2 hrs), Copenhagen (hrly, 3.5 hrs), Hamburg (5/day, 5.5 hrs).

Ferries: Day and night, ferries sail between Hirtshals, Denmark, and Kristiansand, Norway. On board, you'll find a decent *smørgåsbord*, music, duty-free shopping, and a bank (no fee). The crossing takes 2.5 to 6 hours, depending on the time of day, and the cost ranges wildly from 144 kr to 352 kr (July and weekends are priciest). The charge for a car is 180 kr to 500 kr; a "car package" deal lets five in a car travel for 1,090 kr (summer, Mon–Thu). The overnight boat offers varying levels of comfort and privacy (38 kr for reclining seat, 58 kr for simple curtained *couchette*, 96–104 kr for bed in four-berth room, or 170–220 kr for bed in private double with shower). Call Color Line for information and reservations (Mon–Sat 8:00–22:00, Sun 8:00–21:00, tel. 99 56 19 55 in Denmark; in the United States tel. 212/319-1300, fax 212/319-1390). If you've got a car or want a room, call for a reservation then pay when you arrive at the dock.

Route Tips for Drivers

From the ferry dock at Hirtshals to Århus to Billund: From the dock in Hirtshals, drive E-45 south (signs to Hjørring, Ålborg). It's about a 2.5-hour drive even on the scenic road 507 from Ålborg (signs to Hadsund). E-45 takes you into Århus. (To skip Århus, skirt the center and follow E-45 south.) To get to downtown Århus, follow signs to the center, then Domkirke. Park in the pay lot across from the cathedral. Signs all over town direct you to the open-air folk museum, Den Gamle By. From Århus, continue south on E-45 (leave on Skanderborg Road; follow signs to Vejle, Kolding). For Legoland, take the Vejle S (after Vejle N) exit for Billund.

NORWAY

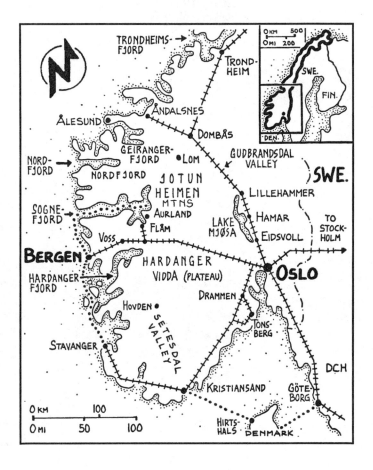

OSLO

Oslo is the smallest and least earthshaking of the Nordic capitals, but this brisk little city offers more sightseeing thrills than you might expect. Sights of the Viking spirit—past and present—tell an exciting story. Prowl through the remains of ancient Viking ships and marvel at more peaceful but equally gutsy modern boats like the *Kon-Tiki*, *Ra*, and *Fram*. Dive into the country's folk culture at the open-air folk museum and get stirred up by Norway's heroic spirit at the Norwegian Resistance Museum.

For a look at modern Oslo, browse through the new yuppie-style harbor shopping complex, tour the striking city hall, take a peek at sculptor Vigeland's people pillars, and climb the towering Holmenkollen ski jump.

Situated at the head of a 60-mile-long fjord, surrounded by forests, and populated by more than 500,000 people, Oslo is Norway's cultural hub and an all-you-can-see *smørgåsbord* of historic sights, trees, art, and Nordic fun.

Planning Your Time

Oslo offers an exciting two-day slate of sightseeing thrills. Ideally, spend two days and leave on the night train to Copenhagen or on the scenic train to Bergen the third morning. Spend the two days like this:

Day 1: Set up. Visit the TI. Tour the Akershus Castle and Norwegian Resistance Museum. Take a picnic on the ferry to Bygdøy and enjoy a view of the city harbor. Tour the *Fram*, *Kon-Tiki*, and Viking ships. Finish the afternoon at the Norwegian Open Air Folk Museum. Boat home. For evening culture, consider the folk music and dance show (20:30 Mon and Thu).

Day 2: At 10:00 catch the city hall tour, then browse through the

National Gallery. Spend the afternoon at Vigeland Park and at the Holmenkollen ski jump and museum. Browse Karl Johans Gate (all the way to the station) and Aker Brygge harbor in the early evening for the Norwegian paseo. Consider munching a fast-food dinner on the harbor minicruise.

Orientation

Oslo is easy to manage, with nearly all its sights clustered around the central "barbell" street (Karl Johans Gate, with the Royal Palace on one end and the train station on the other) or in the Bygdøy district, a 10-minute ferry ride across the harbor.

Tourist Information

The **Norwegian Information Center** displays Norway as if it were a giant booth at a trade show (daily 9:00–19:00, shorter hours off-season, on the waterfront between city hall and Aker Brygge, tel. 22 83 00 50). Stock up on brochures for Oslo and all of your Norwegian destinations. Pick up the free Oslo map, Sporveiskart transit map, *What's on in Oslo* monthly (for the most accurate listing of museum hours and special events), *Streetwise* magazine (hip, fun to read, and full of offbeat ideas), the *Bergen Guide*, and the free annual *Oslo Guide* (with plenty of details on sightseeing, shopping, and eating). Consider buying the Oslo Card (unless your hotel provides it for free). The info center has a handy public toilet and rooms showcasing various crafts and ways you can spend your money. The TI window in the central station is much simpler and deals only with Oslo but can handle your needs just as well (daily in summer 8:00–23:00, less off-season).

Use It is a hardworking youth information center, providing solid, money-saving, experience-enhancing information to young, student, and vagabond travelers (mid-Jun–mid-Aug Mon–Fri 7:30–17:00, closed Sat–Sun; otherwise Mon–Fri 11:00–17:00, Møllergata 3, tel. 22 41 51 32, fax 22 42 63 71, www.unginfo.oslo.no). They have telephones and e-mail, and can find you the cheapest beds in town (no booking fee). Read their free *Streetwise* magazine for ideas on eating and sleeping cheap, good nightspots, the best beaches, and so on.

The **Oslo Card** gives you free use of all city public transit and boats, free entry to all sights, a free harbor minicruise tour, free parking, and many more discounts—and is also a handy handbook (24 hours-150 kr, 48 hours-220 kr, 72 hours-250 kr). Almost any two-day visit to Oslo will be cheaper with the Oslo Card (which costs less than 3 Bygdøy museum admissions, the ski jump, and 1 city bus ride). Students with an ISIC card may be better off without the Oslo Card. The TI's special Oslo Package hotel deal (described under Sleeping, below) includes this card with your discounted hotel room.

Arrival in Oslo

By Train: Oslo S, the modern central train station, is slick and helpful, with a late-hours TI (daily in summer 8:00–23:00, less off-season), room-finding service, and a late-hours bank (fair rates, normal fee). Pick up leaflets on the Flåm and Bergen Railway. For a handy supermarket, head down the escalator across from tracks 13 through 19 to Østbanehallen (Mon–Fri 9:00–21:00, Sat 9:00–20:00, Sun 12:00–20:00).

By Plane: The super speedy "Flytog" train zips travelers from Oslo's Gardermoen Airport to the central train station in 22 minutes (120 kr, 6/hrly, not covered by railpass). InterCity trains cost about half as much and take about twice the time (1/hrly, covered by railpass). "Flybuss" airport buses make several downtown stops including the train station (65 kr, 6/hrly). For a taxi from the airport to downtown, allow 600 kr.

Getting around Oslo

By Public Transit: Oslo's transit system is made up of buses, trams, ferries, and a subway. Tickets cost 20 kr and are good for one hour of use on any combination of the above. Flexicards give eight rides for 105 kr. Buy tickets as you board (bus info tel. 22 17 70 30, daily 8:00–23:00). **Trafikanten**, the public transit information center, is under the ugly tower immediately in front of the station. Their free "Sporveiskart for Oslo" transit map is the best city map around and makes the transit system easy. The similar but smaller "Visitor's Map Oslo" (available at TI) is easier to use and also free. The **Dagskort Tourist Ticket** is a 40-kr, 24-hour transit pass that pays for itself in the second hour. The Oslo **Card** (see "Tourist Information," above) gives you free run of the entire transit system. Note how gracefully the subway lines fan out after huddling at Stortinget. Take advantage of the way they run like clockwork, with schedules clearly posted and followed.

By Bike: Oslo is a good biking town, especially if you'd like to get out into the woods or ride a tram uphill out of town and coast for miles back. Glåmdal Cycle rents bikes (3 hrs/90–130 kr, 6 hrs/140–180 kr, 24 hrs/180–230 kr depending on bike, 20 percent discount for readers of this book; May–Sept Mon–Fri 8:00–21:00, Sat–Sun 10:00–18:00, closes earlier off-season; between Norway Info Center and Akerbrygge Shopping Center, through the iron gates, tel. 23 11 51 08).

Helpful Hints

To get a taxi, call 22 38 80 90, then dial 1. Jernbanetorgets **Apotek** is a 24-hour pharmacy directly across from the train station (on Jernbanetorget, tel. 22 41 24 82). Kilroy Travel is everyone's favorite for student and discounted air tickets (Nedre Slottsgate 23, tel. 23 10 23 10).

Oslo

❶	CITY HOTEL	❼	CASPARI ROOMS
❷	RAINBOW HOTEL ASTORIA	❽	MR. NAESS ROOMS
❸	RAINBOW HOTEL SPECTRUM	❾	ALBERTINE HOSTEL
❹	COCHS PENSJONAT	❿	HARALDSHEIM HOSTEL
❺	ELLINGSEN'S PENSJONAT	⓫	YMCA SLEEP-IN
❻	MEISFJORD ROOMS	⓬	VEGETA VERTSHUS REST.

Sights—Downtown Oslo

Note: Because of Norway's passion for minor differences in
opening times from month to month, I've generally listed only the
peak-season hours. Assume opening hours shorten as the days do.
The high season in Oslo is mid-June to mid-August. (I'll call that
"summer" in this chapter.)

▲▲**City Hall**—Construction on Oslo's richly decorated Rådhuset
began in 1931 and was finished in 1950 in time to celebrate the
city's 900th birthday. Norway's leading artists (including Edvard
Munch) all contributed to what was an avant-garde thrill in its
day. The interior's 2,000 square yards of bold and colorful "social-
ist modernism" murals (which take you on a voyage through the
collective psyche of Norway, from its simple rural beginnings
through the scar tissue of the Nazi occupation and beyond) are
meaningful only with the excellent, free guided tours (offered
Mon–Fri at 10:00, 12:00, and 14:00; open Mon–Sat 9:00–17:00,
Sun 12:00–17:00, until 16:00 in off-season, entry on Karl Johans

side, tel. 22 86 16 00). Ever notice how city halls rather than churches are the dominant buildings in the your-government-loves-you northern corner of Europe? The main hall of Oslo's city hall actually feels like a temple to good government (the altarlike mural celebrates "work, play, and civic administration"). The Nobel Peace Prize is awarded each December in this room.

▲▲**Akershus Fortress Complex**—This parklike complex of sites scattered over Oslo's fortified center is still a military base. But dodging patrolling guards and vans filled with soldiers you'll see war memorials, the castle, a prison, the Nazi resistance museum, an armed forces museum, and cannon-strewn ramparts affording fine harbor views and picnic perches. Immediately inside the gate is an information center with an interesting exhibit on medieval Oslo's fortifications. In summer, free 45-minute tours of the grounds leave from the center (10:00, 12:00, 14:00, 16:00, daily but not Sun morning, tel. 23 09 39 17). There's a small changing of the guard daily at 13:30.

Akershus Fortress—One of the oldest buildings in town, this castle overlooking Oslo's harbor is mediocre by European standards. The big, empty rooms remind us of Norway's medieval poverty. Behind the chapel altar, steps lead down to the tombs of some Norwegian kings. The castle is interesting only with the tour (20 kr for castle entry, May–mid-Sept Mon–Sat 10:00–16:00, Sun 12:30–16:00; open in Jul until 18:00 Mon–Thu; open Sun only in spring and fall; closed in winter; free 50-min English tours offered in summer Mon–Sat at 11:00, 13:00, and 15:00, Sun at 13:00 and 15:00, tel. 22 41 25 21).

▲▲**Norwegian Resistance Museum (Norges Hjemmefront-museum)**—A stirring story about the Nazi invasion and occupation is told with wonderful English descriptions. This is the best look in Europe at how national spirit endured total German occupation (20 kr, Mon–Sat 10:00–17:00, Sun 11:00–17:00, closes 1 hour earlier off-season, next to castle in building overlooking harbor, tel. 23 09 31 38).

Armed Forces Museum—Across the fortress parade ground, a large museum traces Norwegian military from Viking days to post-WWII. The early stuff is very sketchy but the WWII story is fascinating (free, Mon–Fri 10:00–18:00, Sat–Sun 11:00–16:00, shorter hours Sept–May, tel. 23 09 35 82).

▲**National Gallery**—Located downtown, this easy-to-handle museum gives you an effortless tour back in time and through Norway's most beautiful valleys, mountains, and villages, with the help of its romantic painters (especially Dahl). The gallery also has several Picassos, a noteworthy Impressionist collection, some Vigeland statues, and a representative roomful of Munch paintings, including one of his famous *Scream* paintings. His artwork here makes a trip to the Munch museum unnecessary for most.

Greater Oslo

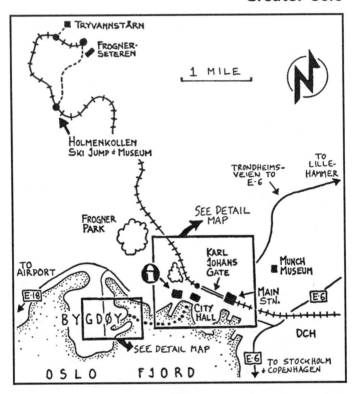

For an entertaining survey of 2,500 years of sculpture, go through the museum gift shop and down the stairs to the right for a room filled with plaster copies of famous works (free, Mon, Wed, Fri 10:00–18:00, Thu 10:00–20:00, Sat 10:00–16:00, Sun 11:00–16:00, closed Tue, Universitets Gata 13, tel. 22 20 04 04).

▲▲**Browsing**—Oslo's pulse is best felt along and near the central Karl Johans Gate (from station to palace), between the city hall and the harbor, and in the trendy harborside Aker Brygge Festival Market Mall—a glass-and-chrome collection of sharp cafés and polished produce stalls just west of the city hall (trams #10 and #15 to/from train station). The buskers are among the best in Europe. Aker Brygge is very lively late evenings.

▲▲▲**Vigeland Sculptures and the Vigeland Museum in Frogner Park**—The 75-acre park contains a lifetime of work by Norway's greatest sculptor, Gustav Vigeland. From 1924 to 1942 he sculpted 175 bronze and granite statues—each nude and unique. Walking over the statue-lined bridge you'll come to the main fountain. Trace the story of our lives in the series of humans intertwined with trees around the fountain. The maze in the pavement around the fountain starts opposite the monolith and comes out, three kilometers later, closest to the monolith. Try following it...you can't go wrong. Vigeland's 60-foot-high tangled tower of 121 bodies called *The Monolith of Life* is the centerpiece of the park. While it seems the lower figures are laden with earthly concerns and the higher ones are freed to pursue loftier, more spiritual adventures, Vigeland gives us permission to interpret it any way we like. Pick up the free map from the box on the kiosk wall as you enter. The park is more than great art. It's a city at play. Enjoy its urban Norwegian ambience. Then visit the Vigeland Museum to see the models for the statues and more in the artist's studio. Photos on the wall show the construction of the monolith (30 kr for museum, Tue–Sat 10:00–18:00, Sun 12:00–19:00, closed Mon; off-season Tue–Sun 12:00–16:00 and free, tel. 22 44 11 36). The park is always open and free. Take bus #20 or #45 or tram #12 or #15—get off at Frogner Plass for the museum or Vigeland Park for outdoor statues—or take the T-bane to "Majorstuen."

Oslo City Museum—Located in the Frogner Manor farm in Frogner Park, this museum tells the story of Oslo. A helpful free English brochure guides you through the exhibits (30 kr, Tue–Fri 10:00–18:00, Sat–Sun 11:00–17:00, closed Mon, shorter hours off-season, tel. 22 43 06 45).

▲▲**Edvard Munch Museum**—The only Norwegian painter to have had a serious impact on European art, Munch (monk) is a surprise to many who visit this fine museum. The emotional, disturbing, and powerfully expressionist work of this strange and perplexing man is arranged chronologically. You'll see paintings, drawings, lithographs, and photographs. Don't miss *The Scream*, which captures the fright many feel as the human "race" does just that (50 kr, daily 10:00–18:00; off-season closes at 16:00 and all day Mon; take T-bane from station to "Tøyen," tel. 22 67 37 74). If the price or location is a problem, you can see a roomful of Munch paintings in the free National Gallery downtown.

Sights—Oslo's Bygdøy Neighborhood

▲▲▲**Bygdøy**—This exciting cluster of sights is on a parklike peninsula just across the harbor from downtown. To get to Bygdøy, either take bus #30 from the station and National Theater or, more fun, catch the ferry from City Hall (20 kr, free with transit pass or Oslo Card, 3/hrly, 8:30–21:00). The Folk Museum and Viking ships are a 10-minute walk from the ferry's first stop, Dronningen. The other museums are at the second stop, Bygdøynes. All Bygdøy sights are within a 15-minute walk of each other. While an overpriced tourist train shuttles visitors around Bygdøy (3/hrly, 50 kr for all-day pass), the *Fram*-Viking ships walk gives you a fine feel for rural Norway.

Bygdøy Neighborhood

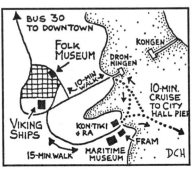

▲▲**Norwegian Folk Museum**—Brought from all corners of Norway, 150 buildings have been reassembled on these 35 acres. While Stockholm's Skansen was the first to open to the public, this museum is a bit older, started in 1885 as the king's private collection. You'll find craftspeople doing their traditional things; security guards disguised in cute, colorful, and traditional local costumes; endless creative ways to make do in a primitive log-cabin-and-goats-on-the-roof age; a 12th-century stave church; and a museum filled with toys and fine folk costumes. The place hops in the summer but is dead off-season. Catch the free one-hour guided walks (call for times). Otherwise, glean information from the 10-kr guidebook and the informative attendants who look like Rebecca Boone's Norwegian pen pals (50 kr, daily Jun–Aug 9:00–18:00; off-season 10:00–17:00 or less). For folk dance performances, tour, and crafts demonstration schedules, call 22 12 37 00.

▲▲**Viking Ships**—Three great ninth-century Viking ships are surrounded by artifacts from the days of rape, pillage, and—ya sure, you betcha—plunder. There are no museum tours, but everything is well described in English, and it's hard not to hear the English-speaking bus tour guides. There was a time when much of a frightened Europe closed every prayer with "And deliver us from the Vikings, Amen." Gazing up at the prow of one of these sleek, time-stained vessels, you can almost hear the screams and smell the armpits of those redheads on the rampage (30 kr, daily summer 9:00–18:00, spring and fall 11:00–17:00, closes in winter at 15:00, tel. 22 43 83 79). To miss the tour-group crowds, come early, late, or at lunchtime.

▲▲**The *Fram***—This great ship took modern-day Vikings Amundsen and Nansen deep into the Arctic and Antarctic, farther north and south than any ship before. For three years the *Fram* was part of an Arctic ice drift. The exhibit is fascinating. Read the ground-floor displays, then explore the boat (25 kr, daily summer 9:00–18:45, shorter hours off-season). You can step into the lobby and see the ship's hull for free. The **polar sloop *Gjøa*** is dry-docked next to the ferry dock. This is the boat Amundsen and a crew of six used from 1903 to 1906 to "discover" the Northwest Passage (*Fram* ticket gets you aboard).

▲▲***Kon-Tiki* Museum**—Next to the *Fram* are the *Kon-Tiki* and the *Ra II*, the boats Thor Heyerdahl built and sailed 4,000 and 3,000 miles, respectively, to prove that early South Americans could have sailed to Polynesia and Africans could have populated Barbados. Both are well displayed and described in English. A short "adventures of Thor Heyerdahl" movie plays constantly (30 kr, daily 9:30–17:00, off-season 10:30–16:00).

▲**Norwegian Maritime Museum**—If you like the sea, this museum is a salt lick, providing a fine look at Norway's maritime heritage (30 kr, 60 kr for a family, daily 10:00–19:00, off-season 10:30–16:00 and sometimes later). Consider viewing the wide-screen nature film on Norway's coast called *The Ocean, A Way of Life* (free, 20 min, on the half hour).

Other Oslo Sights and Activities

▲**Henie-Onstad Art Center**—Norway's best private modern art collection, donated by the famous Norwegian Olympic skater/movie star Sonja Henie (and her husband), combines modern art, a stunning building, a beautiful fjord-side setting, and the great café/restaurant Pirouetten. Don't miss Henie's glittering trophy room near the entrance of the center (about 50 kr, depending on exhibit, Tue–Thu 10:00–21:00, Fri–Mon 11:00–18:00, tel. 67 54 30 50). It's in Høvikodden, eight miles southwest of Oslo (catch bus #151, #161, #251, #252, or #261 from the Oslo train station or from Universitets Plass by the National Theater).

▲▲**Holmenkollen Ski Jump and Ski Museum**—Overlooking Oslo is a tremendous ski jump with a unique museum of skiing. The T-bane #1 gets you out of the city, into the hills and forests that surround Oslo, and to the jump. After touring the history of skiing in the museum, ride the elevator and climb the 100-step stairway to the top of the jump for the best possible view of Oslo—and a chance to look down the long and frightening ramp that has sent so many tumbling into the agony of defeat. The **ski museum**—a must for skiers—traces the evolution of the sport from 4,000-year-old rock paintings to crude 1,500-year-old skis to the slick and quickly evolving skis of our century (60 kr, museum is at ski jump, both open daily Jun–Aug 9:00–20:00 and close earlier off-season).

For a thrill, step into the **Simulator** and fly down the French Alps in a Disneyland-style downhill ski race. My legs were exhausted after the four-minute terror. This stimulator, parked in front of the ski museum, costs 40 kr. (Japanese tourists, who wig out over this one, are usually given a free ride after paying for four.)

To get to the ski jump, ride the T-bane line #1 to the Holmenkollen stop and hike up the road 10 minutes. For a longer walk, ride to the end of the line (Frognerseteren) and walk 10 minutes down to the **Frognerseteren Hovedrestaurant**. This classy, traditional old place, with a terrace that offers a commanding view of the city, is a popular stop for apple cake and coffee or a splurge dinner (café open 10:30–22:30, restaurant open 12:00–15:00 and 16:30–22:00, tel. 22 14 05 50). From the restaurant it's a 30-minute walk downhill through the woods on a gravel path that runs generally parallel to Holmenkollenveien.

The nearby **Tryvannstårnet observatory tower** offers a lofty 360-degree view of Oslo in the distance, the fjord, and endless forests, lakes, and soft hills. It's impressive but not necessary if you climbed the ski jump, which gives you a much better view of the city (Mon–Fri 10:00–20:00, Sat–Sun 10:00–18:00, 10-min walk from Voksenkollen T-bane stop; tel. 22 14 67 11).

Forests, Lakes, and Beaches—Oslo is surrounded by a vast forest dotted with idyllic little lakes, huts, joggers, bikers, and sun worshipers. Mountain bike–riding possibilities are endless (as you'll discover if you go exploring without a guide or good map). For a quick ride, you can take the T-bane (with your bike; it needs a ticket too) to the end of line #1 (Frognerseteren, 30 min from the National Theater, gaining you the most altitude possible) and follow the gravelly roads (mostly downhill but with some climbing) past several dreamy lakes to Sognsvann at the end of T-bane line #3. Farther east, from Maridalsvannet, a bike path follows the Aker River all the way back into town. For plenty of trees and none of the exercise, ride the T-bane #3 to Sognsvann (with a beach towel rather than a bike) and join in the lakeside scene. Other popular beaches (such as Bygdøy Huk—direct boat from city hall pier, and others on islands in the harbor) are described in Use It's *Streetwise* magazine.

Harbor and Fjord Tours—Several tour boats leave regularly from Pier 3 in front of the city hall. A relaxing and scenic 50-minute minicruise with a boring three-language commentary departs hourly and costs only 75 kr (free with Oslo Card, daily 11:00–20:00, tel. 22 20 07 15). They won't scream if you bring something to Munch. The cheapest way to enjoy the scenic Oslofjord is to simply ride the ferries that regularly connect the nearby islands with downtown (free with Oslo Card or transit pass).

▲▲▲**Folk Entertainment**—A group of amateur musicians and dancers (called "Leikarringen Bondeungdomslaget"—Oslo's country youth society) gives a sweet, caring, and vibrant 90-minute show at the Oslo Concert Hall. Several traditional instruments are explained and demonstrated. While folk dancing seems hokey to many, if you think of it as medieval flirting set to music and ponder the complexities of village social life back then, the experience takes you away (140–180 kr, Mon and Thu Jul–early Sept at 20:30, tel. 23 11 31 11). Look for the big, brown, glassy overpass on

Munkedamsveien; the recommended Vegeta Vertshus restaurant is just up the street. For their off-season concert schedule (different locales), call 22 41 40 70.

Tusenfryd/Vikinglandet—A giant amusement complex just out of town offers a world of family fun—sort of a combo Norwegian Disneyland/Viking Knott's Berry Farm. It's one big company. While the Tusenfryd entry includes the Vikings, you can do just the Viking park if you like. Tusenfryd offers more than 50 rides, plenty of entertainment, family fun, and restaurants. Vikinglandet is a Viking theme park. A coach shuttles fun seekers to the park from behind the train station (25 kr, 2/hrly, 20-min ride). The entry, 195 kr, is not covered by the Oslo Card (daily 10:30–19:00 in summer, closed in winter). Tickets for Viking Land cost only 100 kr (tel. 64 97 64 97).

Wet Fun—Oslo offers lots of water fun for 40 kr (kids half price). In Frogner Park, the Frognerbadet has a sauna, outdoor pools, high dives, a cafeteria, and lots of young families (free with Oslo Card, daily late May–mid-Aug Mon–Fri 7:00–19:00, Sat–Sun 11:00–17:00, last entry 1 hour before closing, Middelthunsgate 28, tel. 22 44 74 29). Tøyenbadet is a modern indoor pool complex with minigolf and a 100-yard-long water slide (40 kr, free with Oslo Card, open at odd hours throughout the year, Helgengate 90, a 10-minute walk from Munch Museum, tel. 22 68 24 23). Oslo's free botanical gardens are nearby. (For more ideas on swimming, pick up *Streetwise* magazine.)

Nightlife—They used to tell people who asked about nightlife in Oslo that Copenhagen was only an hour away by plane. Now Oslo has sprouted a nightlife of its own. The scene is always changing. The TI has information on Oslo's many cafés, discos, and jazz clubs. It's the best source of information for local hot spots.

Shopping—For a great selection (but high prices) of sweaters and other Norwegian crafts, shop at Husfliden, the retail center for the Norwegian Association of Home Arts and Crafts (Mon–Wed and Fri 10:00–17:00, Thu 10:00–18:00, Sat 10:00–15:00, Den Norske Husflidsforening, Møllergata 4, behind the cathedral, tel. 22 42 10 75). Shops are generally open 10:00–17:00. Many stay open until 20:00 on Thursday and close early on Saturday and all day Sunday. Shopping centers are open Monday through Friday from 10:00 to 20:00, Saturday from 10:00 to 18:00. The first Saturday of the month is Super Saturday, when shops are open later and have sales.

Sleeping in Oslo
(7 kr = about $1)
Sleep Code: **S** = Single, **D** = Double/Twin, **T** = Triple, **Q** = Quad, **b** = bathroom, **CC** = Credit Card (Visa, MasterCard, Amex).

Yes, Oslo is expensive. In Oslo, the season dictates the best deals. In low season (Jul–mid-Aug, and Fri–Sun the rest of the year), fancy hotels are the best value for softies, when rooms go for 600 kr for a double with breakfast. In high season (business days outside of summer), your affordable choices are dumpy-for-Scandinavia (but still nice by European standards) doubles for around 500 kr in hotels and 350 kr in private homes. For experience and economy (but not convenience), go for a private home. Oslo's Albertine Hostel (see below) is well located, cheap, and normally has beds available.

Like those in its sister Scandinavian capitals, Oslo's hotels are designed for business travelers. They're expensive during our off-season (fall through spring), full in May and June for conventions (get reservations), and empty otherwise. Only the TI can sort through all the confusing hotel "specials" and get you the best deal possible on a fancy hotel—push-list rooms at about half price. Half price is still 600 kr to 700 kr, but that includes a huge breakfast and a lot of extra comfort for a few extra kroner over the cost of a cheap hotel. Cheap hotels, whose rates are the same throughout the year, are a bad value in summer but offer real savings in low season.

The TI's **Oslo Package** advertises 700-kr discounted doubles in business-class rooms (normally priced at 1,200 kr) and includes a free Oslo Card (worth 150 kr/day). The Oslo Package is a good deal for couples and an incredible deal for families with children under 16 who are traveling between early June and late August or on weekends. Two kids under 16 sleep free, breakfast included, and up to four family members get Oslo Cards, covering admission to sights and all public transportation. The clincher is that the cards are valid for four days, even if you only stay at the hotel for one night (technically, you should stay two nights, but this is not enforced). Buy this through your travel agent at home, ScanAm World Tour in the United States at 800/545-2204, or, easier, upon arrival in Oslo (at the TI). If it's late in the day, ask about any half-price last-minute deals.

Use the TI only for these push-list deals, not for cheap hotels or private homes. Some of the cheaper hotels (my listings) tell the TI (which gets a 10 percent fee) they're full when they're not. Go direct. A hotel getting 100 percent of your payment is more likely to have a room. July and early August are easy, but June can be crammed by conventions and September can be tight.

A Laundromat is on Ullevalsvein 15, one kilometer north of the train station (8:00–21:00, tel. 94 22 29 74).

Sleeping in Hotels near the Train Station
Each of these places is within a five-minute walk of the station, in a neighborhood your mom probably wouldn't want you hanging around in at night. The hotels themselves, however, are secure and comfortable. Leave nothing in your car. The Paleet parking garage is handy but not cheap—120 kr per 24 hours.

City Hotel, clean, basic, very homey, and with a wonderful lounge, originated 100 years ago as a cheap place for Norwegians to sleep while they waited to sail to their new homes in America. It now serves the opposite purpose with good if well-worn rooms and a great location (S-395 kr, Sb-510 kr, D-560 kr, Db-695 kr, includes breakfast, CC:VMA, Skippergata 19, enter from Prinsens Gate, tel. 22 41 36 10, fax 22 42 24 29, e-mail: chotea@online.no).

Rainbow Hotel Astoria is a comfortable, modern place, and part of the quickly growing Rainbow Hotel chain that understands which comforts are worth paying for. There are umbrellas, televisions, telephones, and full modern bathrooms in each room. Ice machines! Designed for businessmen, the place has mostly singles. Most "twins" are actually "combi" rooms with a regular bed and a fold-out sofa bed (Sb-470–680 kr, Db/twin-590–780 kr, Db-690–880 kr, rates vary with season, includes buffet breakfast, CC:VMA, 3 blocks in front of the station, 50 yards off Karl Johans Gate, Dronningensgate 21, 0154 Oslo, tel. 22 42 00 10, fax 22 42 57 65).

Rainbow Hotel Spectrum is also conveniently located and a good value (discounted prices Fri–Sun and throughout Jul: "combi" Twin/b-590–780 kr, full doubles-100 kr more, CC:VMA, four blocks to the right as you leave the station on Lilletorget, Brugata 7, 0186 Oslo, tel. 22 17 60 30, fax 22 17 60 80). **Rainbow Hotel Terminus** is similar and closer to the station, but has a less-exciting low-season deal (Fri, Sat, or Sun anytime or reservations within 48 hours any day during the May–Aug period: Sb-470 kr, small bed Db-590 kr, Db-690 kr, regular Db rate-880 kr, includes breakfast, Stenersgate 10, tel. 22 05 60 00, fax 22 17 08 98).

Sleeping in the West End

Cochs Pensjonat has 68 plain rooms (plus 9 remodeled doubles) with fresh paint and stale carpets. It's right behind the palace (S-340 kr, Sb-430–480 kr, D-480 kr, Db-580–640 kr, all Dbs have kitchenettes, no breakfast, CC:VM, tram #11, #13, #17, or #18 to Parkveien 25, tel. 22 33 24 00, fax 22 33 24 10, www.hurra.no \html\cochs_pensjonat.html).

Ellingsen's Pensjonat has no lounge, no breakfasts, and dreary halls. But its rooms are great, with fluffy down comforters. It's located in a residential neighborhood four blocks behind the Royal Palace (a lot of S-280 kr, D-420 kr, Db-460–530 kr, extra bed-110 kr, call well in advance for doubles, Holtegata 25, 0355 Oslo 3, tel. 22 60 03 59, fax 22 60 99 21). Located near the Uranienborg church, it's #25 on the east side of the street (T-bane #19 from the station).

Sleeping in Rooms in Private Homes

The TI at the train station can find you a 300-kr double for a 20-kr fee (minimum two-night stay). My listings are pretty funky, but full of memories.

Marius Meisfjord, a retired teacher deeply interested in imparting Norse culture, rents rooms behind the palace. Beds, which cost 200 kr per person, are in a house stuffed with ancient furniture and pictures of European royalty. This eccentric place feels more like a museum than a B&B, and friendly Mr. Meisfjord looks more like Ibsen than a B&B host (breakfast extra, take tram #12 or #15 to Elisenbergveien, walk 2 blocks to Thomas Heftes Gate 46, tel. 22 55 38 46).

The **Caspari family** rents four comfortable rooms in their home (D-320 kr, no breakfast). Loosely run, it's set in a lush green yard in a peaceful suburb behind Frogner Park, a quick T-bane ride away (get off at Borgen and walk 100 yards more on the right-hand side of the tracks, Heggelbakken 1, tel. 22 14 57 70).

Sleeping in Hostels

Albertine Hostel, a huge student dorm open to travelers of any age, offers the best cheap doubles in town. It feels like a bomb shelter, but each room is spacious, simple, and clean. There are kitchens, free parking, and elevators (Sb-265 kr, Db-340 kr, beds in quads-140 kr, beds in 6-bed rooms-115 kr, sheets-40 kr, towel-10 kr, breakfast-50 kr; catch tram #11, #12, #15, or #17, or bus #27 or #30 from the station; Storgata 55, N-0182 Oslo, tel. 22 99 72 00, fax 22 99 72 20, www.anker.oslo.no). In winter they use the adjacent Anker Hotel reception desk.

Haraldsheim Youth Hostel (IYHF), a huge, modern hostel open all year, is situated far from the center on a hill. It comes with a grand view, laundry, and self-service kitchen. Its 270 beds (four per room) are often completely booked. Beds in the new fancy quads with private showers and toilets are 180 kr per person, including buffet breakfast. (Beds in simple quads-160 kr, includes breakfast, sheets-45 kr, guest membership-25 kr; tram #10 or #11 from station to Sinsen, 4 km out of town, 5-min uphill hike, Haraldsheimveien 4, tel. 22 15 50 43, fax 22 22 10 25.) Eurailers can train (2/hrly, to Grefsen) to the hostel with their railpass.

YMCA Sleep-In Oslo, located near the train station, offers the cheapest mattresses in town in three large rooms with 15 to 30 mattresses each, plus a left-luggage room, kitchen, and piano lounge (earplugs for sale). It's as pleasant as a sleep-in can be (100 kr, Jul–mid-Aug only, reception open daily 8:00–11:00 and 17:00–24:00, no bedding provided, you must bring a sleeping bag, Møllergata 1, entry from Grubbegata, 1 block beyond the cathedral behind Use It, tel. 22 20 83 97). They don't take reservations, but you should call to see if there's room.

Sleeping on the Train

Norway's trains offer 110-kr beds in triple compartments and 210-kr beds in doubles. Eurailers who sleep well to the rhythm of the rails have several scenic overnight trips to choose from (it's light until midnight for much of the early summer at Oslo's latitude). If you have a train pass, use the station's service center (across from the ticket windows) and avoid the long lines.

Eating in Oslo

My strategy is to splurge for a hotel that includes breakfast. A 50-kr Norwegian breakfast is fit for a Viking. Have a picnic for lunch or dinner, using one of the many grocery stores. Basements of big department stores have huge first-class supermarkets with lots of picnic dinner–quality alternatives to sandwiches. The little yogurt tubs with cereal come with collapsible spoons. The train station has a late-hours grocery.

Oslo is awash with clever little budget eateries (modern, ethnic, fast food, pizza, department-store cafeterias). Here are several places for those who want to eat like my Norwegian grandparents:

Kaffistova is an alcohol-free cafeteria serving simple, hearty, and typically Norwegian (read "bland") meals for the best price around. You'll get your choice of an entrée (meatballs) and all the salad, cooked vegetables, and "flat bread" you want (or, at least, need) for around 80 kr (Mon–Fri 12:00–20:30, until 17:00 Sat and 18:00 Sun in summer, closes earlier off-season, Rosenkrantzgate 8).

Norrøna Cafeteria is another traditional budget saver (75-kr *dagens rett*, before 14:00 you'll get the same thing for 65 kr with a cup of coffee tossed in; Mon–Fri until 18:00, later off-season; central at Grensen 19).

Stortorvets Gjæstgiveri offers good Norwegian food. Entrées in the café start at 60 to 90 kr (Grensen 1). For a classier traditional meal with a grand view, consider the **Frognerseteren** restaurant (described above with the ski jump).

Vegeta Vertshus, which has been keeping Oslo vegetarians fat, happy, and low on the food chain for 60 years, serves a huge selection of hearty vegetarian food that would satisfy even a hungry Viking. Fill your plate once (small plate-80 kr, large plate-90 kr) or eternally for 125 kr. How's your balance? One plate did me fine (daily 11:00–23:00, no smoking, no meat, Munkedamsveien 3B, near top of Stortingsgata between palace and city hall, tel. 22 83 42 32).

Lofotstua has a drab interior but cooks up tasty traditional fish dishes (entrées 150–190 kr, Mon–Fri 13:00–22:00, on Kirkeveien between Majorstuen T-bane stop and Frogner Park; exit subway, turn right, and walk 2 blocks on Kirkeveien).

The **Aker Brygge** (harborfront mall) development isn't cheap, but it has some cheery cafés, classy delis, open-till-22:00 restaurants, and markets.

For a grand and traditional breakfast, consider the elegant spread at the **Bristol Hotel** (105 kr, dinner specials 14:00–19:00 for 125 kr, a block off Karl Johans Gate behind the Grand Hotel).

Transportation Connections—Oslo

For train info, call 81 50 08 88 (7:00–23:00, phone tree, press 1 and wait) or use their Web site: www.nsb.no.

By train to Bergen: Oslo and Bergen are linked by a spectacularly scenic seven-hour train ride. Reservations (20 kr) are required on all long and IC (express) trains. Departures are roughly at 7:40, 10:45, 14:55, 16:10, and 23:00 daily in both directions (530 kr; 335 kr if you buy 5 days in advance and don't travel at peak times like Fri or Sun). For more info, see "The Oslo–Bergen Train" section in the Norway in a Nutshell chapter.

By boat to Copenhagen: Consider the cheap quickie cruise that leaves daily from Copenhagen (departs 17:00, returns 9:15 two days later; 16 hrs sailing each way and 7 hrs in Norway's capital). For specifics, see "Transportation Connections" in the Copenhagen chapter.

NORWAY IN
A NUTSHELL

While Oslo and Bergen are the big touristic draws, Norway is essentially a land of natural beauty. There is a certain mystique about the "land of the midnight sun," but you'll get the most scenic travel thrills per mile, minute, and dollar by going west rather than north.

Norway's greatest claims to scenic fame are her deep, lush fjords. A series of well-organized and spectacular bus, train, and ferry connections, appropriately called "Norway in a Nutshell," lays Norway's beautiful fjord country spread-eagled on a scenic platter. You can do it as a day trip from Oslo (or from Bergen) or en route between Oslo and Bergen.

You'll see the seductive Sognefjord, with tiny but tough ferries, towering canyons, and isolated farms and villages marinated in the mist of countless waterfalls. You're an eager Lilliputian on the Norwegian Gulliver of nature.

Today the region enjoys mild weather for its latitude, thanks to the warm Gulf Stream. But 3 million years ago, an Ice Age made this land as inhabitable as the center of Greenland. Like the hairline on Dick Clark, the ice slowly receded. As the last glaciers of the Ice Age cut their way to the sea, they gouged out long grooves—today's fjords. Since the ice was thicker inland and only a relatively thin lip at the coast, the gouging was deeper inland. The average fjord is 4,000 feet deep far inland and only around 600 feet deep where it reaches the open sea.

The entire west coast is slashed by stunning fjords, but the Sognefjord, Norway's longest (120 miles) and deepest (over a mile), is tops. Anything but Sognefjord is, at best, foreplay. This is it, the ultimate natural thrill Norway has to offer.

Aurland, a good home base for your exploration, is on

Norway in a Nutshell

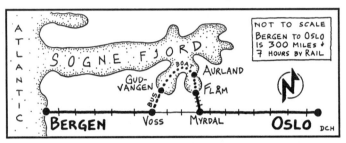

Aurlandsfjord, a remote, scenic, and accessible arm of the
Sognefjord. The local weather is actually decent, with about
24 inches of rain per year, compared to more than six feet annually in nearby Bergen.

Planning Your Time
Even the blitz tourist needs a day for the "Norway in a Nutshell"
trip. This is easily done as a long day trip from Oslo or Bergen.
(All connections are designed for tourists, explained in English,
convenient, and easy—see below.) Ideally, break the trip with an
overnight in Flåm or Aurland, carry on into Bergen, and enjoy a
day in Bergen before sleeping on the night train (past all the
scenery you saw westbound) back to Oslo. Those with a car and
only one day should take the train from Oslo. With more time,
drivers can improve on the "Nutshell" by following the more
time-consuming and thorough version of this scenic *smørgåsbord*
explained in the next chapter.

Norway in a Nutshell
The most exciting single-day trip you could make from Oslo or
Bergen is this circular train/boat/bus/train jaunt through this spectacular chunk of fjord country. Rushed travelers zip in and out by
train from Oslo or Bergen. Those with more time do the Nutshell
segments at their leisure. It's famous, everybody does it, and if
you're looking for the scenic grandeur of Norway, so should you.
    Tourist offices have souvenir-worthy brochures with photos,
descriptions, and exact times. The all-day trip starts by train every
morning from Oslo and Bergen. It's a good day trip or an exciting
way to connect the two cities. Here's the route in a nutshell: Ride
the Oslo–Bergen train to Myrdal (MIUR-doll); take the scenic
Myrdal–Flåm train; hop on the Flåm–Gudvangen cruise; and then
take the Gudvangen–Voss bus. (It's easy. Just follow the crowds.) At
Voss, jump on the Oslo–Bergen train, and head west for Bergen or

east for Oslo. The Nutshell trip is possible all year. Some say it's most beautiful in winter (but not possible as a day trip from Oslo).

Sample "Norway in a Nutshell" Schedules

Confirm all times. Nutshell connections are made even if trains, boats, or buses are running late.

Oslo–Bergen: Train departs Oslo 7:42, arrives Myrdal 12:25, departs Myrdal 12:30, arrives Flåm 13:30, boat from Flåm 14:40, arrives Gudvangen 16:45, bus from Gudvangen 17:15, arrives Voss 18:30, train from Voss 19:00, arrives Bergen 20:18.

Day Trip from Oslo: Same as above through the arrival in Flåm, boat from Flåm 14:00, arrives Gudvangen 15:15, bus from Gudvangen 15:20, arrives Voss 16:40, train from Voss 16:48, arrives Oslo 22:21.

Bergen–Oslo: Train departs Bergen 8:30, arrives Voss 9:43, bus from Voss 10:00, arrives Gudvangen 11:25, boat from Gudvangen 11:30, arrives Flåm 13:40, train from Flåm 16:20, arrives Myrdal 17:20, train from Myrdal 17:33, arrives Oslo 22:21.

Day Trip from Bergen: Same as above through Flåm, train from Flåm 15:00, arrives Myrdal 16:00, departs Myrdal 16:23, arrives Bergen 18:33. There is also a fast boat from Flåm-to-Bergen return option. Tickets and info: Bergen tel. 55 96 69 00 or 81 50 08 88.

Sights—Norway in a Nutshell

▲▲**The Oslo–Bergen Train**—This is simply the most spectacular train ride in northern Europe. The scenery crescendos as you climb over Norway's mountainous spine. After a mild three hours of deep woods and lakes you're into the barren, windswept heaths and glaciers. The line was started in 1894 to link Stockholm and Bergen. But Norway won its independence from Sweden in 1905 so the line served to link the two main cities in the new country.

The railway, an amazing engineering feat completed in 1909, is 300 miles long, peaks at 4,266 feet (which at this Alaskan latitude is far above the tree line), goes under 18 miles of snow sheds, trundles over 300 bridges, and passes through 200 tunnels in just under seven hours. (About 530 kr, second class one-way; about 200-kr cheaper if you buy five days in advance and don't travel on Fri or Sun; reservations required.) Nutshell travelers get off the Oslo–Bergen train at Myrdal and rejoin it later at Voss.

Leaving Oslo you pass through a six-mile-long tunnel and stop in Drammen, Norway's fifth-largest town. The scenery stays mild and woodsy up Hallingdal Valley until you reach Geilo, a popular ski resort. Then you enter a land of big views and tough little cabins. Finse, at about 4,000 feet, is the highest point on the line. From here you enter the longest high-mountain stretch of railway in Europe. Much of the line is protected by snow tunnels.

Detail of Nutshell Route

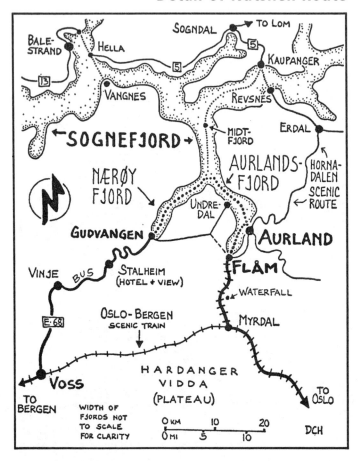

The scenery is most dramatic the hour before and after Myrdal. Just before Myrdal, look to the right and down into Flåm Valley (Flåmsdalen) where the 12-mile-long branch line winds its way down to the fjord.

▲▲**Myrdal–Flåm Train**—This little 12-mile spur line leaves the Oslo–Bergen line at Myrdal (2,800 feet, nothing but a scenic train junction with a decent cafeteria). From Myrdal, the train winds down to Flåm (sea level) in 50 thrilling minutes (110-kr ticket or 50-kr supplement for Eurail and Scanrail pass-holders). It's party time on board, and the engineer even stops the train for photos at the best waterfall. This line has 20 tunnels (more than three miles' worth) and is so steep that the train has five separate braking systems (www.flaamsbana.no).

▲**Flåm**—On the "Norway in a Nutshell" route, this scenic, touristy transit junction at the head of the Aurlandsfjord is little more than a train station, ferry landing, grocery store, souvenir shop (overpriced reindeer pelts—cheaper in Bergen), cluster of hotels and hostels, and a helpful TI (daily Jun–Sept 8:30–15:30, 16:30–20:30, shorter hours off-season, tel. 57 63 21 06). For accommodations, see "Sleeping," below, or, better yet, stay in nearby Aurland (see below). Nightlife in Flåm is sparse. A walk on the sandy beach is fine at twilight, if it's not too windy. Pubs include the more touristy and older Furnkroa at the ferry dock and Heimly Marina's pub, which serves pizza and beer and caters to a younger crowd.

▲▲▲**Flåm–Gudvangen Fjord Cruise**—At Flåm, if you're doing the nonstop Nutshell Suite, follow the crowds and hop on the sightseeing boat. Boats leave Flåm daily at 9:00, 11:05, 14:00, and 14:40, stop at the town of Aurland, then continue to Gudvangen (135 kr one-way, 68 kr for those with an ISIC card, 170 kr round-trip, no railpass discounts; couples ask for "family" discount that lets spouse go for half price). The boat takes you right into the mist of the many fjord waterfalls and close to the goats, sheep, and awesome cliffs.

You'll cruise up the lovely Aurlandsfjord and hang a left at the stunning Nærøyfjord. It's a breathtaking voyage no matter what the weather does. For 90 glorious minutes, camera-clicking tourists scurry around the drool-stained deck like nervous roosters, scratching fitfully for a photo to catch the magic. Waterfalls turn the black rock cliffs into bridal veils, and you can nearly reach out and touch the Nærøyfjord's awesome sheer cliffs. The ride is the ultimate fjord experience. It's one of those fine times, like when you're high on the tip of an Alp and a warm camaraderie spontaneously combusts between all the strangers who came together for the experience.

You can request a stopover in Undredal (see below) or Styvi (which has a farm museum, 20 kr). There's an idyllic six-kilometer shoreline along the 17th-century postal road from Styvi to Bleikindli (ask if the boat stops there, but you'll likely have to walk back to Styvi for a ferry pickup to Gudvangen). If you do get off the boat, you can let the next boat know that you'd like to be picked up by turning on a signal light.

Gudvangen–Voss Bus—Gudvangen is little more than a boat dock and giant tourist kiosk. Norway Nutshellers get off the boat at Gudvangen and catch a bus (60 kr, about a 1-hr ride, 12/day including each ferry landing) up the Nærøydalen (Narrow Valley) to Voss. Try to catch a bus taking the extra-scenic route via Stalheim. At the end of Nærøydalen the bus climbs a corkscrew series of switchbacks before stopping at the Stalheim Hotel for a last grand view back into fjord country.

Voss—A plain town in a lovely lake-and-mountain setting, Voss does have an interesting folk museum (daily Jun–Aug 10:00–19:00, closes earlier off-season), a 13th-century church, and a few other historic sights, but it's basically a home base for summer or winter sports. At Voss, the bus drops you at the train station (on the Oslo–Bergen train line). Drivers should zip right through. You can spend the night, but I wouldn't. **Kringsjå Pensjonat** is nice with a lake view (D-560 kr, Db-700 kr, larger rooms available, includes breakfast, tel. 56 51 16 27), and the **Voss Youth Hostel** is luxurious (tel. 56 51 20 17). **Voss Camping**, on the lake, has huts, bikes, and rowboats (tel. 56 51 15 97). TI tel. 56 52 08 00.

More Fjord Sights

▲▲**Flåm Valley Bike Ride**—While the Myrdal–Flåm train is scenic, the ride doesn't do the view justice. For the best single-day's activity from Flåm, take the train to Myrdal then hike or mountain bike the gravelly construction road back down to Flåm (four hrs, great mountain scenery but no fjord views). Bring a picnic and extra film. The Flåm TI rents bikes (25 kr/hr, 125 kr/day for mountain bikes; costs 55 kr to take bike up to Myrdal on train). You could just hike the best two hours from Myrdal to Berekvam, where you can catch the train into the valley.

▲▲**Aurland**—A few miles north of Flåm, Aurland is more of a town and less of a tourist depot. Nothing exciting, but it's a good, easygoing fjordside home base (see "Sleeping," below). You can hike up the valley or tour the electrical works (public tours show visitors the source of most of Oslo's electricity Jul–mid-Aug Mon–Fri at 11:00 and 13:00). The harborside public library is a pleasant refuge and the 800-year-old church is worth a look.

The local *geitost* (goat's cheese) is sweet and delicious. Aurland has as many goats as people (1,900). The one who runs the tourist office speaks English (mid-Jun–Aug Mon–Fri 8:30–19:00, Sat–Sun 10:00–17:00, shorter hours off-season, tel. 57 63 33 13, fax 57 63 11 48). Pick up the English-language *Bergen Guide*.

Note: Every train (except for the late-night one) arriving in Flåm connects with a bus or boat to Aurland. Fifteen buses and at least four ferries link the towns daily. The Flåm–Gudvangen boat stops at Aurland en route, so it's easy to continue the Nutshell route from Aurland without backtracking to Flåm.

▲**Undredal**—This almost impossibly remote community of 52 families was accessible only by boat until 1985, when the road from Flåm was opened. Undredal has Norway's smallest still-used church (built in the 12th century, holds up to 40 people). The 15-minute drive from Flåm is mostly through a new tunnel. There's not much in the town, which is famous for its goat cheese and church, but I'll never forget the picnic I had on the ferry wharf. If you want the ferry to stop, turn on the blinking light (though some express boats will not stop). You'll sail by Undredal on the Flåm–Gudvangen boat. Undredal Brygge (the harborfront cafeteria) rents four modern, woody rooms (comfortable but on a back street with little character, Db-640 kr, Tb-840 kr, includes breakfast, N-5746 Undredal, tel. & fax 57 63 17 45, e-mail: postmaster@undredalbrygge.no).

▲▲**Sognefjord Scenic Express Boat**—Boats speed between Flåm and Bergen through the Sognefjord. Boats depart Bergen at 8:00 and arrive in Flåm at 13:25; depart Flåm at 15:30 and arrive in Bergen at 20:40 (Sognefjord Express Boat-435 kr one way, 545 kr round-trip, special price not valid on Fri afternoon or Sun, 595 kr round-trip if you return by train, discounted with ISIC card, daily Jun–Aug; all stop in Aurland, tel. 55 90 70 70).

Sleeping on Sognefjord
(7 kr = about $1)
Sleep Code: **S** = Single, **D** = Double/Twin, **T** = Triple, **Q** = Quad, **b** = bathroom, **CC** = Credit Card (Visa, MasterCard, Amex).

Sleeping in Flåm
Heimly Lodge is doing its best to go big time in a small-time town. It's clean, efficient, and the best normal hotel in town (25 rooms in hotel, 7 in annex, S-450 kr, Sb-590 kr, D-650 kr, Db-850 kr, includes breakfast, CC:VMA, bike rental, N-5743 Flåm, tel. 57 63 23 00, fax 57 63 23 40). Their pricing is soft and complex. You can save by sleeping in their annex, providing your own sheets, and skipping breakfast. Their cheap basic deal for a room in the hotel (if available) or the annex is: D-250 kr (if you bring your own sleeping bag); add 50 kr per person for sheets and 75 kr per person for breakfast. Sit on the porch with new friends and watch the clouds roll down the fjord. Located along the harbor 400 yards from the station, they will pick up and drop off at the station/dock for 10 kr round-trip.

Flåm Youth Hostel and Camping Bungalows, recently voted Scandinavia's most beautiful campground, has the cheapest beds in the area. On the river just behind the Flåm train station, the Holand family offers dorm beds in four-bed hostel rooms (95 kr per bed with kitchenette, 40 kr for sheets, 25 kr extra if not a hostel member). They also have some doubles for 350 kr with bedding, four-bed cabins for 380 kr without sheets, and a deluxe cabin for 600 kr (tel. 57 63 21 21, fax 57 63 23 80). Note that the season is boom or bust here, and it can be crowded in July and August.

Sleeping and Eating in Aurland
The **Aabelheim Pension/Vangen Motel** complex, dominating the old center of Aurland, is run from one reception desk (CC:V,

tel. 57 63 35 80, fax 57 63 35 95, e-mail: vangsgas@online.no, Astrid). **Aabelheim Pension** is far and away Aurland's best cozy-like-a-farmhouse place. "Cozy" is *koselig*, a good Norwegian word (six D-375 kr, 70-kr breakfasts are served in a wonderfully traditional dining room, fine old-time living room, open mid-Jun–early Sept). **Vangen Motel**, nestled between Aabelheim and the fjord, is a simple old hotel offering basic rooms, a big self-serve kitchen, and a dining and living area (Ds-450 kr, 350 kr if you BYO sheets, breakfast-70 kr, open all year). The motel has four-bed cabins right on the water for 350 kr without sheets. Deluxe rooms are also available (Db-650 kr, Tb-750 kr).

Aurland Fjord Hotel is big, modern, friendly, and centrally located, with more comfort (sauna, steam bath, TV) and less traditional coziness (30 rooms, Db-990 kr with breakfast, attached restaurant, CC:VMA, tel. 57 63 35 05, fax 57 63 36 22).

At the farmhouse **Skahjem Gård**, Aurland's deputy mayor, Nils Tore, rents out family apartments (a 300-kr hut, 5 newer 500- to 600-kr huts, private bath and kitchenettes, 50-kr extra per person for sheets and towels, 2.5 km up the Oslo road from Aurland, tel. 57 63 33 29, e-mail: nskahjem@online.no). It's a 20-minute walk from town, but Nils will pick up and drop off travelers at the ferry. This is best for families who are driving.

Lunde Camping offers 14 cabins overlooking the river a mile out of Aurland (at the Aurland exit off the big road). Each cabin has four beds in two bunks, a kitchenette, and a river view (350 kr for up to 4 people in summer, 300 kr the rest of the year, 40 kr extra per person for sheets, deluxe cabins for up to 4 people-600 kr, open Apr–Oct, generally full Jun 20–Aug 20, tel. 57 63 34 12, fax 57 63 31 65, Jens Lunde).

Eating in Aurland: The Vangen Motel runs the **Duehuset pub** (long hours, 70–180-kr dinners). For cheap eats on dockside picnic benches, gather a picnic at the late-hours grocery store next to the Vangen Motel (9:00–22:00).

VALLEYS, MOUNTAINS, AND FJORDS

"Norway in a Nutshell" is a great day trip, but with more time and a car, consider meandering from Oslo across the center of the country along a powerfully scenic arc up the tradition-steeped Gudbrandsdalen Valley, over the myth-inspiring Jotunheimen Mountains, and down Norway's greatest troll-thrilling fjord, Sognefjord.

Gudbrandsdalen Valley is the country of Peer Gynt, the Norwegian Huck Finn. This romantic valley of timeworn hills, log cabins, and velvet farms has connected northern and southern Norway since ancient times.

Lillehammer, with Norway's best folk museum, provides an excellent introduction. You might spend the night in a log-and-sod farmstead-turned-hotel, tucked in a quiet valley under Norway's highest peaks.

Next, Norway's highest mountain pass takes you on an exhilarating roller-coaster ride through the heart of Jotunheimen (the "giant's home"), which bristles with Norway's biggest mountains.

The road then hairpins down into fjord country, a softer world of fjords full of medieval stave churches, fishing boats, and brightly painted shiplap villages.

Planning Your Time

While you could enjoyably spend five or six days in this area, on a three-week Scandinavian rampage, this slice of the region is worth three days. By car, I'd spend them like this:

Day 1: Leave Oslo early, spend midday at the Maihaugen Open-Air Folk Museum for a tour and picnic. Drive up Gudbrandsdalen Valley, making a short stop at the Lom church. Evening in Jotunheimen country.

Valleys, Mountains, and Fjords

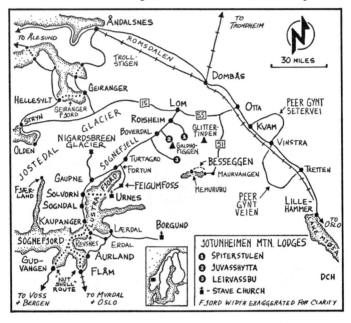

Day 2: Drive out of the mountains, along Lustrafjord, over Hornadalen Pass, and into Aurlandsfjord. Sleep in Aurland.

Day 3: Cruise the Aurland and Nærøy fjords (round-trip) before carrying on to Bergen. (For specifics on Aurland accommodations and fjord cruise, see Norway in a Nutshell chapter.)

Gudbrandsdalen Valley

▲**Lillehammer**—This pleasant winter and summer resort town of 23,000 was the smallest town ever to host the winter Olympics (1994). At Håkon Hall, the 1994 ice hockey arena, you can try a bobsled simulator, visit a museum showcasing Olympics history, and see the "world-famous egg" from the Lillehammer opening ceremonies (50 kr, Mon–Fri 10:00–18:00, less on weekends and off-season, 15-min walk from the station towards Maihaugen, tel. 61 25 21 00). Lillehammer has a happy, old wooden pedestrian zone and several interesting museums, including a popular transportation museum and the Maihaugen Open-Air Folk Museum (see below). Lillehammer's TI is right in the colorful pedestrian shopping zone (Mon–Sat 9:00–19:00, less on Sun and off-season, tel. 61 25 92 99). For accommodations, see "Sleeping," below.

▲▲▲**Maihaugen Open-Air Folk Museum**—Located in Lillehammer, this wonderfully laid out look at the local culture provides an excellent introduction to the Gudbrandsdalen Valley.
Anders Sandvig, a "visionary dentist," started the collection in
1887. The outdoor section has 150 old buildings from the Gudbrandsdalen region, with plenty of free English tours, crafts in
action, and even people living there from ages ago (Williamsburg
style, Jul only).

Indoors, the "We won the land" exhibit gives a look at local
life during the Ice Age, the Vikings, the plague, the Industrial
Revolution, etc. The indoor museum also has the original shops
of 40 crafts- and tradespeople (such as a hatter, cooper, book-
binder, and Dr. Sandvig's old dental office). There's a thorough
English guidebook (50 kr), English descriptions at each house, and
free 45-minute guided tours daily in English (11:00, 13:00, 15:00,
and sometimes 17:00 or on request if you call in advance).

The museum welcomes picnickers and has a café and an outdoor cafeteria (70 kr, daily Jun–mid-Aug 9:00–18:00, shoulder
season 10:00–17:00, in winter the park is open but the houses are
closed, tel. 61 28 89 00; call to be sure you arrive for a tour, especially off-season). Ask on arrival about special events, crafts, or
music, and don't miss the indoor museum. Maihaugen is a steep 30-
minute walk or short bus ride from the Lillehammer train station.

▲**Eidsvoll Manor**—During the Napoleonic period, Denmark was
about to give Norway to Sweden. This ruffled the patriotic feathers
of Norway's Thomas Jeffersons and Ben Franklins, and in 1814
Norway's constitution was written and signed in this stately mansion
(in the town of Eidsvoll Verk, north of Oslo). It's full of elegant furnishings and stirring history (30 kr, daily mid-Jun–mid-Aug 10:00–
17:00, less off-season, tel. 63 95 13 04).

Scenic Drives—Two side trips give visitors a good dose of the
wild beauty of this land. Peer Gyntveien is a 30-kr toll road that
leaves E-6 at Tretten, looping west for 25 miles and rejoining E-6
at Vinstra. This trip sounds romantic, but it's basically a windy,
curvy dirt road over a high desolate heath and scrub-brush plateau
with fine mountain views: scenic, but so is E-6. The second scenic
side trip, which is lesser known but more rewarding, is the Peer
Gynt Seterveg.

▲**Lom**—This isn't much of a town, but it does have a great stave
church, which causes the closest thing to a tour-bus jam this neck
of the Norwegian woods will ever see. Drop by the church; you'll
see its dark spire just over the bridge (25 kr, daily mid-Jun–mid-
Aug 9:00–21:00, shorter hours off-season and during funerals,
fine 5-kr leaflet, check out little footbridge over waterfall). Take
advantage of the TI (in summer, Mon–Fri 9:00–21:00, Sat–Sun
10:00–20:00; shorter hours off-season, tel. 61 21 29 90). I wouldn't
sleep in Lom, but if you would, see "Sleeping," below.

Sleeping in Gudbrandsdalen Valley
(7 kr = about $1)
Sleep Code: **S** = Single, **D** = Double/Twin, **T** = Triple, **Q** = Quad,
b = bathroom, **CC** = Credit Card (Visa, MasterCard, Amex).
Gudbrandsdalen Valley is a very popular vacation valley for
Norwegians, and you'll find loads of reasonable small hotels and
campgrounds with huts (*hytter* means "bungalow," *rom* is "private
room," and *ledig* means "vacancy") for those who aren't quite
campers. These huts normally cost around 200 kr and can hold
from four to six people. Although they are simple, you'll have a
kitchenette and access to a good WC and shower. When available,
sheets rent for an extra 40 kr per person. Local TIs can find you
rooms. Only in the middle three weeks of July will finding a bed
without a reservation prove difficult.

Sleeping in Lillehammer
Gjestehuset Ersgaard is the town's best budget hotel, with a great
view of the valley (13 rooms, D-490 kr, Db-590–650 kr, includes
breakfast, CC:VMA, 2 km east and above town at Nordseterveien
201, tel. 61 25 06 84, fax 61 25 31 09, e-mail: oeilande@online.no).
Sommerstuene rents three rooms with kitchenettes (300–500 kr,
sheets-25 kr, family rooms, Kirkegata 6, 2600 Lillehammer, tel. &
fax 61 25 79 29, e-mail: somstue@interact.no). For cheap beds, try
the **GjesteBu** private hostel (8-bed dorms, bed-80 kr, D-300 kr and
up, sheets-40 kr, Gamleveien 110, 3 blocks from TI, reserve in
advance, tel. & fax 61 25 43 21) or the **IYHF hostel** in the train/
bus station (bed in quad-165 kr for members, sheets extra).

Sleeping in Kvam
Kirketeigen Ungdomssenter ("Church Youth Center") welcomes
travelers year-round. They have camping spots (80 kr per tent or
van), huts (220 kr per 4-person hut), and simple four-bed rooms
(220 kr for 2–4 people with sheets, CC:V). They rent sheets and
blankets for 60 kr (2650 Kvam i Gudbrandsdalen, behind town
church, call in advance, tel. 61 29 40 82, fax 61 29 40 67). **Sinclair
Vertshuset Motel**, 100 meters away, has an inexpensive pizzeria
(Db-690 kr with breakfast but no personality, cheaper off-season,
tel. 61 29 40 24, fax 61 29 45 55). The motel was named after a
Scotsman who led a band of adventurers into this valley, attempting
to set up their own Scottish kingdom. They failed. (All were kilt.)

Sleeping in Lom
About 10 miles north of Røisheim, Lom has plenty of accommodations, such as the rustic **Strind Gård**. This 150-year-old farmhouse offers rooms in sod-roofed huts and in the main house
(D-150–200 kr, T-230 kr, Quint-300 kr, great valley views, 3 km
outside Lom on Route 55 towards Sogndal, tel. 61 21 12 37).

JOTUNHEIMEN MOUNTAINS

▲▲**Sognefjell**—Norway's highest mountain crossing (4,600 feet) is a thrilling drive through a cancan line of northern Europe's highest mountains. In previous centuries, the farmers of Gudbrandsdalen took their horse caravans over this difficult mountain pass on their necessary treks to Bergen. Today the road (Route 55) is still narrow, windy, and otherworldly (and usually closed mid-Oct–May). The 10 hairpin turns between Turtagrø and Fortun are white-knuckle exciting. Be sure to stop, get out, look around, and enjoy the lavish views. Treat each turn as if it were your last.

Scenic Drives and Hikes—From the main road near Bøverdal and Røisheim, you have several options springing from three toll roads. The Bøverdal hostel has good information and a fine 1:150,000 hiking map.

Spiterstulen: From Røisheim, this 18-km toll road (60 kr) takes you to the Spiterstulen mountain hotel/lodge (1,100 meters). This is the best destination for serious all-day hikes to Norway's two mightiest mountains, Glittertinden (2,470 meters) and Galdhopiggen (a 4-hr hike up and a 3-hr hike down, doable without a guide).

Juvasshytta: This toll road, starting from Bøverdal, takes you the highest you can drive and the closest you can get to Galdhopiggen by car (1,840 meters). At the end of the 50-kr toll road there are daily guided six-hour hikes across the glacier to the summit and back (60 kr, 10:00 and 11:30 in the summer, 6 km each way, hiking shoes a good idea, easiest ascent but very dangerous without a guide). You can sleep in the Juvasshytta lodge (D-525, Ds-480 kr, D without sheets-350 kr, 145 kr beds in quads, sheets-35 kr, breakfast-75 kr, dinner-145 kr, tel. 61 21 15 50).

Leirvassbu: This 18-km, 30-kr toll road is most scenic for "car hikers." It takes you to a lodge (owned by the Elvesæter Hotel people; see "Sleeping," below) at 1,400 meters with great views and easy walks. A serious (4-hr round-trip) hike goes to the lone peak, Kyrkja (2,030 meters).

Besseggen: This ridge offers an incredible opportunity to hike between two lakes separated by five feet of land and a 1,000-foot cliff. To get to the trailhead, drivers detour down road #51 after Otta south to Maurvangen. Turn right to Gjendesheim to park your car. From Gjendesheim, catch the boat to Memurubu. The path starts at the boat dock. Hike along the ridge with a blue lake on one side and a green lake on the other, and keep your balance. The six-hour trail leads back to Gjendesheim. (This is a thrilling but potentially dangerous hike, and it's a major detour: Gjendesheim is about an hour, or 55 miles, from Røisheim.)

▲▲**Jostedalsbre's Nigardsbreen Glacier Hike**—Jostedalsbre is the most accessible branch of mainland Europe's largest glacier (185 square miles), and the Nigardsbreen Glacier Hike offers a good opportunity for a hands-on glacier experience. It's an easy drive up Jostedal from Lustrafjord.

From Gaupne, drive up road #604 for 23 miles just past Gjerde, where the private 20-kr toll road continues two miles to the lake. Before the toll road (and 2.5 km past Gjerde), look for Breheimsenteret, an information center on the glacier and its history, at the entrance to the Nigard Glacier valley (daily in summer 9:00–19:00, May–mid-Jun and mid-Aug–Sept 10:00–17:00, tel. 57 68 32 50). From here take the special boat (20 kr roundtrip, 2/hrly, 15 min, mid-Jun–mid-Aug 10:00–18:00) to a spot just 20 minutes from the glacier.

The walk is steep and slippery. Follow the red marks. There are 90-minute guided "family" walks of the glacier (90 kr, 40 kr for kids, daily departures 12:00–14:30 depending on demand, minimum age 5, I'd rate them PG-13 myself, you get clamp-on crampons). Tougher glacier hikes are also offered (starting at 210 kr including boots, real crampons, and more, daily 10:30 and 13:00, 4 hours, but you'll need to be at the Glacier Center nearly 2 hours early to buy tickets and pick up your gear, book by telephone the day before). For information on the glacier, check the Web site: www.jostedal.com.

Respect the glacier. It's a powerful river of ice, and fatal accidents are not uncommon. The guided walk is the safest, and exciting enough. Use the Gaupne TI to confirm your plans (tel. 57 68 15 88). If this is your first glacier, it's worth the time and hike even without the tour. If glaciers don't give you tingles and you're feeling pressed, it's not worth the long drive.

Sleeping in Jotunheimen
(7 kr = about $1)
Røisheim and Elvesæter are just hotel road stops in the wild. Bøverdal, two miles up the road, is a tiny village with a hostel.

Røisheim, in a marvelously remote mountain setting, is a storybook hotel comprised of a cluster of centuries-old, sod-roofed log farmhouses. Filled with antiques, Norwegian travelers, and the hard work of its owners, Røisheim is a cultural end in itself. Each room is rustic but elegant (Db-1,250 kr with breakfast, CC:VM, Lars and Christina Aanes). Some rooms are in old log huts with low ceilings and heavy beams. A full three-course traditional dinner (one that Norway's royalty travels far to eat) is served at 19:00 (375 kr). Call ahead so they'll be prepared. (Open mid-May–Sept, 6 miles south of Lom on the Sognefjell Road 55 in Bøverdalen, tel. 61 21 20 31, fax 61 21 21 51, e-mail: r-dref-a @online.no.)

Elvesæter Hotel is as Old World romantic as Røisheim but cheaper and less impressed with itself (Sb-500 kr, Db-680 kr with breakfast, wonderful 190-kr buffet dinners, open Jun–Sept,

CC:VMA, a few minutes farther up Road 55, just past Bøverdal, tel. 61 21 20 00, fax 61 21 21 01, e-mail: pllien@online.no). They also offer apartments with kitchens and all bedding (3–6 people, 700–900 kr without breakfast). The Elvesæter family has done a great job of retaining the historic character of their medieval farm, even though the place is big enough to handle large tour groups. They have the dubious distinction of being, as far as I know, the only hotel in Europe that charges for its advertising flier (5 kr). It's scenic—but not that scenic.

Bøverdalen Youth Hostel, just a couple of miles from Røisheim, is in another galaxy price-wise (90 kr per bed in 4- to 6-bed rooms, D-230 kr, the usual extra for sheets and non-members, hot and self-serve meals, open late May–Sept, tel. & fax 61 21 20 64). It's in the center of a little community (store, campground, and toll road up to Galdhopiggen area). The hostel is a comfortable budget value. An added advantage is that you'll be encountering real hikers rather than car tourists.

LUSTRAFJORD

This arm of the famous Sognefjord is rugged country. Only 2 percent of this land is fit to build or farm on. Lustrafjord is ringed with tiny villages where farmers sell cherries and giant raspberries. Urnes, perched on the east bank of Lustrafjord, has an ancient stave church and a less ancient ferry dock (ferries connect with sleepy Solvorn on the west bank, car crossings at the bottom of each hour 10:00–17:50, pedestrian ferries more often, 10-min ride, 30 kr round-trip).

▲▲**Urnes Stave Church**—A steep but pleasant 20-minute walk takes you from the town of Urnes to Norway's oldest stave church (1150), the most important artistic and historic sight in the region (40 kr, daily early Jun–late Aug 10:30–17:30, ask for an English tour).

Solvorn—Ten miles east of Sogndal, on the west bank of the Lustrafjord, Solvorn is a sleepy little Victorian town. Its tiny fjerry crosses the fjord regularly to Urnes (10-min ride, 40 kr round-trip). For accommodations, see "Sleeping," below.

Sogndal—About a 10-minute drive from the Mannheller ferry, Sogndal is the only sizable town in this region. It's big enough to have a busy shopping street and a helpful TI (tel. 57 67 30 83). See "Sleeping," below.

Honorable Mention—As you drive along Lustrafjord, check out these towns and sights: Skjolden, a village at the north tip of Lustrafjord, has a good TI (tel. 57 68 67 50) with advice on fjord ferries and glacier hikes, and a cozy youth hostel on the river (90 kr per bed, D-230 kr, open mid-May–mid-Sept, tel. 57 68 66 15). From the little town of Nes on the west bank of the Lustrafjord, look across the fjord at the impressive Feigumfoss

Waterfall. Drops and dribbles come from miles around for this 200-yard tumble. Viki Fjord Camping, located directly across from Feigumfoss Waterfall, has great fjordside huts (tel. 57 68 64 20). Dale, a village on the west bank, boasts a 13th-century stone Gothic church with 14th-century frescoes. It's unique and worth a peek.

Kaupanger–Gudvangen by Car Ferry—Ferries take tourists through an arm and elbow of the Sognefjord. Marvel at the staggering Nærøyfjord. Boats leave Kaupanger daily at 9:20, 12:05, 16:00, and 18:50 (2-hr trip, ferry info tel. 57 75 70 00 or 94 50 65 20). Kaupanger is a ferry landing set on the scenic Sognefjord, and little more. The little stave-type church at the edge of Kaupanger merits a look.

▲▲Sogndal/Mannheller/Fodnes/Lærdal/Hornadalen/Aurland Scenic Drive—This drive takes you over an incredible mountain pass, offers classic aerial fjord views, and winds into the pleasant fjordside town of Aurland. Near Sogndal, catch the Mannheller–Fodnes ferry (2/hrly, 15 min, no reservations so arrive early in summer) and drive through the tunnel to Lærdal. While the 24-kilometer-long tunnel (world's longest) from Lærdal under Hornadalen to Aurland opens in 2000, the scenic route over the pass is worth the messy pants. Leave E-68 at Erdal (just west of Lærdal) for the breathtaking 90-minute drive to Aurland over 4,000-foot-high Hornadalen. This summer-only road passes remote mountain huts and terrifying mountain views before its 12-hairpin zigzag descent into the Aurlandsfjord. Stop at the first fjord viewpoint as you begin your descent; it's the best.

Shortcut scenically and directly from Kaupanger to Gudvangen by ferry (4/day, 185 kr for car and driver, 53 kr per adult passenger) to get a quick taste of all this fjord scenery.

Sleeping on Lustrafjord
(7 kr = about $1)

Sleeping in Solvorn
Walaker Hotel, a former inn and coach station, has been run by the Walaker family for 307 years (that's a lot of pressure on the next generation). In the main house, tradition drips like butter through the halls and living rooms. The rooms are simple but good, a warm family feeling pervades, and there are only patriotic hymns on the piano. The Walaker, set right on the Lustrafjord (in the perfect garden to get over a mental breakdown), is open mid-April to mid-October. Oda and Hermod Walaker are a wealth of information, and they help serve fine food (S-460 kr, Sb-550–880 kr, D-720 kr, Db-1,080 kr, includes breakfast, dinners are worth the 290-kr splurge, CC:VM, tel. 57 68 42 07, fax 57 68 45 44, e-mail: walaker.hotel@sf.telia.no).

Sleeping in Sogndal

For budget rooms, try the home of **Bjarne and Ella Skielde-stad** (175 kr per person, 125 kr if you bring your sleeping bag; kitchenette; on main drag at Gravensteinsgate 10, tel. 57 67 21 83), **Loftenes Pensjonat** (late Jul–late Aug, D-590 kr, Db-650 kr, includes breakfast, CC:VM, near the water, tel. 57 67 15 77), or the excellent **youth hostel** (beds in 3- and 4-bed rooms-90 kr, S-160 kr, D-210 kr, sheets and guest membership extra, breakfast-50 kr, members' kitchen—bring your own pots, at fork in the road as you enter town, closed 10:00–17:00 and mid-Aug–mid-Jun, tel. 57 67 20 33).

Transportation Connections

Cars are better, but if you're without wheels: **Oslo to Lilleham-mer** (11 trains/day, 2.5 hrs), **Lillehammer to Otta** (6 trains/day); a bus meets some trains (confirm schedule at the train station in Oslo) for travelers heading on to **Lom** (1 hr, 62 kr) and from **Lom to Sogndal** (2 buses/day).

Route Tips for Drivers

Oslo across Norway to Jotunheimen: It's 2.5 hours from Oslo to Lillehammer and four hours after that to Lom. Wind out of Oslo following signs for E-6 (not to Drammen, but for Stockholm and then to Trondheim). In a few minutes you're in the wide-open pastoral countryside of eastern Norway. Norway's Constitution Hall is a five-minute detour off E-6, a couple of miles south of Eidsvoll in Eidsvoll Verk (follow the signs to Eidsvoll Bygningen). Then E-6 takes you along Norway's largest lake (Mjøsa), through the town of Hamar, over a toll bridge (15 kr), and past more lake scenery into Lillehammer. The old E-6 stays east of the lake, is only marginally slower, and avoids the toll bridge. Signs direct you uphill from downtown Lillehammer to the Maihaugen museum. There's free parking near the pay lot (10 kr) above the entrance. Then E-6 enters the valley of Gudbrandsdalen. From Lilleham-mer, cross the bridge again and follow signs to E-6/Dombås and Trondheim. At Otta, exit for Lom.

Mountain driving tips: Use low gears and lots of patience both up (to keep it cool) and down (to save your brakes). Uphill traffic gets the right-of-way, but drivers, up or down, dive for the nearest fat part whenever they meet. Ask backseat drivers not to scream until you've actually been hit or have left the road.

Ferry travel: Car ferries and express boats connect towns along the Sognefjord and Bergen. Ferries cost roughly $4 per hour for walk-ons and $14 per hour for a car, driver, and passenger. Reservations are generally not necessary (and sometimes not possible), but in summer, especially on Friday and Sunday, I'd get one to be safe (free and easy, tel. 55 90 70 70).

From Gudvangen to Bergen (85 miles): From Gudvangen, drive up the Nærøydalen (Narrow Valley) past a river bubbling excitedly about the plunge it just took. You'll see the two giant falls just before the road marked "Stalheimskleiva." Follow the sign (exiting left) to the little Stalheimskleiva road. This incredible road doggedly worms its way up into the ozone. My car overheated in a few minutes. Take it, but take it easy. (The main road gets you there easier—through a tunnel and 1.3 km back up a smaller road.) As you wind up, you can view the falls from several turnouts. At the top, stop for a break at the friendly but very touristy Stalheim Hotel. This huge eagle's-nest hotel is a stop for just about every tour group that ever saw a fjord. Here, genuine trolls sew the pewter buttons on the sweaters, and the priceless view is free.

The road continues into a mellower beauty, past lakes and farms, toward Voss. Tvindefossen, a waterfall with a handy campground/WC/kiosk picnic area right under it, is worth a stop. Unless you judge waterfalls by megatonnage, this 150-yard-long fall has nuclear charms. The grassy meadow and flat rocks at its base were made especially for your picnic lunch.

The highway takes you through Voss and into Bergen. From Monday through Friday, 6:00 to 22:00, drivers pay a 5-kr toll to enter Bergen. (If you plan to visit Edvard Grieg's home and the nearby Fantoft stave church, now is the ideal time since you'll be driving right by. Both are overrated but almost obligatory, a headache from downtown, and open until 17:30.)

BERGEN

Bergen— Norway's capital in the 12th and 13th centuries, permanently salted with robust cobbles and a rich sea-trading heritage— has a rugged charm. Bergen's wealth and importance came thanks to its membership in the heavyweight medieval trading club of merchant cities called the Hanseatic League. Bergen still wears her rich maritime heritage proudly.

Famous for lousy weather, Bergen gets an average of 80 inches of rain annually (compared to 30 inches in Oslo). A good year has 60 days of sunshine. With 221,000 people, Bergen has its big-city tension, parking problems, and high prices. But visitors stick mainly to the old center.

Enjoy her salty market, then stroll the easy-on-foot old quarter. From downtown Bergen, a funicular zips you up a little mountain for a bird's-eye view of this sailors' town.

To celebrate the millennium, Bergen reigns as Europe's City of Culture in the year 2000. Events all year highlight the city's culture and arts (for information, contact the City of Culture Bergen 2000, Vågsallmenningen 1, P.O. Box 434, N-5001 Bergen, tel. 55 55 20 00, www.bergen2000.no).

Planning Your Time

Bergen can be enjoyed even on the tail end of a day's scenic train ride from Oslo before returning on the overnight train. But that teasing taste will make you wish you had more time. On a three-week tour of Scandinavia, Bergen is worth a whole day. Start that day at the harborfront fish market and spend the rest of the morning in the Bryggen quarter (the tour is a must).

Bergen, a geographic dead end for most travelers, is an efficient place to end your Scandinavian tour. Consider flying home from here. (Ask your travel agent about the economic feasibility of this "open jaws" option.)

Orientation

The action is on the waterfront. Virtually everything in this chapter is within a few minutes' walk of the fish market. The busy Torget (market square and fish market) is at the head of the bay. Facing the sea from here, Bergen's TI and historic "Hanseatic" quarter (Bryggen) line the harbor on the right, and boats from Flåm and Stavanger tie up at the left side of the harbor. Two blocks from the market square or Torget (behind Bryggen), a funicular stands ready to whisk you to the top of Mount Fløyen.

Tourist Information

The TI covers Bergen and west Norway, has information and tickets for tours and concerts, and maintains a daily events board. They change money at 4 percent less than the banks, but they don't charge the typical 15-kr-per-check fee for traveler's checks or cash. They're OK if you're exchanging less than $100 or if you're stuck with small checks in Norway (daily Jun–Aug 8:30–22:00, May and Sept daily 9:00–20:00, off-season Mon–Sat 9:00–16:00, closed Sun, on the harborfront, across from fish market at Vågsallmenningen 1, a 10- to 15-minute walk from the train station, tel. 55 32 14 80, www.Bergen-travl.com). From late May through late August, there's also a TI at the train station (daily 7:15–23:00). Pick up a free *Bergen Guide*, which lists all sights, hours, and special events and has a fine map. The **Bergen Card** gives you 24 hours of city buses, the Mount Fløyen funicular, and admission to many sights for 130 kr (48 hours for 200 kr). But check carefully to see if it will pay off for you, as it doesn't cover the Hanseatic Museum or Troldhaugen.

Arrival in Bergen

By Train or Bus: Bergen's train and bus stations are on Strømgaten, facing a park-rimmed lake. Walk around the lake to Ole Bulls Plass, then take a right on the wide street called Torgelmenning, which leads down to Torget (a 10- to 15-minute walk from the station), where you'll find Bergen's famous and fragrant fish market and the waterfront.

By Plane: The SAS bus runs between Bergen's Flesland Airport and downtown Bergen, stopping at the SAS hotel in Bryggen, Hotel Norge, and the bus station at platform 17 (45 kr, 40 min). Taxis take up to four people and cost about 200 kr for the 30-minute ride. SAS info tel. 81 00 33 00.

Getting around Bergen

Most sights can be seen on foot. Buses cost 17 kr per ride or 90 kr for a 48-hour Tourist Ticket (purchase as you board). The best

Bergen

● RAINBOW HOTEL BRISTOL
● HOTEL BRYGGEN ORION
● KLOSTER PENSION
● PARK PENSION
● HESKJA ROOMS
● OLSNES ROOMS
● SKANSEN PENSJONAT
● VÅGENES ROOMS

● MONTANA HOSTEL
● BRYGGESTUENE, TRACTEURSTED & ENHJØRNINGEN RESTAURANTS
● ZACHARIASBRYGGEN RESTAURANTS
● FISH MARKET
● KAFFISTOVA RESTAURANT
● SAS / HOTEL NORGE BUFFET
● HOTEL NEPTUN RESTAURANT

buses for a city joyride are #1 (along the coast) and #4 (into the hills). The *Beffen*, a little orange ferry, chugs across the harbor every half hour (15 kr, Mon–Fri). This three-minute "poor man's cruise" has great harbor views. For a taxi call 55 99 70 00.

Sights—Bergen's Hanseatic Quarter

Called "the German wharf" until WWII, and now just called "the wharf," or "Bryggen" (BREW-gun), this is Bergen's old German trading center. From 1370 to 1754 German merchants controlled Bergen's trade. In 1550 it was a German city of 2,000 workaholic merchants—walled and surrounded by 8,000 Norwegians. Bryggen, which has burned down several times, is now gentrified and boutiquish but still lots of fun. Explore. You'll find plenty of sweater shops, restaurants, planky alleys, leaning old wooden warehouses, good browsing, atmospheric eating, and two worthwhile museums within a five-minute walk of each other.

▲▲▲**Walking Tour**—Local guides take visitors on an excellent 90-minute walk through the old Hanseatic town (30 min in Bryggens Museum, 30-min walk through old quarter and Schøtstuene, and 30 min in Hanseatic Museum). This is a great way to get an understanding of Bergen's 900 years of history. Tours cost 60 kr and leave from the Bryggens Museum (next to big and modern SAS Hotel). When you consider that the tour cost includes entry tickets to the Hanseatic and Bryggens Museums and the medieval assembly rooms called the Schøtstuene (worthwhile only with a guide), the tour is virtually free (daily at 11:00 and 13:00 Jun–Aug; you can reenter museums; tel. 55 31 67 10).

▲▲**Hanseatic Museum**—This wonderful little museum is in an atmospheric old merchant house furnished with dried fish, old ropes, an old oxtail (used for wringing spilled cod-liver oil back into the bucket), sagging steps, and cupboard beds from the early 1700s, one with a medieval pinup (35 kr, daily in summer 9:00–17:00, off-season daily 11:00–14:00, good guided tours, tel. 55 31 41 89).

▲▲**Bryggens Museum**—This modern museum on the archaeological site of the earliest Bergen (1050–1500), with interesting temporary exhibits upstairs, offers little English information. To understand the exhibits you can borrow the museum guidebook, take the free 30-minute Walkman tour, or join the guided walk explained above. You can see the actual excavation for free from the window just below St. Mary's Church (20 kr, 10:00–17:00, less off-season, tel. 55 58 80 10). The museum has a good, inexpensive cafeteria with soup-and-bread specials.

St. Mary's Church—Dating from about 1150, this is Bergen's oldest building and one of Norway's finest churches (10 kr, summer Mon–Fri 11:00–16:00, off-season Tue–Fri 12:00–13:30).

▲▲**Fish Market**—This famous, bustling market has become touristy but still offers lots of smelly photo fun (Mon–Fri 7:00–16:00, until 19:00 Thu in summer, Sat until 15:00, less off-season). Don't miss it. This could be the only outdoor fish market that accepts credit cards.

More Sights—Bergen

▲**Håkon's Hall/Rosenkrantz Tower**—These reminders of Bergen's medieval importance sit barren and boldly out of place on the harbor just beyond Bryggen. Håkon's Hall was a royal residence 700 years ago when Bergen was the political center of Norway. Tours of both start in Håkon's Hall and leave on the hour (15 kr, mid-May–Aug 10:00–16:00, 45-min tours, last tour at 15:00 daily, off-season 12:00–15:00, tel. 55 31 43 80). There's a great harbor view from the tower's rooftop.

▲▲**Fløibanen**—Just two blocks up from the fish market you can ride the funicular to the top of "Mount" Fløyen (1,000 feet up in eight minutes) for the best view of the town, surrounding islands, and fjords all the way to the west coast. The top is a popular picnic or pizza-to-go dinner spot (Peppe's Pizza is a block away from the base of the lift) and the jumping-off point for many peaceful hikes. Sunsets are great here. It's a pleasant walk back down into Bergen. But to save your knees, you can get off at the "Promsgate" stop halfway down and then wander through the delightful cobbled and shiplap lanes (40 kr round-trip, departures each way on the half hour and often on the quarter hour until 23:00). This is actually used by locals commuting into and out of downtown.

▲▲**Wandering**—Bergen is a great strolling town. The harborfront is a fine place to kick back and watch the pigeons mate. Other good areas to explore are Klostergate, Marken, Knosesmanet, Ytre Markevei, and the area behind Bryggen. The modern town also has a pleasant ambience, especially around Ole Bulls Plass.

▲▲**Aquarium**—Small but great fun if you like fish, this aquarium, wonderfully laid out and explained in English, claims to be the second-most-visited sight in Norway. A pleasant 20-minute walk from the center, it has a cheery cafeteria with fresh fish sandwiches (75 kr, daily 9:00–20:00, off-season 10:00–18:00, feeding times 11:00, 14:00, and 18:00, bus #4, tel. 55 55 71 71).

▲**Old Bergen**—Gamle Bergen is a Disney-cute gathering of 40 18th- and 19th-century shops and houses offering a cutesy, cobbled look at "the old life." The town is free, and some of the buildings are art galleries and gift shops. English tours (40 kr) departing on the hour get you into the 20 or so museum buildings (daily mid-May–Aug 10:00–17:00, tel. 55 25 78 50). Take bus #9, #20, or #22 from Bryggen (direction Lonborg) to Gamle Bergen (first stop after the second tunnel).

▲▲**Art Museums**—If you need to get out of the rain (or want to see more of Dahl, the realist Krogh, Munch, and other Norwegian painters), check out Rasmus Meyer's Collection (35 kr, Rasmus Meyers Alle 3). The Stenersen Collection next door has some interesting modern art, including Munch and Picasso (35 kr). Both are free with the Bergen Card.

▲**Various City Tours**—The TI sells tickets to several tours, including a daily 90-minute introductory tour at 17:00 (90 kr) and a daily two-hour tour at 14:30 (125 kr). These tours, which leave from the TI, are barely worthwhile for a quick orientation. More fun and informative, if you're into city tours, are the harbor tours (14:30, from the fish market, aboard the *White Lady*, tel. 55 25 90 00) and the tacky tourist train with English-language headphone narration. Both tours cost 80 kr for 50 minutes and leave on the hour from the harborfront.

▲**Fantoft Stave Church**—The huge, preserved-in-tar, most-touristy-stave-church-in-Norway burned down in 1992. It was rebuilt and reopened in 1997, but it can never be the same. Situated in a quiet forest next to a mysterious stone cross, this replica of a 12th-century wooden church is bigger, but no better, than others covered in this book. But it's worth a look if you're in the neighborhood, even after hours, for its evocative setting (30 kr, daily 10:30–14:00, 14:30–18:00 in season, offers nothing in English).

▲**Edvard Grieg's Home, Troldhaugen**—Norway's greatest composer spent his last 22 years here (1885–1907), soaking up inspirational fjord beauty and composing many of his greatest works. In a very romantic Victorian setting, the ambience of the place is pleasant, even for nonfans, and essential to anyone who knows and loves Grieg's music. The house is full of memories, and his little studio hut near the water makes you want to sit down and modulate. Unfortunately, it gets the "Worst Presentation for a Scandinavian Historical Sight" Award, since it's mobbed with tour groups, offers nothing in English, and uses no imagination in mixing Grieg's music with the house (40 kr, daily mid-Apr–Sept 9:00–18:00, less off-season, closed Dec, tel. 55 91 17 91). Ask the TI about concerts in the concert hall at the site (130 kr, plus 50 kr for shuttle bus from TI, Wed and Sun at 19:30, Sat at 14:00 late Jul–Aug; arrive one hour early for tickets).

The TI's free *Bergen Guide* gives bus directions to Troldhaugen (the bus leaves you with a 30-min walk). The daily three-hour bus tour (10:00, 220 kr) is worthwhile for the informative guide and easy transportation. If you've seen other stave churches and can't whistle anything by Grieg, skip them.

Shopping—The Husfliden Shop is a fine place for handmade Norwegian sweaters and goodies (good variety and quality but expensive, just off the market at 3 Vågsalmenning). Like most shops, it's open Monday through Friday from 9:00 to 16:30, Thursday until 19:00, and Saturday from 9:00 to 14:00. Major shops are closed on Sunday, but shop-til-you-drop tourists manage to find plenty of action even on the day of rest.

Folk Evenings—The "Fana Folklore" show is Bergen's most advertised folk evening. An old farm hosts this touristy collection of cultural clichés, with food, music, dancing, and colorful costumes. While many think it's too gimmicky, and many think it's lots of fun, *nobody* likes the meager dinner (200 kr includes short bus trip and meal; Jun–Aug Mon, Tue, Thu, and Fri 19:00–22:30, tel. 55 91 52 40).

The **Bergen Folklore show** is a smaller, less gimmicky program, featuring a good music-and-dance look at rural and traditional Norway. Performances are downtown at the Bryggens

Museum (Jun–Aug Tue and Thu at 21:00, 1 hr, 95-kr tickets sold by TI and at the door, tel. 55 31 95 50).

Scenic Boats and Trains from Bergen—The TI has several brochures on tours of the nearby Hardanger and Sogne fjords. There are plenty of choices. For all the specifics on "Norway in a Nutshell," a scenic combination of buses, ferries, and trains that can be done in a day from Bergen (8:30–18:30, reservation required), see the Norway in a Nutshell chapter.

Sleeping in Bergen
(7 kr = about $1)
Sleep Code: **S** = Single, **D** = Double/Twin, **T** = Triple, **Q** = Quad, **b** = bathroom, **CC** = Credit Card (Visa, MasterCard, Amex).

There are two kinds of demands on the hotel scene in Bergen: Business travelers fill up the fancy hotels outside of summer and weekends, and tourists take the budget places from July through mid-August. If you want a simple, comfy place in summer, reservations are advisable. If you just show up in summer, unless you're unlucky and hit some convention, you'll get a great deal on a business-class hotel. While Bergen lacks the great summer discounts found in other big Nordic cities, if you can handle showers down the hall and cooking breakfast yourself in the communal kitchens, several pensions offer better rooms with homey atmospheres and fine central locations for half the hotel prices.

The private homes I list are cheap, central, and quite professional. The cheapest dorm/hostel-style beds don't cost much less than the private homes, and unless the shoestring you're traveling on is really frazzled or you like to hang out with other vagabonds and hostelers, I'd stick with the private rooms. The TI is helpful in finding the least expensive rooms (for a 25-kr fee).

Consider the **Bergen Package**, which gives you a bed, a big breakfast, and a Bergen Card (worth 130 kr) for from 395 kr per person (double occupancy) depending on the fancy hotel you choose (good only Fri–Sun or mid-Jun–Aug, order in United States from Scan-Am World Tours, tel. 800/545-2204, or purchase upon arrival). The arithmetic: Db + card for 650 kr. If you'd each buy a card anyway, that gives you an 800-kr double with buffet breakfast for about 410 kr . . . wow.

Laundromat: Jarlens Vaskoteque (Mon–Fri 10:00–18:00, Sat 9:00–15:00, closed Sun, Lille Ovregate 17, near Korskirken, tel. 55 32 55 64).

Sleeping in Hotels and Pensions
If you must have a uniformed person behind the key desk, the prestigious old **Hotel Hordaheimen** is central, just off the harbor, and a good budget-hotel bet (Db-1,070 kr, 720 kr on off-season weekends, or 890 kr in summer with reservations no more

than 48 hours in advance, CC:VMA, C. Sundts Gate 18, tel. 55 23 23 20, fax 55 23 49 50). Run by the same alcohol-free, give-the-working-man-a-break organization that brought you Kaffistova restaurants, their cafeteria, open late, serves traditional, drab, inexpensive meals.

Rainbow Hotel Bristol, a big, modern, all-the-comforts place in the center of town, is one of a chain of hotels which offers less character but more comfort for the krone (two price tiers—regular: Sb-885 kr, Db-1,190 kr; mid-Sept–mid-May Fri/Sat/Sun night: Sb-550 kr, Db-750 kr; includes breakfast, extra bed-150 kr, a block off Ole Bulls Plass at Torglamenningen 11, N-5014 Bergen, tel. 55 23 23 44, fax 55 23 23 19). **Hotel Bryggen Orion** beyond Bryggen near Håkon's Hall offers similar comfort, location, and value (Bradbenken 3, tel. 55 31 80 80, fax 55 32 94 14).

Kloster Pension, in a funky cobbled neighborhood four blocks off the harbor, has basic doubles including breakfast (S-320 kr, D-480 kr, Db-620 kr, Strange Hagen 2, tel. 55 90 21 58, fax 55 23 30 22).

Park Pension is classy and in a wonderful central but residential neighborhood. People who have the money for a cheap hotel but want Old World, lived-in elegance love this place (40 rooms, 20 of them in classy old hotel, 20 in nearby annex; Sb-700 kr, Db-850 kr, Db suite-990 kr, extra bed-200 kr, includes breakfast, summer and weekend discounts, prices drop 200–250 kr in winter, CC:VMA, Harald Hårfagres Gate 35, tel. 55 54 44 00, fax 55 54 44 44).

Rosenberg Gjesthus has a friendly staff and spartan but clean rooms with hardwood floors; it might close in 2000, so call ahead (Sb-525 kr, Db-600 kr, breakfast-25 kr, cash only, Rosenbergsgate 13, tel. 55 23 10 70, fax 55 23 10 71, e-mail: anysath@online.no).

Rent-a-Room is a simple pension near the train station (S-295 kr, Sb-350 kr, D-390 kr, Db-500 kr, communal kitchen, Nygårdsgate 31, tel. 55 32 72 53).

Sleeping in Rooms in Private Homes
Since the Bergen hotel owners don't quite understand the magic of the marketplace, there are more private homes opening up to travelers than ever. While (for a price) the TI would love to help you out, here are several you can book direct. They are cheap, quite private, and lack a lot of chatty interaction with your hosts. The first two are the most central.

Alf and Elisabeth Heskja are a young couple with four doubles, one shared shower/WC, and a kitchen. This is my home in Bergen, far better than the hostel for budget train travelers (D-290 kr, Skivebakken 17, 5018 Bergen, reserve in advance, tel. 55 31 30 30, fax 55 31 30 90, e-mail: heskja@online.no). It's located five minutes from the train station (down King Oscar's Gate, uphill on D. Krohns Gate, up the stairs at the end of the block) on Skivebakken, the steep, cobbled, "most painted street in Bergen." The Heskjas also rent rooms out of a building at Veiten 2b (a block off Ole Bulls Plass, farther from station but closer to the city action, bigger rooms, not quite as cute but still a fine deal).

The **Olsnes' home** is nearby and offers a shared kitchen (S-180 kr, Sb-200 kr, D-290 kr, Db-340 kr, Skivebakken 24, tel. 55 31 20 44, e-mail: svolsne@online.no, run by Yngve).

Skansen Pensjonat rents eight rooms out of a classy old house situated a steep but scenic five-minute climb above the entrance to the Fløibanen lift overlooking the fish market (S-300–350 kr, D-500 kr, fancy D on corner with view and balcony-600 kr, includes breakfast, 2 showers on ground floor, sinks in rooms, homey family room with TV, one parking place, look for bed symbol above Fløibanen station, Vetrlidsalmenning 29, N-5014 Bergen, tel. 55 31 90 80, e-mail: mail@skansen-pensjonat.no, run by Alvaer family).

The **Vågenes family** has six doubles in a large, comfortable house on the edge of town (D-290 kr, Db with kitchenette-345 kr, breakfast-40 kr, easy parking, J.L. Mowinckelsvei 95, tel. 55 16 11 01). It's 10 minutes from downtown on bus #60. Driving from downtown, cross the Puddefjordsbroen bridge (Road 555), go through the upper tunnel on Road 540, and turn left 200 meters later on J.L. Mowinckelsvei. Continue until you get to Helgeplasset Street, just past the Hagesenter on the right.

Sleeping in Hostels

YMCA Interrail Center offers cheap beds two blocks off the fish market (mid-Jun–mid-Sept 8:00–11:00, 15:00–24:00; one dorm for women, one for men, the others mixed; dorm bed-100 kr, bed in 5-bed room-150 kr, nonmembers-25 kr extra, sheets-40 kr; always a place available, lots of organized budget travel activities, 5 min from station, near center, Nedre Korskirke alm #31, tel. 55 31 72 52, fax 55 31 35 77).

Montana Youth Hostel (IYHF) is one of Europe's best hostels, but its drawbacks are the remote location and relatively high price. Still, the bus connections (#31, 15 min from the center) and the facilities—modern rooms, classy living room, no curfew, huge parking lot, and members' kitchen—are excellent (dorm bed-135 kr, bed in 4-bed room-170 kr, bed in double-235 kr, nonmembers-25 kr extra, sheets-40 kr, includes breakfast, 30 Johan Blydts Vei, tel. 55 29 29 00).

Eating in Bergen

Eating in Bryggen

All of these places are in the old Hanseatic quarter (street numbers are rare but signs are common). They serve traditional Norsk food in candlelit old Norsk ambience (meals 150–220 kr; as usual, more potatoes are yours on request). If you're in the mood for a little Donner or Blitzen, look no farther. To avoid a wait, you may want to call in a reservation.

Bryggestuene and Loft, actually one restaurant with one menu on two levels with two different styles, offers good (but smoky) atmosphere and seafood and traditional meals. Except in summer, they offer a 70-kr *dagens* menu (Mon–Sat 11:00–23:30, opens Sun at 13:00, #11 in Bryggen harborfront, tel. 55 31 06 30). If there's a line downstairs, go upstairs.

Bryggen Tracteursted serves moderately priced Norwegian food in the oldest pub in town (daily from noon, deep in atmospheric center of Bryggen, follow signs from front street, tel. 55 31 40 46).

Enhjørningen, or "The Unicorn," serves some of Bergen's best seafood dinners and offers a delicious 160-kr seafood lunch buffet (available Mon–Sat 12:00–16:00) to readers of this book for a 25 percent discount. For this deal no reservations are taken, but it's easy to find a seat after 14:00 (200 kr for lavish seafood dinners, look for anatomically correct unicorn on old wharf facade, tel. 55 32 79 19).

Facing the Harbor

Perhaps the tastiest and most memorable cheap meal in Bergen would be a seafood picnic picked up right at the **Fisketorvet** (fish market). The stalls are bursting with salmon sandwiches, fresh shrimp, and fish cakes. And for dessert, Baker Brun is right there with *skillingsbolle* (cinnamon rolls) still warm out of the oven. For small and cozy places with the best prices, walk around the Korskirken (church) two blocks off the market square and check out the four or five little no-nonsense eateries.

Zachariasbryggen is a restaurant complex filling a pier at the head of the harbor (on Torget). It thrives with eateries all day and is a lively nightspot. You'll find a **Baker Brun** (open from 9:00, fresh pastries, sandwiches, wonderful shrimp baguettes, seating around back or take-away), Chinese, Italian, and great Mexican food (**Skibet Tex-Mex**, Mon–Sat 12:00–23:00, less Sun and off-season, 150–200-kr dinners, upstairs inside, great harbor view seats, tel. 55 55 96 50). **Zachen**, a piano bar, is open late and is popular with locals.

Kaffistova til Ervingen Cafeteria, overlooking the fish market (in the building with the Eskimo on top), is a good basic food value with fine Norwegian atmosphere in its first-floor self-service cafeteria (50-kr breakfasts, 100-kr dinners, Mon–Fri 8:00–19:00, Sat 8:00–17:00, Sun 11:00–18:00, closes earlier off-season, second floor, Strandkaien 2, tel. 55 32 30 30). **Kafe Bergenhus**, next door, offers similar food and prices (Mon–Sat 11:00–17:00, open

Sun at 13:00). For old Norwegian fare, eat at the borderline-dreary cafeteria in the **Hordaheimen Hotel**, offering cheap 49-kr meals and lots of *lefse*.

From Ole Bulls Plass up to the Theater

Bergen's "in" cafés are stylish, cozy, small, and open very late—great places to experience the local yuppie scene. The trendy **Café Opera** is good (80-kr dinners, 37-kr soup-and-bread specials, often live music Fri and Sat, live locals nightly, English newspapers, chess, across from theater, Engen 18, tel. 55 23 03 15). **Kjøttbørsen**—literally, "meat market"—is a splurge local carnivores enjoy (hearty servings, 200-kr meals, closed Sun–Mon, Vaskerelven 6, tel. 55 31 31 60). **På Folkemunne** is pricey but popular with locals (200-kr meals, Ole Bulls Plass 9). A good place for a drink is **Dickens** on Ole Bulls Plass. It's packed on Friday and Saturday nights.

Radisson SAS/Hotel Norge's "Koltbord" buffet, offered by Bergen's ritziest hotel, is a daily all-you-can-eat buffet in a classy Ole Bull restaurant. You'll find hot dishes, seafood, and desserts rich in both memories and calories (185-kr lunch, enter Mon–Sat 12:00–16:00, Sun 13:00–16:00, tel. 55 57 30 00).

Hotel Neptun is home of the highest-rated restaurant in town (one Michelin star). Its **Bistro Pascal** serves fine food out of the same restaurant at a more affordable price (between harbor and theater at Valkansdorfsgata 8, tel. 55 30 68 00). Students and budget travelers carbo-load at **Pasta Sentral** (50-kr meals, open late, near station at Vestre Strømkai 6).

Transportation Connections—Bergen

Bergen is conveniently connected to **Oslo** only by train (departing Bergen roughly at 7:30, 10:20, 15:00, 15:45, 23:00, arriving Oslo 7 scenic hours later, 25-kr reservation required; an 8:30 departure goes to Voss—perfect for Nutshell route though not a through train to Oslo). Train info tel. 55 96 69 00.

To get to **Stockholm, Copenhagen**, or even **Trondheim**, you'll be going via Oslo unless you fly. Before buying a ticket for a long train trip from Bergen, look into cheap flights. **Kilroy Travels** has a handle on cheap flights (Parkveien 1 in Student Sentret, tel. 55 30 79 00; another office near Ole Bulls Plass at Vaskerelven 16, www.Kilroytravels.com).

By bus to Kristiansand: If you're heading to Denmark, you'll take the ferry from Kristiansand. Catch the Haukeli express bus departing Bergen at 7:30. After a layover in Haukeligrend, take the bus at 15:10, arriving at 19:30 in Kristiansand (560 kr, cheaper for students with ISIC cards, tel. 55 55 90 70 or, within Bergen, dial 177) in time for the overnight ferry to Denmark.

By boat to Newcastle, England: Fjordline sails from Bergen to Newcastle, England (Tue, Fri, and Sun Jun–Aug, tel. 55 54 86 60). The cheapest peak-season crossing for the 22-hour trip is 980 kr on Tuesday or Sunday for a reclining chair ("sleeperette"). Bunks in a four-person cabin cost 1,130 kr. Cars with up to five passengers cost about 3,500 kr.

By boat to Stavanger: FlaggRuten catamarans sail to Stavanger (2–4/day in 4 hrs, 510 kr, 50 percent discount for students or Scanrail/Eurail passholders, tel. 55 23 87 80). From Stavanger, trains run to Kristiansand and Oslo (overnight possible).

By boat to the Arctic: Hurtigrute coastal steamers depart daily in summer at 22:30 for the seven-day trip north up the scenic west coast to Kirkenes on the Russian border. Book cabins well in advance. Call Bergen Lines in the United States: tel. 212/319-1300. Deck space and seats are usually available with short or no notice (info in Bergen, tel. 55 55 72 00, reservations 81 03 00 00, www.hurtigruten.com). For most, the ride is great one way, but a flight back south is a logical last leg.

SOUTH NORWAY'S SETESDAL VALLEY

Welcome to the remote—and therefore very traditional—Setesdal Valley. Probably Norway's most authentic cranny, the valley is a mellow montage of sod-roofed water mills, ancient churches, derelict farmhouses, yellowed recipes, and gentle scenery. The locals practice fiddles and harmonicas, rose painting, whittling, and gold- and silverwork. The famous Setesdal filigree echoes the rhythmical design of the Viking era and Middle Ages.

The Setesdal Valley joined the 20th century with the construction of the valley highway in the 1950s. All along the valley you'll see the unique two-story storage sheds called *stabburs* (the top floor stored clothes; the bottom, food) and many sod roofs. Even the bus stops have rooftops the local goats love to munch.

In the high country, just over the Sessvatn summit (3,000 feet), you'll see herds of goats and summer farms. If you see an "*Ekte Geitost*" sign, that means genuine homemade goat cheese is for sale. (It's sold cheaper and in more manageable sizes in grocery stores.) To some it looks like a decade's accumulation of earwax. I think it's delicious. Remember, *ekte* means all-goat—really strong. The more popular and easier-to-eat regular goat cheese is mixed with cow's-milk cheese.

Each town in the Setesdal Valley has a weekly rotating series of hikes and activities for the regular, stay-put-for-a-week visitor. The upper valley is dead in the summer but enjoys a bustling winter. This is easygoing sightseeing—nothing earthshaking. Let's just pretend you're on vacation.

Planning Your Time

Frankly, without a car, Setesdal is not worth the trouble. There are no trains, bus schedules are as sparse as the population, and the sights are best for joyriding. If you're driving in Bergen and want to get back to Denmark, this route is more interesting than repeating Oslo. On a three-week Scandinavian trip, I'd do it in one long day, as follows: 6:00–Leave Bergen, 8:00–Catch Kvanndal ferry to Utne, 9:00–Say goodbye to the last fjord at Odda, 12:00–Lunch in Hovden at the top of Setesdal Valley, 13:00–Frolic south with a few short stops in the valley, 18:00–Arrive in Kristiansand—dinner and a movie?, 23:00–Board boat for overnight crossing to Denmark.

Sights—Setesdal Valley

These sights are listed from north to south.

Odda—At the end of the Hardanger fjord, just past the huge zinc and copper industrial plant, you'll hit the industrial town of Odda (well-stocked TI for whole region and beyond, tel. 53 64 12 97). Odda brags that Kaiser Wilhelm came here a lot, but he's dead and I'd drive right through. If you want to visit the tongue of a glacier, drive to Buar and hike an hour to Buarbreen. From Odda, drive into the land of boulders. The many, mighty waterfalls that line the road seem to have hurled huge rocks (with rooted trees) into the rivers and fields. Stop at the giant double waterfall (on the left, pull out on the right, drive slowly through it if you need a car wash).

Røldal—Continue over Røldalsfjellet and into the valley below, where the old town of Røldal is trying to develop some tourism. Drive straight through. Its old church isn't worth the time or money. Lakes like frosted mirrors make desolate huts come in pairs. Haukeliseter, a group of sod-roofed buildings filled with cultural clichés and tour groups, offers pastries, sandwiches, and reasonable hot meals (65–85 kr) in a lakeside setting. Try the traditional *rømmegrøt* porridge.

Haukeligrend—The TI is open from 7:00 to 23:00 late June through early August (tel. 35 07 03 67). If you plan to stay here, **Haukelid Turistheim Pensjonat** offers quaint old rooms (in the quaint old half of the building), a feel-at-home Old World living room, a Ping-Pong table, and a cafeteria (D-300 kr, at junction of Roads 39 and 11 in Haukeligrend, about 6 hours out of Bergen, 30 minutes before Hovden, tel. 35 07 01 26). Haukeligrend is a bus/traffic junction, with daily bus service to/from Bergen and to/from Kristiansand.

Hovden—Hovden is a ski resort (2,500 feet high) at the top of the Setesdal Valley, barren in the summer and painfully in need of charm. Locals come here to walk and relax for a week. Good walks offer a chance to see reindeer, moose, arctic fox, and wabbits—so they say. A chairlift takes summer visitors to its nearby 3,700-foot peak (Tue, Thu, and Sat). Hegni Center, on the lake at the south edge of town, rents canoes for 30 kr an hour. A new super indoor spa/pool complex, the Hovden Badeland (100 kr, daily 11:00–19:00 in summer) provides a much-needed way to

Setesdal Valley

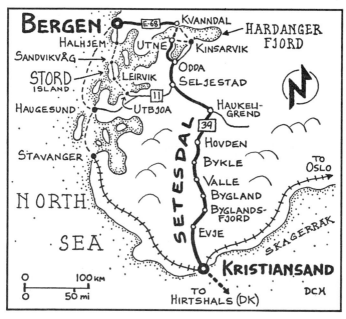

spend an otherwise dreary (and very likely) drizzly early evening here. The TI is open all year (Mon–Fri 8:00–17:00, summer Sat 9:00–13:00, tel. 37 93 96 30).

Hovden Fjellstoge is a big old ski chalet with an inviting ski-lodge atmosphere (large dining room and open fire in the living room). It offers clean, modern bunk-bed doubles for 400 kr, as well as dorms (dorm bed-130 kr, 25 kr extra if you're not a hostel member, sheets-60 kr, breakfast-60 kr, restaurant open 12:00–20:00, tel. 37 93 95 43). Built in 1911, this is the oldest place in town. It's also the only cozy and reasonable place to stay in this booming winter resort of sprawling ranch-style ski hotels.

▲**Dammar Vatnedalsvatn**—Just south of Hovden is a two-mile side trip to a 400-foot-high rock-pile dam. Great view, impressive rockery. This is one of the highest dams in northern Europe. Read the chart. Sit out of the wind a few rows down the rock pile and ponder the vastness of Norwegian wood.

▲**Bykle**—The most interesting folk museum and church in Setesdal are in the teeny town of Bykle. The 17th-century church interior has two balconies—one for men and one for women (10 kr, mid-Jun–mid-Aug Mon–Fri 10:00–18:00, Sat–Sun 12:00–18:00).

The **Huldreheimen Museum**, a wonderful little open-air museum, is a typical 800-year-old *seterhouse* used when the cattle spent the summer high in the mountains. Follow the sign up a road to a farm high above the town, park, then hike a steep 150 yards into Norway's medieval peasant past. You'll get a fine view, six houses filled with old stuff, and a good English brochure (15 kr, mid-Jun–mid-Aug Mon–Fri 10:00–18:00, Sat–Sun 12:00–18:00).

Grasbrokke—On the east side of the main road (at the "Grasbrokke" sign) you'll see an old water mill (1630). A few minutes farther south is a "Picnic and WC" sign. Exit onto that little road. You'll pass another old water mill with a fragile rotten-log sluice. At the second picnic turnout (just before this roadlet returns to the highway, you'll find a covered picnic table for rainy lunches), turn out and frolic along the river rocks.

Flateland—One mile east, off the main road, is the Setesdal museum (Rygnestadtunet), offering more of what you saw at Bykle (20 kr, 2 buildings, daily mid-Jun–mid-Aug 11:00–17:00). Unless you're a glutton for culture, I wouldn't do both.

▲Valle—This is Setesdal's prettiest village (but don't tell Bykle). In the center you'll find fine silver- and goldwork, traditional dinners in the cozy Bergtun Hotel (130–180 kr, summer only), homemade crafts next to the TI, old-fashioned *lefse* cooking demonstrations (in the small log house by the campground), and a fine suspension bridge for kids of any age who still like to bounce (and for anyone interested in a great view over the river of the strange mountains that look like polished, petrified mudslides). European rock climbers, tired of the over-climbed Alps, often entertain spectators with their sport. Is anyone climbing? (TI open mid-Jun–mid-Aug, Mon–Fri 10:00–17:00, Sat 10:00–14:00, closed Sun except in Jul 10:00–14:00; off-season Mon–Fri 7:30–15:00, tel. 37 93 73 12.)

If you stay in Valle, try the **Bergtun Hotel**. Run by Halvor Kjelleberg, it's a real folksy, sit-a-spell Setesdal lodge full of traditional furniture, paintings, and carvings in each charming room (open mid-Jun–mid-Aug, D-500 kr, some rooms have bunks, extra bed-100 kr, includes breakfast, Valle i Setesdal, tel. 37 93 77 20, fax 37 93 74 37).

Nomeland—Sylvartun, the silversmith with the valley's most aggressive publicity department, demonstrates the Setesdal specialty in a 17th-century traditional log cabin and a free little gallery/museum. He also gives a free 30-minute fiddle concert weekdays in July at 13:00. On Monday and Thursday at 14:30 you can see a 30-minute folk dance show (40 kr).

Grendi—The Ardal Church (1827) has a rune stone in its yard. Three hundred yards south of the church is a 900-year-old oak tree.

Evje—A huge town by Setesdal standards (3,500 people), Evje is famous for its gems and mines. Fancy stones fill the shops here.

Only rock hounds would find the nearby mines fun; for a small fee you can hunt for gems. The new super-for-rock hounds Setesdal Mineral Park is on the main road, three kilometers south of town. For modern, bright, functional doubles in Evje, stay with the **Haugen family** (2-bunk rooms for 200 kr, 280 kr with sheets, pleasant garden, kitchenette, huge stuffed moose in the garage) on Arendal Road (last house on the left, look for "Rom" sign, tel. 37 93 08 88, fax 37 93 01 14).

KRISTIANSAND

This "capital of the south" has 67,000 inhabitants, a pleasant grid-plan Renaissance layout (Posebyen), a famous zoo with Norway's biggest amusement park (10 km toward Oslo on the main road), a daily bus to Bergen, and lots of big boats going to England and Denmark. It's the closest thing to a beach resort in Norway. The Posebyen neighborhood, around the bustling pedestrian market street, is the shopping/eating/browsing/people-watching town center. Stroll along the Strand Promenaden (marina) to Christiansholm Fortress.

The TI is at Dronningensgate 2 (Mon–Fri 8:00–20:00, Sat 9:00–20:00, Sun 12:00–20:00, off-season Mon–Fri 8:30–15:30 only, tel. 38 12 13 14). The bank at the Color Line terminal opens for each arrival and departure (even the midnight ones) and is reasonable. The cinema complex is within two blocks of the Color Line docks and the TI (50 kr, 7 screens, showing movies in English, check schedules at TI or cinema).

Sleeping and Eating in Kristiansand

Your best modern, comfy, and cozy bet is **Hotel Sjøgløtt**. Friendly Helene Ranestad gives this small hotel lots of class (S-350 kr, Sb-490 kr, D-530 kr, Db-690 kr, includes breakfast, CC:VM, near harbor on quiet street at Østre Strandgt 25, tel. & fax 38 02 21 20). **Villa Frosbusdal B&B**, once a shipbuilder's mansion, has friendly hosts and modern bathrooms (Frosbusdalen 2, tel. 38 07 05 15). Otherwise, Kristiansand hotels are expensive and nondescript. Consider the traditional **Bondeheimen** (Sb-640 kr, Db-820 kr, includes breakfast, CC:VMA, tel. 38 02 44 40, fax 38 02 73 21). **Rainbow Hotel Norge** is more modern and expensive but reduces its rates to 820 kr for a double on Friday, Saturday, and Sunday and from mid-June through mid-August (regular rates: Db-940 kr, Dronningensgate 5, tel. 38 02 00 00, fax 38 02 35 30).

Villa Frobusdal Hotel, outside the city center, is a 1917 villa and classy B&B run by the friendly Herigstads (Sb-550 kr, Db-690 kr, includes breakfast, Frobusdalen 2, access from E-18 going east, tel. 38 07 05 15, fax 38 07 01 15). The **hostel** is cheap but not central (tel. 38 02 83 10).

In the town center you'll find plenty of *kafeterias*, a **Peppe's**

Pizza (open until 23:00, salad bar, on Gyldenløvesgate), and
budget ethnic restaurants. For the best dinner in town, splurge at
Bak Gården (dinner-250 kr, closed Sun, Tollbodgaten 5, hiding
in the center, tel. 38 02 79 55).

Transportation Connections—Kristiansand

By boat to Hirtshals, Denmark: The Color Line ferry sails
from Kristiansand in Norway to Hirtshals in Denmark (usually
daily departures at about 8:00, 13:45, 15:00, 21:45, and 01:00,
mid-Jun–late Aug; 2–4 departures daily other months). Fast boats
take 2.5 hours, regular boats take 4 hours, and the overnight ride
is slower, to arrive at 6:30. Passengers pay 144 kr to 352 kr (Jul
and weekends are most expensive). A car costs 200 kr to 500 kr.
The "car package" lets five in a car travel for 1,090 kr (summer
Mon–Thu). There are decent *smørgåsbords*, music, duty-free
shopping, a desk to process your Norwegian duty-free tax rebates,
and a bank for small changes (no fee).

When you can commit yourself to a firm date, call Color
Line to make a reservation. They accept telephone reservations
payable when you get to the dock. Color Line's information and
reservation line is open daily from 8:00 to 23:00 (tel. 81 00 08 11).
If it's more convenient, contact their New York office c/o Bergen
Line (tel. 212/319-1300, fax 212/319-1390). Ask about specials.
Round-trip fares can be lower than one-way fares.

Take the night boat to save the cost of a hotel. Enjoy an
evening in Kristiansand, then sleep (or vomit) as you sail to
Denmark. Beds are reasonable (reclining seats euphemistically
called "sleeperettes"-40 kr, simple *couchettes*-100 kr, bed in a four-
berth room-110 kr, private double with shower-170–220 kr per
person). You owe yourself the comfort of a private room if you're
efficient enough to spend this night traveling. I slept so well that
I missed the Denmark landing and ended up crossing three times!
After chewing me out, the captain said it happens a lot. Set your
alarm or spend an extra day at sea.

Route Tips for Drivers

Bergen to Kristiansand (10 hours): Your first key connection
is the Kvanndal–Utne ferry (a 2-hr drive from Bergen, departures
hrly 6:00–23:00, tel. 55 23 87 80 to confirm times, reservations not
possible or even necessary if you get there 20 minutes early, breakfast in cafeteria). If you make the 8:00, your day will be more
relaxed. Driving comfortably, with no mistakes or traffic, it's two
hours from your Bergen hotel to the ferry dock. Leaving Bergen is
a bit confusing. Pretend you're going to Oslo on the road to Voss
(signs for Nestune, Landas, Nattland, R-7). About a half-hour out
of town, after a long tunnel on Road 7, leave the Voss road and
head for Norheimsund. This road, as treacherous for the famed

beauty of the Hardanger Fjord it hugs as for its skinniness, is faster and safer if you beat the traffic (which you will with this plan).

The ferry drops you in Utne, where a lovely road takes you to Odda and up into the scenic mountains. From Haukeligrend, turn south and wind up to Sessvatn at 3,000 feet. Enter Setesdal Valley. Follow the Otra River downhill for 140 miles south to the major port town of Kristiansand. Skip the secondary routes. As you enter Kristiansand, follow signs for Denmark.

SWEDEN

STOCKHOLM

If I had to call one European city home, it would be Stockholm. Surrounded by water and woods, bubbling with energy and history, Sweden's stunning capital is green, clean, and underrated.

Crawl through Europe's best-preserved old warship and relax on a canal-boat tour. Browse the cobbles and antique shops of the lantern-lit Old Town and take a spin through Skansen, Europe's first and best open-air folk museum. Marvel at Stockholm's glittering city hall, modern department stores, and art museums.

While progressive and sleek, Stockholm respects its heritage. In summer, mounted bands parade daily through the heart of town to the royal palace, announcing the changing of the guard and turning the most dignified tourist into a scampering kid. The Gamla Stan (Old Town) celebrates the midsummer festivities (late June) with the vigor of a rural village, forgetting that it's part of a gleaming 20th-century metropolis.

Planning Your Time

On a two- to three-week trip through Scandinavia, Stockholm is worth two days. Efficient train travelers sleep in and out for two days in the city with only one night in a hotel. (The Copenhagen train arrives at about 8:00 and departs at about 22:00 or 23:00.) To be even more economical and efficient, you could use the luxury Stockholm–Helsinki boat as your hotel for two nights (spending a day in Helsinki) and have two days in Stockholm without a hotel (e.g., Copenhagen; night train to Stockholm, day in Stockholm; night boat to Helsinki, day in Helsinki; night boat to Stockholm, day in Stockholm; night train to Copenhagen). That schedule may sound crazy, but it gives you three interesting and inexpensive days of travel fun.

Spend two days in Stockholm this way:
Day 1: Arrive by train (or the night before by car), do station chores (reserve next ride, change money, pick up map, *Stockholm This Week*, and a Stockholm Card at the Hotellcentralen TI), check into hotel, 10:30–Catch 50-minute bus tour from Opera, 11:30–Tour Vasa warship and have a picnic, 13:30–Tour Nordic Museum, 15:00– Skansen Open-Air Museum (ask for tour), 19:00–Folk dancing, possible *smørgåsbord*, and popular dancing, or wander Gamla Stan.
Day 2: 10:00–City hall tour, climb city hall tower for a fine view, 12:00–Catch the changing of the guard at the palace, tour royal palace and armory, explore Gamla Stan, or picnic on one-hour city boat tour, 16:00–Browse the modern city center around Kungsträdgården, Sergels Torg, Hötorget market and indoor food hall, and Drottninggatan area.

Orientation (tel. code: 08)

Greater Stockholm's 1.8 million residents live on 14 islands that are woven together by 54 bridges. Visitors need only concern themselves with five islands: **Norrmalm** is downtown, with most of the hotels, shopping areas, and the train station. **Gamla Stan** is the old city of winding lantern-lit streets, antique shops, and classy, glassy cafés clustered around the royal palace. **Södermalm**, aptly called Stockholm's Brooklyn, is residential and not touristy. **Skeppsholmen** is the small, central, traffic-free park island with the Museum of Modern Art and two fine youth hostels. **Djurgården** ("deer garden"), now officially a national city park, is Stockholm's wonderful green playground with many of the city's top sights (bike rentals just over bridge as you enter island).

Tourist Information

Hotellcentralen is primarily a room-finding service (in the central train station), but its friendly staff adequately handles all your sightseeing and transportation questions. This is the place for anyone arriving by train to arrange accommodations, buy the Tourist Card or Stockholm Card (see below), and pick up a city map, *Stockholm This Week* (which lists open hours and directions to all the sights, special events, and much more), and brochures on whatever else you need (city walks, parking, jazz boats, excursions, bus routes, shopping, and so on). While *This Week* has a decent map of the sightseeing zone, the 15-kr map covers more area and bus routes. It's worth the extra money if you'll be using the buses (daily Jun–Sept 7:00–21:00, May 8:00–19:00, off-season 9:00–18:00, tel. 08/789-2425 or 08/789-2456, fax 08/791-8666, www.stoinfo.se).

Sverige Huset (Sweden House), Stockholm's official TI (a short walk from the station on Kungsträdgården), is good but usually more crowded than Hotellcentralen. They've got pamphlets on

Stockholm's Islands

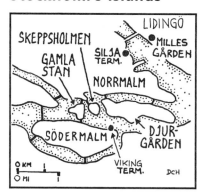

everything; an "excursion shop" for transportation, day-trip, and bus-tour information and tickets; and an English library and reading room upstairs with racks of information on various aspects of Swedish culture and one state's attempt at cradle-to-grave happiness (Jul–Aug Mon–Fri 8:00–19:00, Sat–Sun 9:00–17:00, less off-season, Hamngatan 27, T-bana: Kungsträdgården, tel. 08/789-2490 for info, 08/789-2415 for tickets).

The **City Hall TI** is smaller but with all the information and a bit less chaos (May–Oct daily 9:00–17:00, off-season Fri–Sun 9:00–15:00, closed Jan, at the Stadshuset or City Hall, tel. 08/5082-9000).

Arrival in Stockholm

By Train: Stockholm's central train station is a wonderland of services, shops, and people going places. The Hotellcentralen TI is as good as the city TI nearby. If you're sailing to Finland, check out the Viking Line office. The FOREX long-hours exchange counter changes traveler's checks for a 15-kr fee (2 offices, upstairs and downstairs, in the station).

By Plane: Stockholm's Arlanda Airport is 45 kilometers north of town. Shuttle buses run between the airport and City Terminal, which is next to the station (6/hrly, tel. 08/600-1000). Airport info tel. 08/797-6000 (SAS tel. 020/727-727, British Air tel. 020/770-098).

Helpful Hints

There are three kinds of public phones: coin-op, credit card, and phone card. For operator assistance, call 0018. Numbers starting with 020 are toll free. For around-the-clock medical help, call 08/463-9100. There's a 24-hour pharmacy near the central station at Klarabergsgatan 64 (tel. 08/454-8130). To get a taxi within three minutes, call Taxi Stockholm (tel. 08/150-000) or Taxi Kurir (tel. 08/300-000). Rent bikes, inline skates, and boats at Skepp & Hoj on Djurgådsbron Bridge next to Vasa Museum (summer 9:00–21:00, tel. 08/660-5757). For Internet access, try Fröken Matildas (open until 23:00, Stora Nygatem 6 in Gamla Stan, tel. 08/206-020).

Greater Stockholm

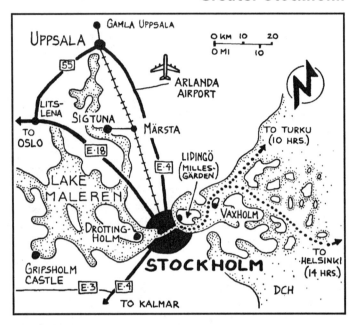

GAMLA UPPSALA

UPPSALA

55

ARLANDA AIRPORT

LITS-LENA   SIGTUNA

TO OSLO

E·18   MÄRSTA

E·4

LIDINGÖ (MILLES-GÅRDEN)

LAKE MALEREN

VAXHOLM

TO TURKU (10 HRS.)

DROTTING-HOLM

GRIPSHOLM CASTLE

E·3   E·4

STOCKHOLM

TO KALMAR

TO HELSINKI (14 HRS.)

DCH

0 KM 10   20
0 MI   10

Getting around Stockholm

By Bus and Subway: Stockholm complements her many sightseeing charms with great information services, a fine bus and subway system, and special passes that take the bite out of the city's cost (or at least limit it to one vicious budgetary gash).

Buses and the subway work on the same tickets. Ignore the zones since everything I mention (except Drottningholm and Carl Millesgården) is in Zone One. Each 14-kr ticket is valid for one hour (10-packs cost 95 kr). The subway, called T-bana or Tunnel-bana, gets you where you want to go quickly. Ride it just for the futuristic drama of being a human mole and to check out the modern public art (for instance, in Kungsträdgården station, transit info tel. 08/600-1000). The **Tourist Card**, which gives you free use of all public transport and the harbor ferry (24 hrs/60 kr, 72 hrs/ 120 kr, sold at TIs and newsstands), is not necessary if you're getting the Stockholm Card (see below). The 72-hour pass includes admission to Skansen, Gröna Lund, and the Kaknäs Tower.

It seems too good to be true, but each year I pinch myself and the **Stockholm Card** is still there. This 24-hour, 199-kr pass (sold at TIs and ship terminals) gives you free run of all public transit, free entry to virtually every sight (70 places), free parking, a handy sightseeing handbook, and the substantial pleasure of doing everything without considering the cost (many of Stockholm's sights are worth the time but not the steep individual ticket costs). This pays for itself if you do Skansen, the Vasa, and the Royal Palace and Treasury. If you enter Skansen on your 24th hour (and head right for the 55-kr aquarium), you get a few extra hours. (Parents get an added bonus: Two children under 18 go along for 35 kr with each adult pass.) The same pass comes in 48-hour (398 kr) and 72-hour (498 kr) versions.

By Harbor Shuttle Ferry: Throughout the summer, ferries connect Stockholm's two most interesting sightseeing districts. They sail from Nybroplan and Slussen to Djurgården, landing next to Vasa and Skansen (20 kr, not covered by Stockholm Card, 3/hrly).

Sights—Downtown Stockholm

▲**Kungsträdgården**—The King's Garden Square is the downtown people-watching center. Watch the life-size game of chess and enjoy the free concerts at the bandstand. Surrounded by the Sweden House, the NK department store, the harborfront, and tour boats, it's the place to feel Stockholm's pulse (with discretion).

▲▲**Sergels Torg**—The heart of modern Stockholm, between Kungsträdgården and the station, is worth a wander. Enjoy the colorful, bustling underground mall and dip into the Gallerien mall. Visit the Kulturhuset, a center for reading, relaxing, and socializing designed for normal people (but welcoming tourists), with music, exhibits, hands-on fun, and an insight into contemporary Sweden (free, Wed and Fri–Sat 11:00–17:00, Tue and Thu 11:00–19:00, Sun 12:00–17:00, often open later, closed Mon, tel. 08/700-0100). From Sergels Torg, walk up the Drottninggatan pedestrian mall to Hötorget (see "Eating," below).

▲▲**City Hall**—The Stadshuset is an impressive mix of 8 million bricks, 19 million chips of gilt mosaic, and lots of Stockholm pride. One of Europe's finest public buildings (built in 1923) and site of the annual Nobel Prize banquet, it's particularly enjoyable and worthwhile for its entertaining tours (40 kr, daily Jun–Aug at 10:00, 11:00, 12:00, and 14:00; Sept at 10:00, 12:00, and 14:00; off-season at 10:00 and 12:00; just behind the station, bus #48 or #62, tel. 08/5082-9059). Climb the 350-foot tower (an elevator takes you halfway) for the best possible city view (15 kr, daily 10:00–16:30 May–Sept only). The city hall also has a TI and a good cafeteria with complete lunches for 60 kr (Mon–Fri 11:00–14:30).

▲**Orientation Views**—Try to get a bird's-eye perspective on this wonderful urban mix of water, parks, concrete, and people from the city hall tower (see above), the Kaknäs Tower (at 500 feet, the tallest building in Scandinavia, 25 kr, daily May–Aug 9:00–22:00, daily Sept–Apr 10:00–21:00, bus #69 from Nybroplan or

Stockholm

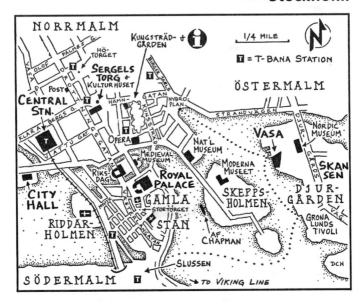

Sergels Torg, tel. 08/789-2435), the observatory in Skansen, or the Katarina elevator (5 kr, Mon–Sat 7:30–21:00, Sun 10:00–21:00, circa 1930s, ride 40 meters to the top; near Slussen subway stop—walk behind Katarinavagen for grand views, a classy residential neighborhood, and a lively Mosebacke evening of strolling, dancing, and beer gardens).

▲**Quickie Orientation Bus Tour**—Several different city-bus tours leave from the Royal Opera House. Your choices: 50 minutes for 90 kr with a Swedish/English guide (mid-Jun–mid-Aug 10:30–18:30 at half past the hour), 90 minutes for 130 kr (mid-Apr–Oct at 10:00, 12:00, 14:00; in summer also at 11:00, 13:00, 15:00, 17:00; tel. 08/411-7023), or a 75-minute Old Town walk (75 kr, daily in summer at 11:30 and 14:30). For a free self-guided tour, follow the Gamla Stan walk laid out below.

▲**City Boat Tour**—For a good floating look at Stockholm, and a pleasant break, consider a sightseeing cruise. Tour boats leave regularly from in front of the Grand Hotel (tel. 08/240-470). The "Historical Canals of Stockholm" tour offers the best informative introduction (90 kr, 1 hour, departing on the half hour 10:30–16:30 mid-Jun–mid-Aug). The "Under the Bridges" tour goes through two locks and under 15 bridges (live guide, 140 kr, 2 hours, hrly departures mid-Apr–mid-Oct). The "Royal Canal" tour is a scenic joyride through lots of greenery (90 kr, 1-hour tape-recorded spiel, departing on the half hour 10:30–18:30 mid-May–Aug).

▲**National Museum**—Though mediocre by European standards, this museum is small, central, uncrowded, and user-friendly. The highlights of the collection are several Rembrandts, Rubens, a fine group of Impressionists, and works by the popular and good-to-get-to-know local artists Carl Larsson and Anders Zorn (60 kr, Tue–Sun 11:00–17:00, Tue and Thu until 20:00, closed Mon, tel. 08/5195-4300). A free and worthwhile CD guides you through a 50-minute tour of the collection's highlights. In summer, free guided tours in English begin at 13:00.

Museum of Modern Art—Newly reopened after a major renovation, this bright and cheery gallery is as far out as can be, with Picasso, Braque, and lots of goofy Dada art (such as the *Urinal* and the *Goat with Tire*). It's in a pleasant park on Skeppsholmen (60 kr, Tue–Thu 11:00–22:00, Fri–Sun 11:00–18:00, closed Mon, tel. 08/5195-5200).

Sights—Stockholm's Gamla Stan

▲▲**Gamla Stan self-guided walk**—Stockholm's old island core is charming, fit for a roll of film, and full of antique shops, street lanterns, painted ceilings, and surprises. While you could just happily wander, try this guided walk first:

Slottsbacken: Start at the base of the palace (bottom of Slottsbacken) where a statue of King Gustav III gazes at the palace, formerly the site of Stockholm's first castle. Walk up the broad cobbled boulevard. Behind the obelisk stands the Storkyrkan, Stockholm's cathedral (and most interesting church, which we'll visit later in the walk). Opposite the palace (orange building on left) is the Finnish church (Finska Kyrkan), which originated as the royal tennis hall. Walk behind the church into the shady churchyard where you'll find the three-inch-tall "iron boy," the tiniest statue in Stockholm (often with a little gift). Continue through the yard onto Trädgårdsgatan, which leads (turn right) to the old stock exchange.

Stortorget: Left of the stock exchange is the oldest square in town, Stortorget. The town well is now dry but this is still a popular meeting point. Scan the fine old facades. This square has a notorious history. It was the site of Stockholm's bloodbath of 1520—during a royal power grab, most of the town's aristocracy was beheaded. Rivers of blood were said to have run through the streets. Later, this was the location of the town's pillory. At the far end of the square (under the finest gables) turn right and follow Trangsund toward the cathedral.

Cathedral: Just before the church you'll see my favorite phone booth (Rikstelefon) and the gate to the churchyard being guarded by statues of Caution and Hope. Enter the cathedral

(10 kr, daily 9:00–18:00, until 16:00 off-season, pick up free English flyer describing interior). The fascinating interior is paved with centuries-old tombstones; more than 2,000 people are buried under the church. In front on the left is an impressive sculpture of *Saint George and the Dragon* made of oak, gilded metal, and elk horn (1489). Near the exit is a painting with the oldest existing depiction of Stockholm (from 1535, showing a walled city filling only today's Gamla Stan).

Prastgatan: Exiting through the churchyard, continue down Trangsund. At the next corner go downhill on Storkyrkobrinken and take the first left—where the priests used to—on Prastgatan. Enjoy a quiet wander down this peaceful lane. After two blocks (at Kakbrinken) you'll see a cannon on the corner guarding a prehistoric rune stone. (In case you can't read ancient Nordic script, it says: "Torsten and Trogun erected this stone in memory of their son.") Continue farther down Prastgatan until you see the German-strength brick steeple of the Tyska Kyrkan (German church). This is a reminder of the days when German merchants worked here. Wander through its churchyard and out the back onto Svartmangatan. Follow it downhill to its end at a couple of benches and an iron railing overlooking Österlånggatan.

Österlånggatan: From this perch, survey the street to the left and right. Notice how it curves. This marks the old shoreline. In medieval times piers stretched out like many fingers into the harbor. Gradually, as land was reclaimed and developed, these piers were extended and what were originally piers became lanes leading to piers farther away. Walk left along Österlånggatan. At the cobbled Y in the road head uphill (up Kopmanbrinken) past a copy of *George and the Dragon*. (Or, for a quick finish, Österlånggatan takes you back to your starting point at the palace.)

Shopping, Jazz, and Food: From Kopmantorget (the statue), Kopmangatan leads past fine antique shops (some with their medieval painted ceilings still visible) back to Stortorget. Crossing the square, follow the crowds downhill two blocks to Stora Nygatan. This is Gamla Stan's main commercial drag, a festival of distractions that keeps most visitors from seeing the historic charms of the Old Town—which you just did. Now you can shop and eat.

▲▲**Military Parade and Changing of the Guard**—Starting at the Army Museum (daily at 12:00), the parade marches over either Norrbro Bridge or Strombron Bridge and up to the palace courtyard where the band plays and the guard changes (every other day the band is mounted . . . on horses). These days, the royal family lives out of town at Drottningholm, but the guards are for real. If the guard by the cannon in the semicircular courtyard looks a little lax, try wandering discreetly behind him.

▲▲**Royal Palace**—The palace is a complex of sights. Drop by the info booth in the semicircular courtyard (at the top where the guard changes) for an explanatory brochure with a map marking the different entrances. In a nutshell: The Apartments of State are lavish, as worthwhile as any; the Royal Treasury is the best in northern Europe; the chapel is no big deal; skip Gustav III's Museum of Antiquities; and plan to spend some time in the awesome Royal Armoury. An 80-kr combo ticket covers the apartments, treasury, and antiquities (more info below). To add the Royal Armory, get the 100-kr combo ticket (tel. 08/5877-1000, www.royalcourt.se).

▲▲**Apartments of State**—The stately palace exterior encloses 608 rooms (one more than Britain's Buckingham Palace) of glittering Baroque and rococo decor. Clearly the palace of Scandinavia's superpower, it's richly decorated (18th century) and steeped in royal history. The guided tour is heavy and tedious; the place is more interesting on your own—pick up English descriptions where available and don't miss the Bernadotte rooms (50 kr, daily Jun–Aug 10:00–16:00; off-season Tue–Sun 12:00–15:00, closed Mon; free English-language tours at 12:00 and 13:15).

▲▲**Royal Treasury**—You'll find great crowns, scepters, jeweled robes, and plenty of glitter that's gold. Nothing is explained, so get the 2-kr description at the entry (50 kr, May–Aug 10:00–16:00, off-season 12:00–15:00, no samples, often tours at 11:00 and 14:15, tel. 08/402-6000).

Gustav III's Museum of Antiquities—In the 1700s, Gustav III traveled through Italy and brought home an impressive gallery of classical Roman statues. This was a huge deal if you'd never been out of Sweden. It's worth a look only if you've never been to the rest of Europe. Nothing is explained in English (50 kr, same hours as Apartments).

▲▲▲**Royal Armoury (Livrust Kammaren)**—This, the oldest museum in Sweden, has the most interesting and best-displayed collection of medieval royal armor I've seen anywhere in Europe. The incredible, original 17th-century gear includes royal baby wear, outfits kings wore when they were killed in battle or assassinated, and five centuries of royal Swedish armor—all wonderfully described in English. An added bonus is a basement lined with royal coaches, including coronation coaches, all beautifully preserved and richly decorated (60 kr, daily 10:00–16:00; winter Mon–Sat 11:00–16:00, closed Mon; tours daily in summer at 11:00, entry at bottom of Slottsbacken at base of palace, tel. 08/5195-5544).

Riksdaghuset—You can tour Sweden's parliament buildings if you'd like a firsthand look at its government (free hrly tours in English Jun–Aug, usually Mon–Fri at 12:30 and 14:00, some Sat–Sun at 13:30, enter at Riksgatan 3a, but call 08/786-4000 to confirm times).

Museum of Medieval Stockholm (Medeltidsmuseet)—This may be grade-schoolish, but it gives you a good look at medieval

Stockholm (40 kr, daily Jul–Aug 11:00–16:00, Tue–Thu until 18:00; Sept–Jun Mon–Sat 11:00–16:00, Wed until 18:00, closed Mon; free 30-min English tours at 14:00 daily in summer enlivens the exhibits; enter from park in front of Parliament, tel. 08/5083-1790). The Stromparterren park, with its Carl Milles statue of the *Sun Singer* greeting the day, is a pleasant place for a sightseeing break (but an expensive place for a potty break—use the free WC in the museum). **Riddarholm Church**—This final resting place for about 600 years of Sweden's royalty is pretty lifeless (20 kr, daily May–Aug 10:00–16:00, Sept Sat–Sun 12:00–15:00, closed in winter, tel. 08/402-6130). In a futile attempt to make this more interesting, they'll loan you the church guidebooklet. The cathedral next to the palace (see "Gamla Stan self-guided walk," above) is far more interesting.

Sights—Stockholm's Djurgården

▲▲▲**Skansen**—Europe's original and best open-air folk museum, Skansen is a huge park gathering more than 150 historic buildings (homes, churches, shops, and schoolhouses) transplanted from all corners of Sweden. Tourists can explore this Swedish-culture-on-a-lazy-Susan, seeing folk crafts in action and wonderfully furnished old interiors (lively only in the summer). In the town quarter (top of the escalator), craftspeople such as potters are busy doing their traditional thing in a re-created Old World Stockholm. Seek out the glassblowers if you'll be missing Sweden's glass country to the south.

Spreading out from there, the sprawling park is designed to show northern Swedish culture and architecture in the northern part of the park (top of park map) and southern Sweden in the south (bottom of map). Free one-hour guided walks (from Bollnästorget info stand at top of escalator) paint a fine picture of old Swedish lifestyles (usually daily at 14:00 and 16:00 Jun–Aug). There's fiddling nightly (except Sun) at 18:15; folk dancing demonstrations daily in summer at 19:00, Sunday at 14:30 and 16:00; and public dancing to live bands three nights a week (20:30–23:30, call for evening theme—jazz, folk, rock, or disco). Admission to the aquarium is the only thing not covered on your entry ticket (55 kr, opens daily at 10:00, closes between 16:00 and 20:00 depending on season and day of the week, call for times, tel. 08/660-1082).

Kids love Skansen, especially its zoo (ride a life-size wooden Dala-horse and stare down a hedgehog) and Lill' Skansen (Punch 'n' Judy, Mon–Fri at 12:00 and 14:00, minitrain, and pony ride fun daily from 11:00 till at least 16:00). There are lots of special events and several restaurants. The main restaurant serves a grand *smørgåsbord* (200 kr) and the Ekorren café offers the least expensive self-service lunches with a view. Tre Byttor (next to Ekorren) serves 18th century–style food in a candlelit setting. Another cozy inn, the old-time Stora Gungan Krog, at the top of the escalator, has better food (60- to 90-kr indoor or outdoor lunches with a salad and cracker bar).

Skansen is great for people watching and picnicking, with open and covered benches all over (especially at Torslunden and Bollnästorget, where peacenik local toddlers don't bump on the bumper cars). Get the map or the 30-kr museum guidebook that has the same map, and check the live crafts schedule at the information stand at Bollnästorget to confirm your Skansen plans.

Use the west entrance (Hazeliusporten) if you're heading to or from the Nordic Museum. (60 kr; winter weekdays-30 kr, weekends-40 kr; daily May–Aug 10:00–22:00, buildings 11:00–17:00; winter 10:00–16:00, some buildings 11:00–15:00; take bus #47 or #44 from the station; call 08/5789-0005 for recording of the day's tour, music, and dance schedule, or tel. 08/442-8000.) You can miss Gröna Lund, the second-rate amusement park across the street.

▲▲▲*Vasa*—Stockholm turned a titanic flop into one of Europe's great sightseeing attractions. This glamorous but unseaworthy warship—top-heavy with a tacked-on extra cannon deck—sank 20 minutes into her 1628 maiden voyage when a breeze caught the sails and blew her over in the Stockholm harbor. After 333 years she rose again from the deep (with the help of marine archaeologists) and today is the best-preserved ship anywhere, housed in a state-of-the-art museum. The masts on the roof are placed to show their actual height.

Catch the 25-minute English-subtitled movie (in English at 11:30 and 13:30, other languages with English subtitles every half hour) and, for more information, take the free 25-minute English tours (at the bottom of each hour from 10:30, fewer tours off-season, call for times) to best enjoy and understand the ship. Learn about ship's rules (bread can't be older than eight years), why it sank (heavy bread?), how it's preserved, and so on. Private tours are easy to freeload on, but the displays are so well described that a tour is hardly necessary. (60 kr, daily mid-Jun–mid-Aug 9:30–19:00; off-season 10:00–17:00, winter Wed until 20:00, tel. 08/666-4800.) Take bus #47 to the big brick Nordic Museum or catch the boat from Nybroplan or Slussen, or walk from Skansen.

▲▲**Nordic Museum**—This museum, built to look like a Danish palace, offers a look at how Sweden lived over the last 500 years. Ask for a free audio guide when you enter. Highlights include the Food and Drink section, with its stunning china and crystal table settings; the Nordic folk art (2nd and 3rd floors); the huge statue of Gustav Vasa, father of modern Sweden, by Carl Milles (top of 2nd flight of stairs); and the Sami (Lapp) exhibit in the basement (Tue–Sun 10:00–21:00, summer Tue and Thu until 21:00, closed Mon, free guided tour in English Tue–Thu at 15:00 and 17:00, or ask for a free audio guide when you enter, tel. 08/51 95 6000).

It's worth your time if you have the Stockholm Card, but it's overpriced at 60 kr per admission.

▲**Thielska Galleriet**—If you liked the Larsson and Zorn art in the National Gallery and/or if you're a Munch fan, this charming mansion on the water at the far end of the Djurgården park is worth the trip (40 kr, Mon–Sat 12:00–16:00, Sun 13:00–16:00, bus #69 from the central station, tel. 08/662-5884).

Sights—Outer Stockholm

▲▲**Carl Millesgården**—The home and garden housing a museum and the major work of Sweden's greatest sculptor is dramatically situated on a cliff overlooking Stockholm. Milles' entertaining, unique, and provocative art was influenced by Rodin. There's a classy café and a great picnic spot (60 kr, daily May–Sept 10:00–17:00; off-season Tue–Sun 12:00–16:00, closed Mon, tel. 08/446-7590.) Catch the T-bana to Ropsten, then take any bus (except #203 and #213) to the first stop (Torsvik). It's a five-minute walk from there (follow the signs).

▲▲**Drottningholm**—The queen's 17th-century summer castle and present royal residence has been called, not surprisingly, Sweden's Versailles. The adjacent, uncannily well-preserved Baroque theater is the real highlight, especially with its 50-kr guided tours (Jun–Aug English theater tours normally depart half past each hour 11:30–16:30, fewer tours off-season). Get there by a relaxing but overpriced boat ride (85 kr round-trip, two hrs) or take the subway to Brommaplan and bus #301 to #323 to Drottningholm. (50-kr entry, palace open daily May–Aug 12:00–16:30, Sept 12:00–15:30, tel. 08/402-6280 for palace tours in English, Jun–Aug often at 11:00, Sept at 12:00.)

The 18th-century Drottningholm court theater performs perfectly authentic operas (about 30 performances each summer). Tickets for this popular, time-tunnel musical and theatrical experience cost 100 kr to 470 kr, and go on sale each March. For information, contact Drottningholm's Theater Museum (Box 27050, 10251 Stockholm, tel. 08/660-8225, fax 08/665-1473).

▲▲**Archipelago**—The world's most scenic islands (24,000 of them!) surround Stockholm. Europeans who spend their vacations here rave about them. If you cruise to Finland, you'll get a good dose of this island beauty. Otherwise, consider the hour-long cruise (80 kr each way, buy tickets on boat) from Nybroplan downtown to Vaxholm. The TI has a free archipelago guidebooklet.

Sauna

Sometime while you're in Sweden or Finland, you'll have to treat yourself to Scandinavia's answer to support hose and a face-lift. (A sauna is actually more Finnish than Swedish.) Simmer down with the local students, retired folks, and busy executives. Try to cook as calmly as the Swedes. Just before bursting, go into the shower room. There's no lukecold, and the trickle-down theory doesn't apply—only one button, bringing a Niagara of liquid ice. Suddenly your shower stall becomes a Cape Canaveral launch pad, as your body scatters to every corner of the universe. A moment later you're back together. Rejoin the Swedes in the cooker, this time with their relaxed confidence; you now know that exhilaration is just around the corner. Only very rarely will you feel so good.

Any TI can point you toward the nearest birch twigs. Good opportunities include a Stockholm–Helsinki cruise, any major hotel you stay in, some hostels, or (cheapest) a public swimming pool. In Stockholm, consider Eriksdalsbadet (Hammarby Slussväg 8, near Skanstull T-bana, tel. 08/5084 0275). Use of its 50-meter indoor/outdoor pool and first-rate sauna costs 55 kr.

For a classier experience, the newly refurbished Centralbadet lets you enjoy an extensive gym, "bubblepool," sauna, steam room, and an elegant Art Nouveau pool from 1904 (Mon–Fri-79 kr, Sat-99 kr, long hours, last entry 20:30, closed Sun, Drottninggatan 88, 5 minutes up from Sergels Torg, tel. 08/242-403). The steam room is mixed; the sauna is not. Bring your towel into the sauna—not for modesty but to separate your body from the bench. Massage and solarium cost extra, and the pool is more for floating than for jumping and splashing. The leafy courtyard is a relaxing place to enjoy their restaurant (reasonable and healthy light meals).

Shopping

Modern design, glass, clogs, and wooden goods are popular targets for shoppers. Browsing is a free, delightful way to enjoy Sweden's brisk pulse. Cop a feel at the Nordiska Kompaniet (NK, also meaning "no kroner left") just across from the Sweden House or close by in the Gallerian mall. The nearby Åhlens is less expensive. Swedish stores are open weekdays from 10:00 to 18:00 and Saturdays until 15:00, but are closed on Sundays. Some of the bigger stores (like Åhlens and NK) are open later on Saturdays and on Sunday afternoons. Take a short walk to Norrmalms Torg to the new bank branch of Scandia Insurance for its ATMs, Internet access, and free coffee, tea, or chocolate.

For a *smørgåsbord* of Scanjunk, visit the Loppmarknaden (northern Europe's biggest flea market) at the planned suburb of Skärholmen (free on weekdays, 10 kr on weekends, Mon–Fri 11:00–18:00, Sat 9:00–15:00, Sun 10:00–15:00, busiest on weekends, T-bana: Skärholmen, tel. 08/710-0060).

Sleeping in Stockholm
(7 kr = about $1, tel. code: 08)
Sleep Code: **S** = Single, **D** = Double/Twin, **T** = Triple, **Q** = Quad, **b** = bathroom, **CC** = Credit Card (Visa, MasterCard, Amex).

Stockholm Hotels

N = T-BANA STATION

1/4 MILE

NORRMALM

ÖSTERMALM

CENTRAL Stn.

SÖDERMALM → TO VIKING LINE TERMINAL

❶ QUEEN'S HOTEL		❾ SUNDIN ROOMS
❷ BENTLEY'S HOTEL		❿ LICHTSTEINER ROOMS
❸ STUREPARKENS GÄSTVÅNING		⓫ AF CHAPMAN HOSTEL
❹ HOTEL GUSTAV VASA		⓬ SKEPPSHOLMEN HOSTEL
❺ DROTTNING VICTORIAS ORLOGSHEM		⓭ ZINKENSDAMM HOSTEL
❻ PRIZE HOTEL		⓮ BRYGGHUSET HOSTEL
❼ RICA CITY HOTEL		⓯ KRISTINA RESTAURANG
❽ HOTELLJÄNST ROOM FINDING		⓰ HERMITAGE REST.

"Summer rates" mean mid-June to mid-August, and Friday and Saturday (sometimes Sunday) the rest of the year. Prices include breakfast unless otherwise noted.

Stockholm has plenty of money-saving deals for the savvy visitor. Its hostels are among Europe's best ($15 a bed), and plenty of people offer private accommodations ($50 doubles). Peak season for Stockholm's expensive hotels is business time—workdays outside of summer. Rates drop by 30 to 50 percent in the summer or on weekends. If business is slow, ask for a discount. To sort through all of this, the city has helpful, English-speaking room-finding services with handy locations and long hours (see Hotell-centralen and Sweden House, above).

The **Stockholm Package** (limited to Jun–Aug and Fri and Sat throughout the year) offers business-class doubles with buffet breakfasts from 870 kr, includes two free Stockholm Cards, and lets two children up to 18 years old sleep for free. Assuming you'll be getting two Stockholm Cards anyway (398 kr), this gives you a $200 hotel room for about $50. This is for real (summertime is that dead for business hotels). The procedure (through either TI) is easy: a 100-kr advance-booking fee (you can arrange by fax, pay when you arrive) or a 40-kr in-person booking fee if you just drop in. Arriving without reservations in July is never a problem. It gets tight during the Water Festival (10 days in early Aug) and during a convention stretch for a few days in late June.

My listings are a good value only outside of Stockholm Package time, or if the 790 kr for a double and two cards is out of your range and you're hosteling. Every place listed here has staff who speak English and will explain their special deals to you on the phone. If money is limited, ask if they have cheaper rooms. It's not often that a hotel will push their odd misfit room that's 100 kr below all the others. And at any time of year, prices can be soft.

About the only Laundromat in central Stockholm is Tvätto-maten, at Västmannagatan 61 on Odenplan (60 kr, full serve-80 kr, Mon–Fri 8:30–18:30, Sat 9:30–15:00, closed Sun, across from Gustav Vasa church, bus #53 from Upplandsgaten to Central Station, T-bana: Odenplan, helpful manager, tel. 08/346-480).

Sleeping in Hotels

Queen's Hotel is cheery, clean, and just a 10-minute walk from the station, located in a great pedestrian area across the street from the Centralbadet (city baths, listed on all maps). With a fine TV and piano lounge, coffee in the evenings, and a staff that enjoys helping its guests, this is probably the best cheap hotel in town (summer and Fri–Sat rates: S-525 kr, Ss-550 kr, Sb-675 kr, D-575–680 kr, Ds-625 kr, Db-775 kr, winter rates: D-575–680 kr, Ds-625 kr, Db-1,100–1,250 kr, CC:VMA, Drottninggatan 71A, tel. 08/249-460, fax 08/217-620, e-mail: queenshotel@queenshotel.se). Their simple rooms have no sinks. If you're arriving early from the train or boat, you're welcome to leave your bags and grab a 45-kr breakfast.

Bentley's Hotel is an interesting option with old-English flair and renovated rooms (summer rates include winter Sundays: very small Db-750 kr, Db-775 kr, Db suite-915 kr, winter Db-1,175 kr, CC:VMA, 2 blocks up the street from Queen's at Drottninggatan 77, 11160 Stockholm, tel. 08/141-395, fax 08/212-492). Klas and Agi Källström attempt to mix elegance, comfort, and simplicity into an affordable package. Each room is tastefully decorated with antique furniture but has a modern full bathroom.

The proud little **Stureparkens Gästvåning** is a carefully run, traditional-feeling place with lots of class and 10 thoughtfully appointed rooms. (S-460 kr, D-695–750 kr, Db-950 kr, 2-night minimum, elevator, CC:VM, near T-bana: Stadion, across from Stureparken at Sturegatan 58, tel. 08/662-7230, fax 08/661-5713). They rent an apartment for 1,500 kr per night (7-night minimum).

Hotel Gustav Vasa has classy Old World rooms in a listed building with a family-run feel on a convenient square just 15 minutes on foot from the center (Ss-575 kr, Sb-650 kr, D-680 kr, Db-900 kr, includes breakfast, rates up to 150-kr higher outside of summer and weekends, they have some cheaper tiny doubles, family deals, CC:VMA, elevator, subway to Odenplan, exit Väst-mannagatan, to Västmannagatan 61, tel. 08/343-801, fax 08/307-372, e-mail: gustov.vasa@wineasy.se).

Drottning Victorias Orlogshem, formerly a hotel for navy personnel, now accepts the public. It offers functional, quiet rooms with hardwood floors and naval decor in a great neighborhood behind the National Museum and a block off the central harbor (35 rooms, Sb-500 kr, Db-700 kr, Tb-900 kr, extra bed-150 kr, family deals, breakfast-40 kr, only twin beds, Teatergatan 3, 11148 Stockholm, tel. 08/611-0113, fax 08/611-3150).

Prize Hotel is unique—a super-modern, happy place with tight 'n' tidy rooms two blocks from the station in Stockholm's World Trade Center. Designed for business travelers, it has mostly singles (with wall-beds that fold down to make doubles) and major summer and weekend discounts (not worth the high-season price; low prices Fri, Sat, and Jun 8–Aug 8: Sb-680 kr, Db-835 kr; high-season price: Sb-1,195 kr, Db-1,350 kr; they have a few real doubles for the same price as their wall-bed doubles; low rates offered during slow winter times; breakfast-55 kr, CC:VMA, Kungsbron 1, tel. 08/566-22200, fax 08/5662-2444, e-mail: prize.sth@prize.se, www.prize.se).

Rica City Hotel is also unique. Filling the top floors of a downsized department store and a leader in environmental friendli-ness, this modern place offers hardwood floors and all the comforts in a "one-star delux" package (200 rooms, discount rates weekends and Jun 20–Aug 9: Sb-700 kr, Db-880 kr, Qb-970–1,280 kr, some rooms lack windows but have good ventilation: Sb-550 kr, Db-700 kr, all D are twins shoved together, high-season Db-1,360 kr, breakfast-50 kr, CC:VMA, free loaner bikes, overlooking Hötorget market at Kungsgatan 47, tel. 08/723-7220, fax 08/723-7299).

Sleeping in Rooms in Private Homes

Stockholm's centrally located private rooms are nearly as expen-sive as discounted hotels—a deal only in the high season. More reasonable rooms are a few T-bana stops just minutes from the center. Stockholm's TIs refer those in search of a room in a private house to **Hotelljånst** (near station, Vasagatan 15, tel. 08/104-467, fax 08/213-716). They can set you up for about 450 kr per double without breakfast for a minimum two-night stay. Go direct—you'll save your host the listing service's fee. Be sure to get the front door security code when you call, as there's no intercom connection with front doors.

Else Mari Sundin, an effervescent retired actress, rents her homey apartment just two blocks from the bridge to Djurgården (Db-700 kr for up to 4 people, bus #47 or #69 to Torstenssons-gatan 7, go through courtyard to "garden house" and up to 2nd floor, tel. 08/665-3348, 0884 door code). Since she lives out of town, this can be complicated. But once you're set up, it's great.

Mrs. Lichtsteiner offers rooms with kitchenettes and has a family room with a loft (S-from 300 kr, D-from 400 kr without breakfast, a block from T-bana: Rådhuset, exit T-bana direction Polishuset, at Bergsgatan 45, once inside go through door on left and up elevator to 2nd floor, tel. 08/746-9166, call ahead to get the security code, e-mail: rooms@user.bip.net).

Sleeping in Hostels
Stockholm has Europe's best selection of big-city hostels offering good beds in simple but interesting places for 100 kr. If your budget is tight, these are right. Each has a helpful English-speaking staff, pleasant family rooms, good facilities, and good leads on budget survival in Stockholm. All will hold rooms with a phone call. Hosteling is cheap only if you're a member (guest membership: 40 kr per night; necessary only in IYHF places); bring your own sheet (paper sheets rent for 30 kr, cotton sheets-50 kr) and plan on a picnic for breakfast (or pay 45 kr). Several of the hostels are often booked up well in advance but hold a few beds for those who are left in the lurch.

Af Chapman (IYHF), Europe's most famous youth hostel, is a permanently moored cutter ship. Just a five-minute walk from downtown, this floating hostel has 140 beds—two to eight per stateroom. A popular but compassionate place, it's often booked far in advance, but saves some beds each morning for unreserved arrivals (given out at 7:00) and gives away unclaimed rooms each evening after 18:00. If you call at breakfast time and show up before 12:00, you may land a bed, even in summer (130 kr per bed, D-300 kr, bike rental-90 kr/day or 50kr/half day, open Apr–mid-Dec, sleeping bags allowed, has a lounge and cafeteria that welcomes nonhostelers, reception open 24 hours, rooms locked 11:00–15:00, STF Vandrarhem Af Chapman, Skeppsholmen, 11149 Stockholm, tel. 08/08/679-5015 for advance booking).

Skeppsholmen Hostel (IYHF), just ashore from the Af Chapman, is open all year. It has better facilities and smaller rooms (150 kr per bed in doubles, 130 kr in triples or quads, only 100 kr in dorms, nonmembers-40 kr extra, tel. 08/463-2266), but it isn't as romantic as its seagoing sister.

Bed and Breakfast is Stockholm's newest cozy hostel, with only 20 beds (145 kr per bed in 8- to 12-bed rooms, breakfast-20 kr, sheets-40 kr, near Rådmansgatan T-bana stop, just off Sveavägen at Rehnsgatan 21, tel. & fax 08/152-838). Friendly

Bjørn and Daniela also offer eight single (295 kr) and double (395 kr) rooms with breakfast.

Zinkensdamm Hostel (IYHF) is a big, basic hostel in a busy suburb, with 135-kr dorm beds (40 kr extra for sheets and non-members), plenty of 360-kr doubles without sheets, a Laundromat, and the best hostel kitchen facilities in town (STF Vandrarhem Zinken, open 24 hours all year, restaurant, Zinkens Väg 20, T-bana: Zinkensdamm, tel. 08/616-8100, fax 08/616-8120, e-mail: info:zinkensdamm@Sweden.hotels.se). This is a great no-nonsense, user-friendly value.

Vandrarhemmet Brygghuset, in a former brewery near Odenplan, is small (57 beds in 12 spacious rooms), bright, clean, and quiet, with a Laundromat and a kitchen. Since this is a private hostel, its two- to six-bed rooms are open to all for 130 kr per bed (no sleeping bags allowed, sheets rent for 45 kr). Sheetless doubles are 320 kr. (Open Jun–mid-Sept 7:00–12:00, 15:00–23:00, 02:00 curfew, Norrtullsgatan 12 N, tel. 08/312-424.)

Stockholm has 12 campgrounds (located south of town) that are a wonderful solution to your parking and budget problems. The TI's "Camping Stockholm" brochure has specifics.

Eating in Stockholm

Stockholm's elegant department stores (notably NK and Åhlens, near Sergels Torg) have cafeterias for the kroner-pinching local shopper. Look for the 50-kr "rodent of the day" (*dagens rätt*) specials. Most museums have handy cafés. The café at the **Af Chapman** hostel serves a good salad/roll/coffee lunch in an unbeatable deck-of-a-ship atmosphere—if the weather's good (open to the public Jun 28–Aug 2 11:30–18:00, off-season closed at 16:00). **Restaurang Al Forno** on Drottningsgatan, across from Queen's Hotel, has tasty 50-kr pizzas and pasta.

In Gamla Stan: The Old Town (Gamla Stan) has lots of restaurants. Try the wonderfully atmospheric **Kristina Restaurang** (Västerlånggatan 68, tel. 08/208-086). In this 1625 building, under a leather ceiling steeped in a turn-of-the-century interior, you'll find good dinners from 145 kr, including a salad and cracker bar and a cheaper "summer" menu. They serve a great 55-kr lunch (Mon–Fri 11:00–15:00) that includes an entrée, salad bar, bread, a drink, and live jazz. You can enjoy the music over just a beer or coffee, too. **Hermitage** has good vegetarian food and daily specials (Stora Nygatan 11). **Paganini** has a good mix of Swedish and Italian food, and great people watching if you snare a window seat (80-kr lunch specials, Västerlånggatan 75, tel. 08/406-0607).

Picnics

With higher taxes almost every year, Sweden's restaurant industry is suffering. You'll notice many fine places almost empty. Swedes joke that the "local" cuisine is now Chinese, Italian, and hamburgers. Here more than anywhere, budget travelers should picnic.

Stockholm's major department stores and the many small corner groceries are fine places to assemble a picnic. **Åhlens** department store has a great food section (open until 21:00, near Sergels Torg). The late-hours supermarket downstairs in the central train station is picnic friendly, with fresh, ready-made sandwiches (Mon–Fri 7:00–23:00, Sat–Sun 9:00–23:00).

The market at **Hötorget** is a fun place to picnic shop, especially in the indoor, exotic, and ethnic **Hötorgshallen** (fun café and restaurant in fish section). The outdoor market closes at 18:00, and many merchants put their unsold produce on the push list (earlier closing and more desperate merchants on Sat).

For a classy vegetarian buffet, often with a piano serenade, try **Ørtagården**— literally "the herb garden"—above the colorful old Østermalms food market at Østermalmstorg (70-kr lunch Mon–Fri until 17:00, 85-kr dinner evenings and weekends, Nybro-gatan 31, tel. 08/662-1728).

Transportation Connections—Stockholm

By train to: Uppsala (40/day, 40 min), Kalmar (12/day, 5 hrs, including evening service 18:18–23:00), **Copenhagen** (6/day, 8 hrs, night service 22:30–7:05), **Oslo** (2/day, 7 hrs, plus a 15-hour night train via Göteborg: 20:12–10:52). Train info tel. 020/757-575 (toll free in Sweden) or 08/227-940 (outside Sweden).

By boat to: Helsinki (daily/nightly boats, 16 hrs; see Helsinki chapter), **Turku** (daily/nightly boats, 11 hrs).

Estline runs a regular ferry from Stockholm to **Tallinn, Estonia** (every night at 18:00, arriving at 9:30 the next morning, 410 kr each way, 720 kr round-trip with a bed in a quad, cheaper off-season). It offers a 39-hour tour (no visa necessary, round-trip, simple two-bed cabins, two breakfasts) from 290 kr per person in a four-person cabin (tel. 08/667-0001).

Parking in Stockholm: Only a Swedish meatball would drive his car in Stockholm. Park it and use the public transit. But parking is confusing, a major hassle, and expensive. Unguarded lots generally aren't safe. Take everything into your hotel or hostel, or pay for a garage. The TI has a "Parking in Stockholm" brochure. Those hosteling on Skeppsholmen feel privileged with their 25-kr-a-day island parking pass. Those with the Stockholm Card can park free in a big central garage or at any meter for the duration of the ticket. Ask for your parking card and specifics when you get your Stockholm Card. There's a safe and reasonable (10 kr per day) lot at Rop-sten, the last subway station (near the Silja Line terminal). Those sailing to Finland can solve all parking worries by long-term parking on arrival in Stockholm at either terminal's safe and reasonable parking lot (70 kr per day).

NEAR STOCKHOLM: UPPSALA AND SIGTUNA

Uppsala

Uppsala is a compact city with a cathedral and university that win "Sweden's oldest/largest/tallest" awards. Allow the better part of a day, including the train from Stockholm.

The sights of historic Uppsala, along with its 30,000 university students, cluster around the university and cathedral. Just over the river is the bustling shopping zone.

Tourist Information: The Uppsala TI is near the cathedral (Mon–Fri 10:00–18:00, Sat 10:00–15:00, Sun 10:00–14:00; closed Sun off-season, tel. 018/274-800). Pick up their free, entertaining, and helpful *Uppsala Guide*.

Sights—Uppsala

▲▲**Uppsala Cathedral**—One of Scandinavia's largest and most historic cathedrals, it has a breathtaking interior, the tomb of King Gustavus Vasa, and twin 400-foot spires. Ask about a guided tour. Otherwise, push the English button and listen to the tape-recorded introduction in the narthex opposite the TI table (daily 8:00–18:00).
University—Scandinavia's first university was founded here in 1477. Linnaeus and Celsius are two famous grads. Several of the old buildings are open. A historic (but not much to see) silver-bound Gothic Bible is on display with other rare medieval books in the Carolina Rediviva (library). The anatomy theater in the Gustavianum is thought provoking. Its only show was a human dissection.
Gamla Uppsala—Old Uppsala is rooted deeply in history but now almost entirely lost in the sod of centuries. Look at the postcards of Gamla Uppsala's 15 grassy burial mounds from downtown. That's all you'll see if you go out there. Easy by car, but not worth the headache by bus (#2, #5, #20, #24, or #54).
Other Uppsala Sights—Uppland Museum is on the river by the waterfall (20 kr, Wed–Sun 12:00–17:00). Near the Carl Linnaeus Garden and Museum, the 16th-century castle on the hill has slice-of-castle-life exhibits.

Eating in Uppsala

Browse through the lively **Saluhallen**, the riverside indoor market near the cathedral. The university district abounds with inexpensive eateries. Try **Kung Kral** for great food; ask about a five-shot sampler of schnapps (St. Persgata 4, tel. 018/125-090).

Sigtuna

Between Stockholm and Uppsala you'll pass Sigtuna. Possibly Sweden's cutest town, Sigtuna is basically fluff. You'll see a medieval lane lined with colorful wooden tourist shops, a pleasant TI, a café, a romantic park, a lakeside promenade, an old church, and some rune stones. The TI organizes walking tours in English (40 kr, 2/day except Mon, Jul–mid-Aug and weekends May–Jun, tel. 08/5925-0020 for schedule). If it's sunny, Sigtuna is worth a browse and an ice-cream cone, but little more. Sigtuna is one hour from Stockholm (2 trains/hrly to Marsdal, then catch bus #570 or #575).

Route Tips for Drivers

Stockholm to Oslo: From downtown, follow Sveavägen West to Nortull/Gottberg/E-3/E-4 South. Take the second E-18 (immediately after the first). From Uppsala to Oslo, it's about 325 miles—that's seven hours of mostly freeway. Leaving Uppsala, follow signs for Route 55 and Nörrköping. When you hit E-18, just follow the Oslo signs. You'll pass *loppmarkets* (flea markets), Ester's Café (before Arjang), and hostel signs (90-kr dorm beds).

Arjang, just before the Norwegian border, is worth a stop if you don't make it to Oslo. The Arjang TI (Mon–Fri 9:00–20:00, less on weekends and off-season, tel. 0573/14136) books rooms (D-240 kr plus a 50-kr fee). Hotel Karl XII is cheap (D-300 kr, Db-400 kr, Sveavägen 22, near marketplace, tel. 0573/10156, fax 0573/711-426).

At the border, change money at the little TI kiosk (left side, under flags, daily in summer 10:00–19:00, fair rates, standard 20-kr-per-traveler's-check fee). If you change a traveler's check, convert your extra Swedish paper and coins for no extra fee. Pick up the Oslo map and *What's On*.

The freeway zips you into downtown Oslo. Follow "E-18" signs to Sentrum, then Sentral Stasjon (train station) and Paleet P (a central parking garage). If you're going directly to a room on the west end, keep left, following signs to Oslo V, veering right toward the palace immediately after passing the harborfront and twin brick towers of the city hall. If your hotel is near the station, don't take the Sentrum O exit; instead, follow the sign for Paleet P. (At the Paleet P parking garage, turn right on Fred Olsens Gate, 1.5 blocks for the Sjømannshjem.)

SOUTH SWEDEN: VÄXJÖ AND KALMAR

Outside of Stockholm, the most interesting region in Sweden is Småland. This Swedish province is famous for its forests, lakes, great glass, and the many immigrants it sent to the United States. More Americans came from this area than any other part of Scandinavia, and the immigration center in Växjö tells the story well. Between Växjö and Kalmar is Glass Country, a 70-mile stretch of forest sparkling with glassworks. Of the prestigious glassworks that welcome curious visitors, Kosta's best. Historic Kalmar has a rare Old World ambience and the most magnificent medieval castle in Scandinavia. From Kalmar, you can cross one of Europe's longest bridges to hike through the Stonehenge-type mysteries of the strange island of Öland.

Planning Your Time

By train, on a three-week Scandinavian trip, I'd skip this area in favor of the slick night train from Copenhagen to Stockholm (and side trips to Helsinki and Estonia). If you're driving, the sights described below make that same trip an interesting way to spend a couple of days. While I'm not so hot on the Swedish countryside (OK, blame my Norwegian heritage), you can't see only Stockholm and say you've seen Sweden. Växjö and Kalmar give you the best possible dose of small-town and countryside Sweden. (I find Lund and Malmö, both popular side trips from Copenhagen, really dull. And I'm not old or sedate enough to find a sleepy boat trip along the much-loved Göta Canal appealing.) Drivers can spend three days getting from Copenhagen to Stockholm this way:
Day 1: Leave Copenhagen after breakfast, tour Frederiksborg Castle, picnic under Kronborg Castle, 14:00–Take ferry (or bridge, as of July 2000) to Sweden, then drive northeast, 18:00–Set up in Växjö.

South Sweden: Växjö and Kalmar

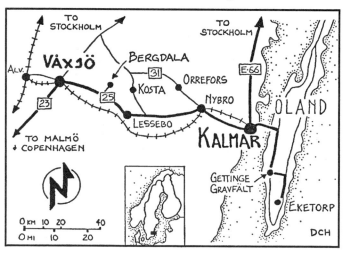

Day 2: Tour Växjö's House of Emigrants, drive into Glass Country, tour Kosta glassworks (or the smaller, more traditional Bergdala works), 14:30–Set up in Kalmar in time to tour the castle and its provincial museum, evening in Kalmar.

Day 3: 8:00–Begin five-hour drive north along the coast to Stockholm, 10:30–Break in Västervik, 12:00–Stop in Söderköping for picnic lunch and a walk along the Göta Canal, 13:30–Continue drive north, 16:00–Arrive in Stockholm and possibly catch the night boat to Helsinki.

Thinking ahead to your Helsinki cruise: boat tickets may be cheaper (off-weekend) and your drive to Oslo more reasonable (earlier start) if you do the Helsinki excursion immediately after Kalmar, before seeing Stockholm.

VÄXJÖ

A pleasant but rather dull town of 70,000, Växjö (vek-fwuh) is in the center of Småland. A stroll through downtown Växjö is perhaps the purest Swedish experience you can have.

The town is compact, with the train station, town square, two important museums, and the TI all within two blocks of each other. Växjö has an easy-to-enjoy pedestrian center, and the nearby lake is encircled by a pleasant three-mile path. Train travelers not interested in glass can make this a convenient three-hour stopover en route to Kalmar. A farmers' market bustles on the main square on Wednesday and Saturday mornings.

Tourist Information: The busy TI is at the train station (mid-Jun–Aug Mon–Fri 9:30–18:00, Jul until 18:30, Sat 10:00–14:00, Sun 11:00–15:00; Sept–mid-Jun Mon–Fri 9:00–16:30, tel. 0470/41410).

Sights—Växjö

▲▲**House of Emigrants (Utvandrarnas Hus)**—This tidy brick box is a user-friendly archive filled with letters home to the old country, ships' registers, and Minnesotans pondering their roots. A large part of the 1,300,000 Swedes who moved to the United States came from this neck of the Swedish woods. If you have Swedish roots, this place is really exciting. Even if you don't, this small exhibit is more interesting than you might expect. In 1900 Chicago was the second-largest Swedish town. Back then, one in six Swedes lived in the United States. The *Dream of America* exhibit tells the story of the "American Fever" experienced from the 1850s to the 1920s (30 kr, Jun–Aug Mon–Fri 9:00–18:00, Sat–Sun 11:00–16:00, off-season closes weekdays at 16:00, tel. 0470/20120.) The emigration festival, three days around the second Sunday in August, is a real hoot, as thousands of Minnesotans storm Växjö.

Upstairs is an excellent library and research center. You're welcome to take a peek. Interview an American Swede at work. Root-seekers (10,000 a year from the United States) are welcome, encouraged to write well in advance (Box 201, S-35104, Växjö, for research form and information), and advised to bring whatever information they have—such as ship names and birthdates. (Research center open Mon–Fri 9:00–16:00, members-50 kr/3 hrs, nonmembers-100 kr/3 hrs, membership-150 kr/year.)

The Liv Ullman movie about the emigration, *The Immigrants*, and its sequel, *The New Land*, make for great pre-trip viewing.

▲**Småland and Swedish Glass Museum**—This offers a good look at local forestry, a prehistoric exhibit, a wonderful traditional costume display (top floor), and a look at the local glass industry (40 kr, Mon–Fri 11:00–17:00, Sat–Sun 11:00–17:00, closed Mon off-season, next to House of Emigrants).

Domkyrka—Växjö's fine church (dedicated to the 11th-century English missionary, Saint Sigfrid) features some fine sacred art—in glass, of course. The thoughtfully written 15-kr brochure describes it well. The church offers concerts many Thursday evenings in July and August at 20:00 (50 kr).

Linneparken—This lovely park, located behind the cathedral, is dedicated to the great Swedish botanist Carl von Linne (a.k.a. Carolus Linnaeus). It has an arboretum, lots of well-categorized perennials, and a big children's playground.

Swimming—From the House of Emigrants you can see the town's super-modern lakeside swimming hall (Simhall), a five-minute walk away (25 kr including sauna, plus a little more if you want to tan or use exercise room, towel-10 kr, call for open-swim hours, tel. 0470/41204).

Sleeping in Växjö
(7 kr = about $1, tel. code: 0470)
Sleep Code: **S** = Single, **D** = Double/Twin, **T** = Triple, **Q** = Quad, **b** = bathroom, **CC** = Credit Card (Visa, MasterCard, Amex). Rates include breakfast.

Sleeping in Hotels and Motels
Hotel Esplanad is your best central hotel value. This quiet, comfortable old hotel, run by Birgit, is just three blocks from the town center (summer rates are mid-Jun–mid-Aug and Fri–Sun nights: S-265 kr, Sb-420 kr, D-350 kr, Db-450 kr; high-season rates: D-520 kr, Db-690 kr; CC:VM, N. Esplanaden #21A, 35231 Växjö, tel. 0470/22580, fax 0470/26226). From the station, walk five blocks up Kungsgatan and turn left on N. Esplanaden; it's two blocks to the hotel. From the freeway, follow "Centrum" signs into town. At the Royal Corner Hotel, turn left; 200 yards later, at the first light, turn right onto N. Esplanaden. The yellow hotel is on the right.

Best Western Hotel Statt, in the town center, is more traditional and borderline luxurious (small Sb-845–995 kr, Db-1,195 kr; summer and weekend rates can stretch during slow times: small Sb-590 kr, Db-690 kr; CC:VMA, a block in front of station at 6 Kungsgatan, tel. 0470/13400, fax 0470/44837, www.hotelstatt.se).

Hotell Teaterparken, in the Konserthus complex, has sleek rooms that are a good value when discounted (in summer and on winter weekends: Sb-500 kr, Db-700 kr, CC:VMA, V. Esplanaden 10-12, tel. 0470/39900, fax 0470/47577).

Sleeping in Rooms in Private Homes
For a 50-kr fee, the TI can find private rooms for about 140 kr per person, 125 kr if you have sheets. Breakfast is usually 50 kr extra. To save money and be assured of a good value, go or call direct to the following places.

Eva and Håkan Edfeldt are a professional couple with a teenage son. They live in a woodsy 80-year-old house in a folksy old neighborhood (150 kr per person, one double and one triple share a bathroom on the top floor up some steep stairs, 30-kr breakfast baskets in the room, kitchenette, Telestadsgatan 6, 35235 Växjö, tel. 0470/19242 or 0470/88279). The whole family speaks great English. Their home is a 12-minute walk from the station: Take the bridge over the tracks, jog right and follow Värendsgatan to the lake, and turn right at Skånegatan, which ends at the Edfeldts' driveway.

The **Emigrant's Cabin** is remotely situated deep in a forest near a lake, 200 meters from a tiny road, and 25 miles from Växjö. This hundred-year-old rustic cabin has no modern conveniences. Consider a peaceful escape/adventure here (book in advance, 500 kr per night for two to four people, minimum two nights, includes a rowboat, emergency cell phone, "guided visit" to a grocery store, and round-trip drive from Växjö by the owners, the Edfeldts—see previous listing). While I haven't done this, after hearing this charming couple describe the experience, it's high on my list.

Siv Kidvik, a more comfortable, newer home run by an older couple, is fine for families with a car and has a great garden and four rooms (D-175 kr, children half price, breakfast-35 kr, kitchenette, Kastanjevägen 70, tel. 0470/17053, speak slowly and clearly). Drive north from the center on Linnegatan, which becomes Sandsbrovägen. At the end of the cemetery before the Shell Tankomat station, go right on Lillestadsvägen. Take the first left onto Gamla Norrvägen, then the first left again onto Kastanjevägen.

Sleeping in the Hostel

Växjö has a fine **hostel** on a lake two miles out of town (110-kr beds in 2- to 4-bed rooms, nonmembers pay 40 kr extra, breakfast-45 kr, open 8:00–10:00, 17:00–20:00, STF Vandrarhem Evedal—IYHF, 35263 Växjö, telephone reservations required in summer, tel. 0470/63070, fax 0470/63216). Take bus #1C from the TI to the last stop (summer only, last ride 16:15, first ride 9:15, so hitch a ride into Växjö with a fellow hosteler).

Eating in Växjö

After-hours Växjö has precious little charm. You might consider dining out. These splurges are recommended by locals: **Lager Lunden** (180-kr meals, in front of Statt Hotel), **PM** (100- to 200-kr meals, modern European cuisine in bistro ambience popular with discerning yuppies, friendly service and good meals, across from theater at V. Esplanaden 9, tel. 0470/45445), **Spisen** (60-kr lunch specials, 100- to 200-kr dinners, traditional Swedish, a bit smoky, across from station, tel. 0470/12300), and **Café Momento** in the Småland museum (Swedish-French). The restaurant in **Hotell Teaterparken** has light meals for 60 kr to 100 kr.

Transportation Connections—Växjö

By train to: Copenhagen (10/day, 5 hrs, change in Alvesta), **Kalmar** (11/day, 90 min). While there are buses from Växjö to Kosta and bus tours of the Glass Country from Växjö, the glass-works aren't worth the time and trouble unless you have a car. Instead, take a careful look at the glass exhibit in the Växjö museum and train straight to Kalmar.

Sights—Between Växjö and Kalmar

Lessebo Paper Mill—The town of Lessebo has a 300-year-old paper mill that's kept working for visitors to see. If you've never seen handmade paper produced, this mill is worth a visit. Get the English brochure. (Mon–Fri 7:00–16:00, Sat 11:00–15:00, tours in English at 9:30, 10:30, 13:00, and 14:15 in summer; the mill makes paper 7:00–11:15, 12:30–15:00; otherwise it's open but dead, tel. 0478/47691.) By car, Lessebo is an easy stop between Växjö and Kosta. Just after the Kosta turnoff, you'll see a black-and-white "Handpapersbruk" sign.

▲▲**The Kingdom of Crystal**—This is Sweden's Glass Country. Frankly, these glassworks cause so much excitement because of the relative rarity of anything else thrilling in Sweden, outside of greater Stockholm. Pick up the Glasriket "Kingdom of Crystal" brochure in Växjö or Kalmar. The following three glassworks give tours and welcome visitors. Bergdala is cutest; Kosta treats its tourists best; Orrefors is the most famous. The fourth glassworks makes art.

Bergdala has a glassworks that offers a fine close-up look at actual craftsmen blowing and working the red-hot glass, a good shop (with Bergdala's tempting blue-ringed cereal bowls), and a fine picnic area with covered tables in case it's wet (Mon–Fri 9:00–14:30, Sat 10:00–15:00, Sun 12:00–15:00, no action 12:00–12:30, 30 min east of Växjö, exit Road 25 at "Bergdala" sign, drive three miles north, tel. 0478/31650).

Kosta is your best major glassworks stop. This town boasts the oldest of the *glasbruks*, dating back to 1742. Today the glassworks is a thriving tourist and shopping center (open year-round Mon–Fri 9:00–18:00, Sat 9:00–16:00, Sun 11:00–16:00, actual glassblowing is seen only on workdays but not from 10:00–11:00, tel. 0478/34500, book tours at tel. 0478/34529). On arrival, report to the information desk to get your English tour. Tours start in the historic and glass display rooms, then go to the actual blowing room, where guides are constantly narrating the ongoing work.

Making great strides toward getting the lead out, Kosta's crystal is already 80 percent lead free. Visitors show the most enthusiasm in the shopping hall, where crystal "seconds" and discontinued models are sold at good prices. This is duty-free shopping, and they'll happily mail your purchases home. Kosta's best picnic tables (rainproof) are at the Gamla Kosta museum. Kosta is a well-signposted 15-minute drive from Lessebo. In town, follow signs for "Glasbruk."

Orrefors has the most famous of the several renowned glassworks in Glass Country, but its glassworks are quite a tourist racket and offer mediocre 30-minute tours (hrly, tel. 0481/34195 to confirm tour times, www.orrefors.se). Most visitors just observe the work from platforms. There's glassblowing action from 8:00 to

15:00 except during the 10:30-to-11:30 lunch break. Like Kosta, their shop sells nearly perfect crystal seconds at deep discounts (Jun–mid-Jul Mon–Fri 9:00–18:00, Sat 10:00–16:00, Sun 12:00–16:00; off-season closes an hour earlier). Don't miss the dazzling "museum" (open same hours as shop).

Transjö Glashytta offers a much different experience. Set up in an old converted farm just 10-minutes south of Kosta, this tiny glassworks does expensive but fine art pieces (tel. 0478/50700 for hours and specifics).

KALMAR

Kalmar feels formerly strategic and important. In its day, the town was called "the gateway to Sweden"—back when the Sweden/Denmark border was just a few miles to the south. Today it's just a sleepy has-been and a gateway only to the holiday island of Öland. Kalmar's salty old center, fine castle, and busy waterfront give it a wistful sailor's charm. The town is great on foot or by bike.

History students remember Kalmar as the place where the treaty establishing the Kalmar Union was signed. This 1397 "three crowns" treaty united Norway, Sweden, and Denmark and created a huge kingdom—impressive for its day, as most of Europe was fragmented and bickering. But the union, which was dominated by Denmark, lasted only a little more than a hundred years. When Gustav Vasa came to power in 1523, it was dissolved.

Tourist Information: The TI is central and helpful (mid-Jun–mid-Aug Mon–Fri 9:00–20:00, Sat 10:00–17:00, Sun 12:00–18:00, closing at 17:00 other months and closed on winter weekends, from station walk two blocks down Sodra Langgatan and turn right on Larmgatan to #6, tel. 0480/15350, www.kalmar .com). Get the handy town map and city guide, and confirm your sightseeing plans. The TI sells a 30-kr brochure, "A Walk Around Kalmar," outlining the town's historical sights, the old town, park, and castle. Guided tours in English (40 kr) leave from the TI at 18:00 on Wednesdays in July.

Bike Rental: Kalmar, with its cheery lanes, surrounding parks, and brisk harborfront, makes for happy biking. Team Sportia, a big sport shop near the station, rents fine bikes for 50 kr per day (Mon–Fri 10:00–18:00, Sat 10:00–15:00, closed Sun; leaving station, turn left on Stationsgatan and walk 300 meters to the roundabout, tel. 0480/21244). The Frimurare Hotellet rents bikes to its guests for 30 kr. The TI has a "Vasa Stigen" flier outlining a pleasant bike/hike past the castle and around the Stensö Peninsula.

Arrival in Kalmar: Arriving by train couldn't be easier. Get a reservation for your departure at the station (lockers available). The TI and town are dead ahead, bikes are to your left, and the castle is behind you.

Kalmar

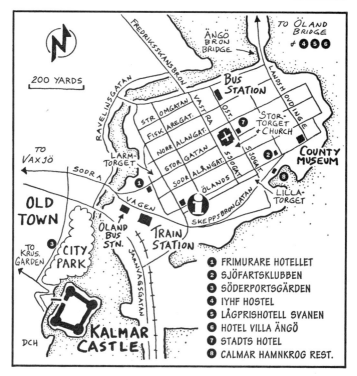

200 YARDS

TO VAXJÖ

OLD TOWN

1 FRIMURARE HOTELLET
2 SJÖFARTSKLUBBEN
3 SÖDERPORTSGÄRDEN
4 IYHF HOSTEL
5 LÅGPRISHOTELL SVANEN
6 HOTEL VILLA ÄNGÖ
7 STADTS HOTEL
8 CALMAR HAMNKROG REST.

Sights—Kalmar

▲▲**Kalmar Castle**—This moated castle is one of Europe's great medieval experiences. The stark exterior, cuddled by a lush park, houses a fine Renaissance palace interior, which is the work of King Gustavus Vasa and his sons. You'll walk up steps made of Catholic gravestones into faded but grand halls alive with Swedish history. The elaborately furnished rooms are entertainingly explained in English (60 kr, student-30 kr, mid-Jun–mid-Aug Mon–Sat 10:00–18:00, Sun 12:00–18:00; shoulder season 12:00–18:00; Nov–Mar 11:00–15:30, tel. 0480/451491). English tours are worthwhile for the goofy medieval antics of Sweden's kings (free, 45 min, daily in summer at 11:30 and 14:30). Check out the eerie exhibit on the women's prison; find the book with English descriptions. The castle lawn is an ideal picnic spot.

▲**Krusenstiernska Garden**—This early-19th-century middle-class home is lovingly cluttered with old family photos, toys, and

Gustavian-style furniture. A helpful English leaflet gives a room-by-room inventory. The garden, with its breezy café selling traditional homemade cakes, is also a treat (15 kr, garden open Mon–Fri 10:00–18:00, Sat–Sun 12:00–16:00; museum open Mon–Fri 13:00–17:00, Sat–Sun 13:00–16:00, closed off-season, 200 yards in front of castle at St. Dammgatan 11, tel. 0480/411-552). Between this house, the castle, and the station is Kalmar's Gamla Stan (old town), a toy village of well-painted wooden homes, tidy yards, and perfect fences.

▲Kalmar Town—The old town of Kalmar is more interesting than its grid plan. Stroll the Storgatan spine to the main square, Stortorget, where you'll find the biggest Baroque church in Sweden. The quieter lanes and Lilla Torget have fine old wooden homes. The ramparts survive and mark the old harbor line. The 20th-century extension is filled with parked cars and a modern shopping center.

▲▲Kalmar County (Läns) Museum—The second floor of this museum displays the impressive salvaged wreck of the royal ship *Kronan*, which sank nearby in 1676. Lots of interesting soggy bits and rusted pieces giving a here's-the-buried-treasure thrill are well described in English. (For maximum info, borrow the *Kronan* English booklet.) While the actual ship has yet to be recovered, this museum gives a much more intimate look at life at sea than Stockholm's grander Vasa exhibit. See the excellent 12-minute film (to avoid a delay, request an English showing as you enter). The third floor is worth a quick look for its Jenny Nystrom exhibit (a turn-of-the-century Kalmar artist who gained fame for her cute Christmas decorations featuring gidgets, elves, and pixies), a little old-time Kalmar city-life exhibit, and a cozy cafeteria (daily, same hours as museum, 45-kr salad buffet). From the harborfront museum's door you can see the distant half of the long bridge leading to the island of Öland (50 kr, daily mid-Jun–mid-Aug 10:00–18:00, off-season closes at 16:00, tel. 0480/451300).

Maritime History Museum (Sjöfartsmuseum)—This humble little three-room exhibit behind the Läns Museum is a jumble of model boats, charts, and paraphernalia interesting only to sailors who speak Swedish (25 kr, May–Aug Mon–Fri 11:00–16:00, Sat–Sun 12:00–16:00, Södra Långgatan 81, tel. 0480/86690).

▲Island of Öland—Until recently, this was Europe's longest bridge (free, 4 miles), connecting Öland with Kalmar and the mainland. The island, 90 miles long and only 8 miles wide, is a pleasant local resort known for its birds, windmills, flowers, beaches, and prehistoric sights. Public transportation is miserable, and the island is worthwhile only if you have a car and three extra hours. A 60-mile circle south of the bridge will give you a good dose of the island's windy rural charm.

   Gettlinge Gravfalt (just off the road about 10 miles up from the south tip) is a wonderfully situated, boat-shaped, Iron Age graveyard littered with monoliths and overseen by a couple of creaky old windmills. It offers a commanding view of the windy and mostly treeless island.

Farther south is the **Eketorp Prehistoric Fort,** a very recon-structed fifth-century stone fort that, as Iron Age forts go, is fairly interesting. Several evocative huts and buildings are filled with what someone imagines may have been the style back then, and the huge rock fort is surrounded by strange, runty, piglike crea-tures that were common 1,500 years ago. A sign reads: "For your convenience and pleasure, don't leave your children alone with the animals." (50 kr, daily May–Aug 10:00–17:00, free English tours usually at 13:00 in summer, tel. 0485/662-000.)

Sleeping in Kalmar
(7 kr = about $1, tel. code: 0480)
The TI can nearly always find you a room in a private home (300 kr per double, 40 kr per person for sheets, and a 50-kr fee per booking, no breakfast). They can also get you special last-minute discounts on fancy hotels. The first three places are great but cheap or open only during summer.

Frimurare Hotellet, newly renovated, fills a grand old build-ing overlooking a fine square. While quite large, it has soul and is run by a friendly family. Rich public areas, broad hardwood floors, chandeliers, and pilasters give it a neoclassical elegance (regular Db rate: 980 kr, mid-Jun–mid-Aug and Fri/Sat/Sun all-year rates: Sb-510 kr, Db-680 kr, family rooms, includes breakfast, CC:VMA, free sauna, bike rental-30 kr/day, yellow building 50 meters in front of train station at Larmtorget 2, 39232 Kalmar; tel. 0480/15230, fax 0480/85887, www.frimurarehotellet.gs2.com).

The **Sjöfartsklubben (Seaman's Club)** opens its shipshape little dorm to tourists June through mid-August. This historic home, built as a girls' school in 1820, now houses student sailors during the school year (13 rooms, S-190 kr, D-300 kr, T-365 kr, Q-430 kr, extra bed-65 kr, sheets-40 kr, no breakfast, kitchen priv-ileges, lively common room, Ölandsgatan 45, reception open same hours as TI, tel. 0480/10810). With harbor views and a lazy gar-den protected by a salty picket fence, this has by far the best cheap beds in Kalmar. If you call Sjöfartsklubben in the off-season, ask to speak to the manager, Lennard Olsson.

Söderportsgärden is a university dorm that opens its doors to tourists mid-June through mid-August (35 simple yet classy rooms, two to a "flat" sharing a bathroom and kitchen, S-350 kr, D-490 kr, includes sheets and breakfast, Slottsvägen 1, tel. 0480/12501). It's beautifully located next to a park, directly in front of the castle.

A 15-minute walk from the center, you'll find a fine **IYHF hostel** and hotel annex. The hostel has two- or seven-bed rooms, laundry, TV, and sauna (145 kr per bed, sheets-45 kr, nonmembers pay 40 kr extra, breakfast-49 kr, closed 10:00–16:30, reservations recommended). The hotel annex, **Kalmar Lågprishotell Svanen**, offers more comfort and privacy (S-380 kr, Sb-410 kr, D-495 kr, Db-525 kr, includes sheets and breakfast, CC:VMA, STF Vandrarhem, Rappegatan 1, 39230 Kalmar, tel. 0480/25560, fax 0480/88293). You'll see a blue-and-white hotel sign and a hostel symbol at the edge of town on Angoleden Street, less than a mile from the train station.

In the same neighborhood, a few blocks farther out, consider **Hotel Villa Ängö**, a big old house with a peaceful garden on the water and homey ground-floor rooms (S-350 kr, D-500 kr, breakfast in summer, basement sauna, Bagensgatan 20, tel. 0480/85415). The management lets the place virtually run itself, leaving the door open and the key waiting for you in the door.

Best Western Stadts Hotel is a 1,300-kr place with an affordable summer price (summer rate: Sb-525 kr, Db-720 kr, includes breakfast, CC:VMA, central at Stortorget 14, tel. 0480/496-900, fax 0480/496-910, e-mail: reservation@calmarstadshotell.se).

Eating in Kalmar

In the old center: I'd stroll the two busy cross streets, Storgatan and Kaggensgatan, to survey the many competitive places—both ethnic and Swedish. **Bistro Matisse** is popular for French cuisine (Kaggensgatan 1). At the intersection of those two streets, upstairs in the Kvasten department store, the **4 Kok** cafeteria serves a hearty *dagens rätt* special (45 kr, 11:00–16:00).

On the modern harborfront: Consider **Calmar Hamnkrog** for classy harbor-view dining (160–200-kr dinners, daily 13:00–23:00, Skeppsbrogatan 30, call 0480/411-020 to reserve seats by a window). For a meal for half the price from the same kitchen, with less ambience but the same harbor views, consider **Däcket** (100-kr dinners, Mon–Sat 17:00–23:00, closed Sun, outside or inside seating).

Near the castle: There are cafeterias in the castle and directly in front of the castle at **Söderportsgården**. For classier dining (or just a coffee break) in the city park with a view of the castle, consider the venerable **Byttan Restaurant** (55-kr lunch special 11:30–14:00, more expensive dinners, closed Sat, closed Sun off-season, you'll pass it as you walk to the castle, tel. 0480/16360).

Near the train station: Oscar Cafe has good three-course meals for 99 kr (open 16:00–22:00, also for lunch in summer, Södra Långgatan 5, one block from station, tel. 0480/15565).

Transportation Connections—Kalmar

By train to: Växjö (11/day, 90 min, reservation not required), **Stockholm** (14/day, 6 hrs, normally a transfer in Alvesta, reservation required; night train possible but with a change, nightly), **Copenhagen** (10/day, 6 hrs, one change, reservation required).

Route Tips for Drivers

Copenhagen to Sweden: See "Route Tips for Drivers" at the end of the Copenhagen chapter.

Helsingborg to Växjö to Kalmar: In Helsingborg, follow signs for E-4 and Stockholm. The road's good, traffic's light, and towns are clearly signposted. At Ljungby, Road 25 takes you to Växjö. Entering Växjö, skip the first Växjö exit and follow the freeway into "Centrum," where it ends.

The 70-mile drive from Växjö to Kalmar is a joy—light traffic with endless forest and lake scenery punctuated by numerous glassworks. The TI's free "Kingdom of Crystal" map lists them all and is your best navigational tool. Leave Växjö on Road 25 to Kalmar. The driving time between Växjö and Kosta is 45 minutes; between Kosta and Kalmar, 45 minutes.

Kalmar to Stockholm: Leaving Kalmar, follow E-22 "Lindsdal" and "Nörrköping" signs. The Kalmar-to-Stockholm drive is 240 miles and takes 5.5 hours. Sweden did a cheap widening job, paving the shoulders of the old two-lane road to get 3.8 lanes. Still, traffic is polite and sparse. There's little to see, so stock the pantry, set the compass on north, and home in on Stockholm.

Make two pleasant stops along the way. Vastervik is 90 miles north, with an 18th-century core of wooden houses (3 miles off the highway, "Centrum" signs lead you to the harbor). Park at the little six-days-a-week-and-great-smoked-fish market on the waterfront next to the seven-days-a-week Exet supermarket and a public WC.

Söderköping is just right for a lunch on the Göta Canal stop. Stay on E-22 past the town center, then turn right at the TI/Kanalbåtarna/Slussen/Kanal P signs. Park by the canal, one block toward the hill from the town square and TI.

Sweden's famous Göta Canal is 110 miles of canals cutting Sweden in half, with 58 locks (*slussen*) working up to a summit of 300 feet. It was built 150 years ago, with more than 7 million 12-hour man-days (60,000 men working about 22 years) at a low ebb in the country's self-esteem—to show her industrial oats. Today it's a lazy three- or four-day tour. Take just a peek at the Göta Canal over lunch, in the medieval town of Söderköping.

The TI on Söderköping's Rådhustorget (a square about a block off the canal) has good town maps, canal information, and Stockholm maps. From there go to the canal. The Toalett sign points to the Kanulbatiquen, a yachters' laundry (40 kr, wash and dry, open daily), shower, shop, and WC, with idyllic picnic tables just over the lock. From the lock, stairs lead up to the Utsiktsplats pavilion (a nice view but not quite worth the hike).

From Söderköping, E-22 takes you to Nörrköping. Follow "E-4" signs through Nörrköping, past a handy rest stop, and into Stockholm. The Centrum is clearly marked. (Viking's ferry terminal for Helsinki is in Södermalm; Silja's is northeast of town in Ropsten.)

FINLAND

HELSINKI

Finland and Estonia are the odd ducks in this book, and, as such, they deserve special comment. First, a brief history lesson. As far as the sightseer is concerned, Finland's history breaks into three parts:

Swedish—Finland was dominated by Sweden before the 1809 Russian takeover. Because of city fires, very little remains of this era.

Russian—Between 1809 and 1917, under fairly benign Russian control, Finland began to industrialize and most of Helsinki's great buildings were built.

Independent—From 1918 on, Finland's bold, trend-setting modern design and architecture blossomed.

Not so long ago, Finland was a dirt-poor agricultural country whose people were eagerly emigrating to northern Minnesota. (Read Toivo Pekkanen's *My Childhood* to learn about the life of a Finnish peasant at the turn of the century.) Since then, though, Finland has built itself up into a modern country with successful timber, paper, and telecommunications industries, despite having to make a devil's bargain with the Soviet Union to preserve its autonomy after World War II. During the Cold War, Finland teetered between the West and the Soviet Union, treading lightly on relations with her giant neighbor to the east. The collapse of the Soviet Union has done to Finland what a good long sauna might do to you.

When the menace of Moscow vanished, so did about 20 percent of Finland's trade. After a few years of adjustment, Finland is on an upswing now. Many Finns used to move to Sweden (where they are the biggest immigrant group), looking for better jobs in the metropolis of Stockholm. Some still nurse an inferiority complex, thinking of themselves as poor cousins to the Swedes. But now, Finland is the most technologically advanced country in Europe, and home to the giant cell-phone company Nokia. Finns are counting on their membership in the European Community and the euro zone to cement the strength of their economy. To visitors, Finland is indistinguishably Scandinavian, and Helsinki is brighter, more compact, and easier to walk around than Stockholm.

Money
There are about 5 Finnish markka (mk) in a U.S. dollar. One markka is about 20 cents.

Finnish
Finnish is a difficult-to-learn Finno-Ugric language originating east of Russia's Ural Mountains and related in Europe only to Estonian (closely) and Hungarian (distantly). Finland is officially bilingual; 6 percent of the country's population speaks Swedish as a first language. You'll notice that Helsinki is called Helsingfors in Swedish. Many street signs list places in both Finnish and Swedish. Nearly every educated young person speaks effortless English—the language barrier is very small.

The only essential word needed for a quick visit is *"Kiitos"* (key-toes)—that's "thank you," and locals love to hear it. *"Kippis"* ("keep peace") is what you say before you down a shot of Finnish vodka or cloudberry liqueur.

SAILING FROM STOCKHOLM TO HELSINKI
The next best thing to being in Helsinki is getting there. Europe's most enjoyable cruise starts with lovely archipelago scenery, a setting sun, and a royal *smørgåsbord* dinner. Dance 'til you drop and sauna 'til you drip. Budget travel rarely feels this hedonistic. Sixteen hours after you depart, it's "Hello, Helsinki."

Planning Your Time
When planning your cruise, consider how much time you'd like to spend in Helsinki (one day is normally enough) and the day you'd like to depart (weekends are more crowded and off-season Fridays are more expensive). Also consider the schedule ripples caused by the ship. If you sleep into and out of Stockholm by train and take two night boats, you'll have two days in Stockholm with no nights. Stockholm is worth two days on a three-week Scandinavian trip, but four in-transit nights in a row is pretty intense. Doable, but intense.

The Cruise Lines: Viking and Silja
Two fine and fiercely competitive lines, Viking and Silja, connect the capitals of Sweden and Finland. Each line offers state-of-the-

Sailing the Baltic Sea

art ships with luxurious *smørgåsbord* meals, reasonable cabins, plenty of entertainment (discos, saunas, gambling), and enough duty-free shopping to sink a ship.

The Pepsi and Coke of the Scandinavian cruise industry vie to outdo each other with bigger and fancier boats. The ships are big—at 56,000 tons, nearly 200 yards long, and with 2,700 beds, they're the largest (and some of the cheapest) luxury hotels in Scandinavia. Many other shipping lines buy their boats used from Viking and Silja.

Which line is best? You could count showers and compare *smørgåsbords*, but both lines go overboard to win the loyalty of the 9 million duty-free-crazy Swedes and Finns who make the trip each year. Viking, with an older, less-luxurious fleet, is cheaper by about 150 kr per trip. Only Silja gives discounts to railpass holders (a hefty 50 percent). But only Viking fully caters to low-budget travelers, selling cheap *"ekonomi"* cabins (shower down the hall) and allowing passengers to pay for deck passage only and sleep for free on chairs, sofas, and under the stars or stairs. Both lines give modest student and senior discounts.

Cruise Schedules

Both lines sail nightly from Stockholm and Helsinki. Going from Stockholm to Helsinki, the boats leave about 17:00 and arrive in Helsinki the next morning about 9:30. From Helsinki to Stockholm, boats leave about 18:00 and arrive in Stockholm about 9:30. Both companies also sail daily between Stockholm and Turku, Finland.

Scenery: The first three hours are filled with island scenery. The first hour after departure is least interesting. The third hour features the most exotic island scenery—tiny islets with cute red huts and happy people. I'd have dinner at the first sitting (shortly after departure) and get out on the deck for the sunset.

Time Change: Finland is one hour ahead of Sweden. Sailing from Stockholm to Helsinki, operate on Swedish time until you go to bed, then reset your watch. Morning schedules are Finnish time (and vice versa when you return).

Cost

Fares vary by season and by day of the week. Mid-June to mid-August is most expensive (and crowded). During the off-season, Friday prices are much higher—sometimes double the regular fare or more; try to plan your trip so you don't travel on a Friday.

Even in high season, a one-way with the cheapest bed that has a private bath (in a below-sea-level, under-car-deck "C" quad) is remarkably cheap: about 450 kr ($65) on Viking, 600 kr ($85) on Silja. Fares drop to about 300 kr on Viking and 430 kr on Silja in low season. Each ship offers a whale of a *smørgåsbord* dinner for an extra 160 kr, and a big breakfast for 60 kr. Reserving your meals in advance saves about 10 percent off the cost and the hassle of hustling for a reservation after you board.

If you're traveling out and back on consecutive days, ask for the round-trip "cruise" fare, which sometimes costs even less than one-way. You have the same cabin both nights and access to your stateroom all day long. If you like, you can sleep in and linger over breakfast long after the boat has docked. But there's too much to do in Helsinki to take advantage of these privileges.

The fares are so cheap because the boats operate tax free and the hordes of locals who sail to shop and drink duty- and tax-free spend a fortune on board. It's a very large operation—mostly for locals. The boats are filled with about 60 percent Finns, 35 percent Swedes, and 5 percent cruisers from other countries. Last year, the average passenger spent nearly as much on booze and duty-free items as for the boat fare—about 600 kr. Finns are big ferryspotters and know all the ships by name. The boats now make a midnight stop in the Åland Islands—a part of Finland that's exempt from European Union membership—specifically to allow duty-free shopping by preserving the international nature of the trip.

Helsinki Harbor Terminals

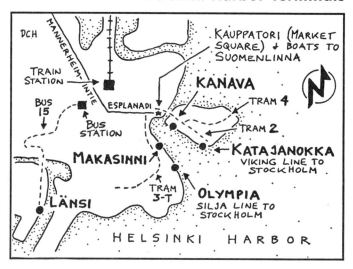

Free Beds

One of the Viking boats (the *Gabriella*) still has free dorm beds for
vagabonds. Get to the boat as soon as it opens (usually 16:00) and
head straight for the bottom. There are 8 to 10 bunks (no sheets)
in a doorless cabin. It's possible to lock up your bags from port to
port in the luggage checkroom. You can check whether you're
sailing on the *Gabriella* in the printed or online Viking timetable.

Reservations

Call the cruise line directly in Scandinavia to reserve your spot
in advance. If you're traveling in summer or on a weekend, make
a reservation as soon as you can commit. The Swedish reservations numbers are 46/8/222-140 (Silja) and 46/8/452-4000
(Viking). You can pay with a credit card and pick up your
reserved ticket at the terminal (come at least one hour before
sailing). Operators speak English. You can also call the Helsinki
reservations numbers (Viking 358/9/123577; Silja 358/203/74552
or, within Finland only, toll-free 9800/52682). Any travel agent
in Scandinavia will also sell you a ticket (same price plus a 30-kr-
or-so booking fee).

Web Sites

Visit Viking at www.vikingline.fi or Silja at www.silja.com/english
(or www.silja.se) for the most up-to-date fare and timetable info.

Terminals

Locations: In Stockholm, the Viking terminal is more central. Take the bus (20 kr) from Central Station's gate #24 or take bus #53 to "London Viaducten." The ship is parked just past the Gamla Stan. For Silja, take the bus (20 kr) from Central Station's gate #35. In Helsinki, both lines are perfectly central, each on opposite sides of the harbor, a 10-minute walk from the market, Senate Square, and shopping district. See the Helsinki map for details. (If staying at Helsinki's Eurohostel, Viking is more convenient.)

Terminal Buildings: These are well organized with cafés, lockers, tourist information desks, lounges, and phones. Remember, 2,000 passengers come and go with each boat. Customs is a snap. Boats open two hours before departure.

Parking: Both lines offer safe and handy 70 kr-per-day parking in Stockholm. Viking's ticket machine takes 5- and 10-kr coins (come with 110 kr for 46 hours, or bring a credit card). For Silja it's wise to reserve a parking spot (tel. 08/662-0046). Keep inserting money until you see the date and time of your return on the meter, then hit the red button and leave the ticket on your dashboard. Park your car here on arrival in Stockholm, take the cruise, and tour Helsinki.

Services Onboard

Meals: The cruise is famous for its *smørgåsbord* dinners, and understandably so. Board the ship hungry. Dinner is self-serve in two sittings, one around 18:00, the other a couple hours later. The scenery is worth being on deck for, but if you call in advance, you can reserve a window seat. If you board without a reservation, go to the headwaiter and make one. Breakfast buffets are 60 kr; dinner buffets are 160 kr (buy with your ticket and save 10 percent). Pick up the "How to Eat a *Smørgåsbord*" brochure. The key is to take small portions and pace yourself. Drinks or free water can be ordered from waiters (free beer and wine on Viking). There are also reasonable or classy restaurants for lighter eaters or those on a budget.

Sauna: Each ship has a sauna. This costs about 60 kr extra. Reserve a time upon boarding. Saunas on Silja are half price or even free in the morning (for those with a cabin towel).

Banking: The change desk on board has bad rates but no fee, which means it's actually a better deal than a Helsinki bank for those changing less than $100 in cash. For a quick visit to Helsinki, just change some of your Swedish kroner. Helsinki banks charge 20 mk to exchange cash and 30 mk for traveler's checks, while the change desk in the boat changes cash for no fee and charges 30 mk for checks. FOREX (with offices at Pohjoises-planadi 27 in Helsinki and in Stockholm's train station) also gives good rates for small exchanges (no fee for cash, 10 mk per traveler's check). While city sightseeing tours can be paid for in kroner, you'll need local currency for public transport, shops, and museums. (5mk = about $1.)

Options

Staying Overnight in Helsinki: This usually increases your boat fare from Stockholm, since the best round-trip deals are only for travel on consecutive nights. In the off-season, though, you can save money if, by staying in Helsinki, you avoid traveling on a Friday night (when boat fares are highest and hotel prices are lowest). Your boat line may be able to get you a $100 double in a $200 hotel when you book your tickets, but you can find a cheaper room by telephoning my budget listings (see below).

Tallinn: You can visit Tallinn as a day trip from Helsinki or as part of a triangle trip: Stockholm-Helsinki-Tallinn-Stockholm or vice versa. For a day trip, you'll need the whole day (too stressful if you arrive from Stockholm in the morning or need to leave in the evening). On a triangle trip, you can sleep on the boat every night if you take one of the evening ferries between Helsinki and Tallinn.

Turku: Consider another "open jaws" plan, sailing from Stockholm into Helsinki and returning to Stockholm from Turku. The cheaper round-trip boat fare saves enough to pay for the two-hour train ride from Helsinki to Turku. Turku boats may have free airplane seats or *couchettes* in the bilge, but the boats are usually smaller and lack cruise-ship excitement. Passengers are rushed on and off, since the boat stays in the port for just one hour.

HELSINKI

Helsinki is the only European capital with no medieval past. In 1746 Sweden built a huge fortress on an island outside its harbor. The town of Helsinki was founded to supply the fortress. After taking over Finland in 1809, the Russians decided to move its capital and university closer to St. Petersburg—from Turku to Helsinki. They hired a young German architect named Carl Ludwig Engel to design new public buildings for Helsinki and told him to use St. Petersburg as a model. This is why the oldest parts of Helsinki (around Market Square and Senate Square) feel so Russian, with stone buildings in yellow and blue pastel with white trim and columns.

Though the city was part of the Russian Empire in the 19th century, most of its residents were still Swedes, and Swedish was the language of business and culture. In the mid-1800s Finland began to industrialize. The Swedish upper class in Helsinki expanded the city, bringing in the railroad and surrounding the old Russian-inspired core of the city with neighborhoods of four- and five-story apartment buildings, including some Art Nouveau masterpieces. Meanwhile, Finns moved from the countryside to Helsinki to take jobs as industrial laborers. The Finnish language slowly acquired equal status with Swedish, and eventually Helsinki became a majority Finnish-speaking city.

Since downtown Helsinki didn't exist until the 1800s, it was more consciously designed and laid out than other European capitals. Europe's most neoclassical city, with its many architectural overleafs, turns guests into fans of architecture and urban planning. Katajanokka, Kruununhaka, and Eira are good walking neighborhoods for architecture and urban history buffs.

Helsinki can be windy and cold, but it makes the best of its difficult situation and will leave you impressed and glad to have dropped in. Start with the two-hour "Hello, Helsinki" bus tour that meets the boat at the dock. Or take the do-it-yourself walking tour—the compact city center is great for roaming and brisk walking. Enjoy Helsinki's ruddy harborfront market, count goose bumps in her churches, and dive into Finnish culture in the open-air folk museum.

Planning Your Time

On a three-week trip through Scandinavia, Helsinki is worth at least the time between two successive nights on the cruise ship—about seven hours. Take the orientation bus tour upon arrival, mingle through the market, buy and eat a picnic, and drop by the TI. People watch and browse through downtown to the National Museum (re-opens in June 2000). For the afternoon, choose between the Open-Air Folk Museum and a boat tour of the harbor. Enjoy a cup of coffee at Café Kappeli before you board. Sail away while sampling another *smørgåsbord* dinner.

Orientation

(Helsinki's tel. code: 09; from outside Finland: 358-9)
Tourist Information: The TI is a half block inland from Market Square, on the right just past the fountain, at the corner of Unioninkatu and Pohjoisesplanadi (Mon–Fri 9:00–19:00, Sat–Sun 9:00–15:00, shorter hours off-season, tel. 09/169-3757, fax 09/169-3839, excellent Web site with maps, timetables, and events: www.hel.fi /english). The TI is friendly, helpful, well stocked in free brochures, and blond(e). Pick up the city map, the public transit map, "Helsinki on Foot" (6 well-described walking tours with maps), the monthly *Helsinki This Week* magazine (lists sights, hours, and events), and *City* magazine (good opinionated restaurant listings, geared for the younger crowd). Ask for the brochure on the scenic #3T tram and go over your sightseeing plans. **Tour Expert**, a travel agency housed at the TI, is efficient and helpful for hotels and excursions, including trips to Tallinn (same hours as TI, fax 09/2288-1599, e-mail: tourexpert@helsinkiexpert.fi).

Money Exchange: FOREX exchange desks are at Pohjoises-planadi 27 (near TI, in summer Mon–Sat 8:00–21:00) and inside the train station (daily 8:00–21:00, no fee for cash, 10 mk fee per traveler's check).

Time: Finland and Estonia are one hour ahead of Sweden and the rest of Scandinavia. Set your watch ahead when you arrive or you'll miss the boat back.

Getting around Helsinki

By Bus and Tram: With the public transit route map and a little mental elbow grease, the buses and trams are easy, giving you the city by the tail. Tickets (8 mk from kiosks, 10 mk from the driver) give you an hour of travel. The Tourist Ticket (25 mk for 24 hours of unlimited travel) pays if you take three or more rides. The single subway line uses the same tickets but is not useful for most visitors.

Tram #3T makes the rounds of most of the town's major sights, letting you stop and go for the cost of your 8-mk ticket. The TI promotes it as a self-guided tour and has a helpful explanatory brochure (not available on board). Bus #24, which goes farther afield to the Sibelius Monument and the open-air museum, also has a great brochure from the TI. Each of these gives you a cheap, go-any-time, once-over-lightly, do-it-yourself tour. In summer the red "Pub Tram" makes a 40-minute circle through the city while its passengers get looped on the (one) beer that comes with the 30-mk ticket (hrly from 11:00–15:00 and 17:00–22:00, leaves from in front of the Fennia building at Mikonkatu 17, across parking lot from train station tower).

If you're staying in Helsinki for more than a few hours, the **Helsinki Card** is a good deal (24 hrs/120 mk, 48 hrs/150 mk, 72 hrs/180 mk). It includes free entrance to sights; free use of buses, trams, and the ferry to Suomenlinna; a 70-mk bus tour; and a 96-page booklet (more information: www.helsinkiexpert.fi). Buy it at the TI or ferry ports.

By Bike: Greenbike rents bikes (at Mannerheimintie 13, behind Kiasma museum and across from the Parliament House, in the low building below street level, tel. 09/8502-2850).

Do-It-Yourself "Welcome to Helsinki" Walk

Start at the harbor. The colorful **produce market** on Market Square thrives from 6:30 to 14:00 daily except Sunday (also summer eves 15:30–20:00). The Russian-style buildings behind it are Helsinki's oldest. With your back to the water, walk left. The fountain features the symbol of Helsinki, the Daughter of the Baltic. Across the street to the right you'll see the **TI**. The round door next to the TI leads into the delightful Jugendsalen. Designed, apparently, by a guy named Art Deco, this free and pleasant information center for locals offers interesting historical exhibits and a public WC (Mon–Fri 9:00–16:00, Pohjoisesplanadi 19).

Make a one-block detour up Unioninkatu to the neoclassical **Senate Square** and **Lutheran Cathedral**. You'll pass the Schroder Sport Shop, with a great selection of popular Finnish-made Rapala fishing lures—ideal for the fisherfolk on your gift list.

In the park across the street from the TI is my favorite café in northern Europe, **Café Kappeli**. When you've got some time, dip into this turn-of-the-century gazebo-like oasis of coffee, pastry, and relaxation. Built in the 19th century, it was a popular hangout for local intellectuals and artists. Today the café offers romantic tourists waiting for their ship a great 10-mk-cup-of-coffee memory (unguarded WC just inside the door).

The TI and Café Kappeli are at the head of the **Esplanade**—two streets, sandwiching a park in the middle, which constitute Helsinki's top shopping boulevard. Walk it. The north (tourist office) side is interesting for window-shopping, people watching, and sun worshiping. You'll pass several stores specializing in Finnish design. Farther down is the huge Academic Bookstore (Akateeminen Kirjakauppa), designed by Alvar Aalto, with a great map and travel section and café. Finally you'll come to the prestigious Stockmann's department store—Finland's Harrods. This biggest, best, and oldest store in town has fine displays of local design. Just beyond is the main intersection in town, that of the Esplanade and Mannerheimintie. Nearby you'll see the famous *Three Blacksmiths* statue. (Locals say, "If a virgin walks by, they'll strike the anvil." It doesn't work. I tried.)

Two blocks to the right, through a busy shopping center, is the harsh (but serene) architecture of the central **train station**, designed by Eliel Saarinen in 1916. The four people on the facade symbolize the peasant farmers with lamps coming into the Finnish capital. Wander around inside. Continuing past the post office and the statue, return to Mannerheimintie, which leads to the large white **Finlandia Hall**, another Aalto masterpiece. Though not open to individuals, there are often guided tours in summer (see "Sights," below). Across the street is the excellent little **Finnish National Museum** (looks like a church, designed by Finland's first three great architects, re-opens in June 2000), and a few blocks behind that is the sit-down-and-wipe-a-tear beautiful rock church, **Temppeliaukio**. Sit. Enjoy the music. It's a wonderful place to end this Welcome to Helsinki walk.

To continue on to the **Sibelius Monument**, set in a lovely park, take bus #24 (direction Seurasaari) from nearby Arkadiankatu street. The same ticket is good on a later #24. Ride to the end of the line—the bridge to Seurasaari Island and Finland's open-air folk museum. When you're ready, a return bus #24 will take you all the way back to the Esplanade.

Sights—Central Helsinki

▲▲▲**Orientation Bus Tour**—A fast, very good two-hour introductory tour leaves daily from both terminals immediately after the ships dock. The rapid-fire two- or three-language tour costs 95 mk (free with Helsinki Card) and gives a good historic overview—a look at all the important buildings from the newly remodeled Olympic Stadium to embassy row, with too-fast 10-minute stops at the Lutheran Cathedral, the Sibelius Monument, and the Church in the Rock (Temppeliaukio). You'll learn strange facts, such as how they took down the highest steeple in town during World War II so the Soviet bombers flying in from Estonia couldn't see their target.

If you're on a tight budget and don't mind missing the more distant sights, you can do the core of this tour on your own, as explained in my city walk (above). But I thoroughly enjoyed listening to the guide. He sounded like an audio shredder that was occasionally turned off so English could come out.

For more time in the Church of the Rock, leave the tour there and consider walking three blocks to the National Museum and Finlandia Hall.

You can pick up the same tour every day at 10:45, 14:00, and 16:00 at the corner of Fabianinkatu and the Esplanade a block from the TI (buy tickets inside TI at Tour Expert). But I like the "pick you up at the boat and drop you at your hotel or back on Market Square" efficiency of the tours that meet the boats. Buy your ticket on board or at the tourist desk in the terminal (availability is no problem).

▲▲**Lutheran Cathedral**—With its prominent green dome overlooking the city and harbor, this church is Carl Ludwig Engel's masterpiece. Open a pew gate and sit to savor neoclassical nirvana. Finished in 1852, the interior is pure architectural truth. Enter on the left side (Mon–Sat 10:00–18:00, Sun 12:00–18:00, off-season closes at 16:00).

Senate Square—From the top of the steps of the Lutheran Cathedral, study Europe's finest neoclassical square. The Senate building is on your left. The small blue stone building, with the slanted mansard roof in the far left corner, is from 1757 and is one of just two pre–Russian conquest buildings remaining in Helsinki. On the right is the university building. Czar Alexander II, a friend of Finland's, is honored by the statue in the square. The huge staircase leading up to the cathedral is a popular meeting and tanning point in Helsinki. The tiny square building across from the cathedral entrance houses a small café.

▲▲**Russian Orthodox Cathedral**—This cathedral hovers above Market Square and faces the Lutheran Cathedral as Russian culture faces Europe's. The inside is a fine icon experience (built 1868, Mon–Sat 9:30–16:00, Tue until 18:00, Sun 12:00–15:00).

▲▲▲**Temppeliaukio Church**—Another great piece of church

Helsinki

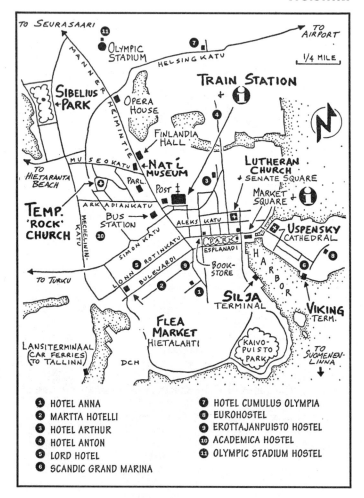

1 HOTEL ANNA
2 MARTTA HOTELLI
3 HOTEL ARTHUR
4 HOTEL ANTON
5 LORD HOTEL
6 SCANDIC GRAND MARINA

7 HOTEL CUMULUS OLYMPIA
8 EUROHOSTEL
9 EROTTAJANPUISTO HOSTEL
10 ACADEMICA HOSTEL
11 OLYMPIC STADIUM HOSTEL

architecture, this was blasted out of solid rock and capped with
a copper-and-skylight dome. It's normally filled with live or
recorded music and awestruck visitors. I almost cried. Another
form of simple truth, it's impossible to describe. Grab a pew.
Gawk upward at a 14-mile-long coil of copper ribbon. Look at
the bull's-eye and ponder God. Forget your camera. Just sit in
the middle, ignore the crowds, and be thankful for peace—

under your feet is an air-raid shelter that can accommodate 6,000 people (Mon–Fri 10:00–20:00, Sat 10:00–16:00, Sun 12:00–13:45, 15:15–17:45). Attend the Lutheran English service (Sun at 14:00, tel. 09/406-091) or one of the many concerts. You can buy individual slides or the picture book.

▲**Sibelius Monument**—Six hundred stainless-steel pipes shimmer over a rock in a park to honor Finland's greatest composer. Notice the face of Sibelius (which the artist was forced to add to silence the critics of this abstract work). Bus #24 stops here (or catch a quick glimpse on the left from the bus) on its way to the open-air folk museum. The #3T tram, which runs more frequently, stops a few blocks away. By the way, music lovers enjoy the English-language tours of the slick new Finnish National Opera (closed in June and July).

▲▲**National Museum**—This grand building was designed by three of Finland's greatest early architects, but there's no telling what the museum will be like when it reopens in June 2000. In the past, the highlight was the Finno-Ugric exhibit downstairs, with a 20-page English guide to help explain the Finns, Estonians, Lapps, Hungarians, and their more obscure Finno-Ugric cousins (tel. 09/40501). The museum café might again serve light meals and Finnish treats such as lingonberry juice and reindeer quiche.

Finlandia Hall—Alvar Aalto's most famous building in his native Finland means little to the nonarchitect without a tour. Take one (once or twice a day in summer only depending on conference schedule, 25 mk, 45 min, call ahead, tel. 09/402-4246).

Kiasma—Finland's new museum of contemporary art doesn't have a permanent collection, but you can check their Web site to find out what's showing (25 mk, Tue 9:00–17:00, Wed–Sun 10:00–22:00, Mannerheiminaukio 2, near train station, www.kiasma.fng.fi).

▲**Harbor tours**—Several boat companies line Market Square, offering 90-minute, 70-mk cruises around the waterfront nearly hourly from 10:00 to 18:00. The narration is slow moving—often tape-recorded and in as many as four languages. But if the weather's good and you're looking for something one step above a snooze in the park, it's a nice break.

▲**Flea Market**—If you brake for garage sales, the Hietalahti Market, Finland's biggest flea market, is worth the 15-minute walk from the harbor or a short ride on tram #6 from Mannerheimintie (Mon–Sat 8:00–14:00, in summer also Mon–Fri 15:30–21:00 and some summer Sun 10:00–16:00).

Sauna—Finland's vaporized fountain of youth is the sauna. Public saunas are a dying breed these days, since saunas are standard equipment in nearly every Finnish apartment and home. Your boat or hotel has a sauna. Your hostel probably even has one. Saunas are generally not mixed—they usually come in pairs. You go in with a towel not to cover your body but to sit on. For hygienic reasons, it's bad form to sit directly on the wooden benches. For a cheap and easy public sauna, go to the swimming pool behind the Olympic Stadium (15 mk, outdoor pool and indoor sauna open Mon–Sat 7:00–20:00, Sun 9:00–20:00). For a real experience, ask at the TI about the Finnish Sauna Society (bus #20 for 20 minutes in a park on the waterfront, men-only most nights, Thu is women's night, reservations required, tel. 09/678-677).

Concerts—Concerts in churches are heavenly. Ask at the TI and keep an eye out for posters. The Kallio Church has a magnificent new organ.

Nightlife—Remember that Finland was the first country to give women the vote. The sexes are equal in the bars and on the dance floor. Finns are easily approachable, and tourists are not a headache to the locals (as they are in places like Paris and Munich). While it's easy to make friends, anything alcoholic is expensive. For the latest on hot nightspots, read the English insert of *City* magazine that lists the "best" of everything in Helsinki. For cheap fun, Suomenlinna and Hietaranta beach is where the local kids hang out (and even skinny-dip) at 22:00 or 23:00. This city is one of Europe's safest after dark.

Sights—Outer Helsinki

A weeklong car trip up through the Finnish lakes and forests to Mikkeli and Savonlinna would be relaxing, but you can actually enjoy Finland's green-trees-and-blue-water scenery without leaving Helsinki. Here are three great ways to get out and go for a walk on a sunny summer day.

▲**Seurasaari Open-Air Folk Museum**—Inspired by Stockholm's Skansen, also on a lovely island on the edge of town, this is a collection of 100 historic buildings from every corner of Finland. It's wonderfully furnished and gives rushed visitors an opportunity to sample the far reaches of Finland without leaving the capital city. Buy the 10-mk guidebook. (The park is free, 20 mk to enter the buildings, Jun–Aug daily 11:00–17:00, Wed until 19:00; late May and early Sept Mon–Fri 9:00–15:00, Sat–Sun 11:00–17:00.) Off-season it's quiet. In winter, the park is open but the buildings are closed. Just you, log cabins, and birch trees—almost not worth a look. Ride bus #24 to the end and walk across the quaint footbridge. Call the museum or ask at the TI about free English tours (daily except Wed at 11:30 and 15:30).

For a 10-mk bottomless cup of coffee in a cozy-like-someone's-home setting, stop by the café in the Tomtebo folklore center at the mainland end of the bridge to Seurasaari (open Jun–Aug only). Great bagels—and Chopin, too. In summer there are also evening folk-dance exhibitions here (usually Thu at 19:00, for info call 09/484-511 or 09/484-234).

▲**Suomenlinna**—This is the island guarding Helsinki's harbor that was fortified by Sweden in the 1740s. It's now a popular park with several museums. You and your imagination get free run of the fortifications and dungeonlike chambers—no cordons or locks (15-min ferry ride, on the half hour from Market Square during daytime hours, same tickets as buses and trams, museums and visitors center open 10:00–18:00 in summer, eat lunch at a café or bring a picnic, www.hel.fi/suomenlinna).

▲**Akseli Gallen-Kallela Museum**—The estate of one of Finland's most famous turn-of-the-century painters is a brisk half-hour walk from the end of tram line #4 (from tram stop, keep to the shore and cross two footbridges to reach museum). Gallen-Kallela illustrated the *Kalevala* (Finland's national epic). His house and studio has been turned into a museum. Check out the cool tower room and ask to see the free 30-minute *Young Finland 1900* video. Have a sandwich in the separate café before walking back (museum admission-35 kr, mid-May–Aug Mon–Thu 10:00–20:00, Fri–Sun 10:00–17:00, rest of year Tue–Sun 10:00–16:00).

Sleeping in Helsinki
(5 mk = about $1, tel. code from outside Finland: 358-9)
Sleep Code: **S** = Single, **D** = Double/Twin, **T** = Triple, **Q** = Quad, **b** = bathroom, **CC** = Credit Card (Visa, MasterCard, Amex).

Standard budget hotel doubles start at $100. But there are many special deals and dorm and hostel alternatives. You have four basic budget options: nice hostels, student dorms turned into "summer hostels," modest but comfortable small hotels, and (on weekends only) expensive business-class hotels at special sale rates. Also remember that the cheapest hotels in Helsinki are actually the ferries to Stockholm and Tallinn.

Hotellikeskus, Helsinki's room-finding service, always knows what wild bargains are available, like luxury-hotel clearance deals that cost only $20 more than the cheapies. Their main office is in the train station (facing the tracks, it's on the left side, next to track 11; Jun–Aug Mon–Sat 9:00–19:00, Sun 10:00–18:00, off-season Mon–Fri only 9:00–17:00, tel. 09/2288-1400, fax 09/2288-1499, e-mail: hotel@helsinkiexpert.fi). If you arrive at the harbor, just visit the Tour Expert desk inside the TI, which is part of the same company as Hotellikeskus and also books rooms. Both offices charge a 30-mk fee per reservation (not per person), 15 mk for hostels.

Sleeping in Hotels
Helsinki hotels have a two-tiered pricing system: low rates on Friday and Saturday nights, and high rates the rest of the week. Most of the listings here are of smaller, less expensive, non-chain hotels that are part of Finland's Private Hotels association (www.privatehotels.fi /helsinki). Some of these (like the Anton) are family owned, while

others are run as fundraising operations by a Finnish nonprofit organization—for example, Hotel Anna by the Finnish Free Church and Martta Hotelli by a Finnish women's foundation.

Hotel Anna, plush and very central, is a good value, especially if you stay in its single rooms (61 rooms, Sb-500 mk/380 mk weekends, Db-680 mk/540 mk weekends, includes breakfast, CC:VMA, near Mannerheimintie and Esplanadi, 15-min walk from the boat, Annankatu 1, tel. 09/616-621, fax 09/602-664, www.hotelanna.com).

At the **Martta Hotelli**, also central, the twin-bedded doubles are the best deal. Check out their Web site for an extra discount (Sb-490 mk/380 mk weekends, Db-590 mk/460 mk weekends, includes breakfast, CC:VMA, Uudenmaankatu 24, 00120 Helsinki, tel. 09/618-7400, fax 09/618-7401, www.webtravel.fi/hotel/martta).

Hotel Arthur is a five-minute walk from the train station and 10 to 15 minutes from Senate Square (144 rooms, Sb-440 mk/350 mk weekends, Db-550 mk/440 mk weekends, includes breakfast, CC:VMA, Vuorikatu 19, 00100 Helsinki, tel. 09/173-441, fax 09/626-880, www.hotelarthur.fi).

Hotel Anton is too far away from the harbor to walk with your luggage, but super-convenient to public transportation. Take trams #1, #2, #3B/3T, #6, #7, or #8 (or ride the metro) to the busy Hakaniemi square, then look for the sign; bus #615 from the airport also stops here (46 rooms, Sb-480 mk/380 mk weekends, Db-580 mk/480 mk weekends, Tb-680 mk/580 mk weekends, includes breakfast, CC:VMA, Paasivuorenkatu 1, 00530 Helsinki, tel. 09/750-311, fax 09/701-4527, www.privatehotels.fi/helsinki/anton). Bill Clinton stayed in room 503 (a single) as a student in 1969.

On weekends—that means Friday and Saturday nights—even Helsinki's more expensive hotels have great deals on doubles. **Lord Hotel**, very central in a striking Art Nouveau building, has doubles for 490 mk (Lönnrotinkatu 29, tel. 09/615-815, fax 09/680-1315). The four-star **Scandic Grand Marina** by the Katajanokka ferry terminal discounts its doubles to 530 mk (tel. 09/16661, fax 09/664-764). If you plan to buy a Helsinki Card (which gives free tram rides), you might like the weekend doubles for only 400 mk at the **Hotel Cumulus Olympia** (far from center but trams #1 and #3B/3T stop outside the door, Läntinen Brahenkatu 2, tel. 09/69151, fax 09/691-5219).

Sleeping in Hostels and Student Dorms
Eurohostel is a wonderful modern hostel located a block from the Viking Terminal or a 10-minute walk from Market Square. Reservations are essential (250 beds, S-185 mk, D-240 mk, T-360 mk, includes sheets, private lockable closets, and morning sauna; 15 mk-per-person discount for hostel members, breakfast-28 mk, doubles can be shared with a stranger of the same sex for 120 mk per bed, CC:VMA, handy tram #2/4 stop around the corner,

Linnankatu 9, 00160 Helsinki, tel. 09/622-0470, fax 09/655-044, www.eurohostel.fi). It's packed with facilities including a TV room, laundry room, a members' kitchen with a refrigerator that lets you lock up your caviar and beer, a cheap cafeteria, and plenty of good budget information on travel around the region.

Erottajanpuisto is a small, friendly, slightly ramshackle hostel with a great location on the top floor of a 19th-century apartment building right in the center of town (15 rooms, S-240 mk, D-295 mk, T-420 mk, dorm bed-140 mk, includes sheets, 15 mk discount for hostel members and in winter, breakfast 25–35 mk, CC:VM, Uudenmaankatu 9, 00120 Helsinki, tel. 09/642-169, fax 09/680-2757, ring bell and go to top floor).

Academica Summer Hostel is a university dorm that's converted into a hostel from June 1 to August 31. It's near the Temppeliaukio church and tram #3B/3T (115 rooms, Sb-240 mk, Db-340 mk, Tb-420 mk, rooms can be shared with strangers for 95–120 mk per person, 15-mk discount for hostel members, CC:VMA, Hietaniemenkatu 14 between Mechelininkatu and Runeberginkatu, tel. 09/1311-4334, fax 09/441-201, www.hyy.fi/hostel).

Olympic Stadium Hostel (Stadionin Retkeilymaja) is big, crowded, impersonal, and a last resort (70 mk per bed in 8- to 12-bed rooms, D-200 mk, 15-mk discount for hostel members, sheets-15 mk, dorm closed daily 10:00–16:00 off-season, tel. 09/496-071). Take tram #7A to the Olympic Stadium.

Eating in Helsinki

Restaurants are a good value for lunch. Finnish companies get a tax break if they distribute lunch coupons to their employees. In 1999, the value of these coupons was 40 mk, and—surprise—most downtown Helsinki restaurants had weekday lunch specials which cost exactly that.

My favorite restaurant in Helsinki is **Konstan Möljä**, featuring an all-you-can-eat buffet on weekdays (40-mk lunch 11:00–14:30; 59-mk dinner starts at 18:00). This family-run restaurant serves Finnish cooking, hearty soup, and home-baked Karelian bread. It's decorated with old photos and mementos of the Karelian timber port of Uuras, now part of Russia (a little out of the way at Hietalahdenkatu 14, two blocks from flea market at the end of Bulevardi; walk or take tram #6 from Mannerheimintie).

Healthy eaters can grab the 40-mk vegan specials at **Lloyd's Vegeteria** (Mon–Sat 11:00–15:00, through the archway at Pohjoisesplanadi 35 just down the Esplanade from the TI). **Holvari**, hidden inside an apartment building a few blocks away at Yrjönkatu 15, also has excellent 40- to 45-mk lunches, but ask them to help you translate the Finnish daily-special menu (the standing à la carte menu is more expensive). A nice surprise: **Eliel restaurant** in the train station has a fine self-service buffet in a splendid architectural setting (daily 11:00–18:00, Mon–Fri-40 mk, Sat–Sun-49 mk, breakfast buffet-35 mk). At the Eurohostel, **Café Pinja** serves good grilled salmon for 40 mk. The Academic Bookstore (upstairs) and Stockmann's (sixth floor) have handy cafés, but neither is a great value.

For dinner, a good option is a picnic assembled from the colorful stalls at the harbor, the nearby bakery, or the redbrick indoor markets at the harbor, **Hietalahti**, and **Hakaniemi**. At the harbor you'll also find several local "tent" cafés and fast-food stalls and delicious fresh fish (cooked if you like), explosive little red berries, and sweet carrots. While the open-air market is the most fun, produce is cheaper in large grocery stores.

In **supermarkets**, buy the semiflat bread (available dark or light) that Finns love—every slice is a heel. Finnish fluid yogurt is also a treat (sold in liter cartons). Karelian pasties (filled with cheese or potato) make a good snack.

Russian food is an interesting but expensive option. The most convenient Russian restaurant is **Kasakka** (near harbor at Meritullinkatu 13, tel. 09/135-6288), but entrées start around 100 mk, and lunch specials (70–110 mk) are not available in summer.

Transportation Connections—Helsinki
The bus and train stations are a couple blocks from each other. They're about a 20-minute walk from the main ferry harbor. Take tram #3T from the harbor to the stations; take tram #3B from the stations to the harbor. It's easy to get to **Turku** (about 2 hrs) or **St. Petersburg, Russia,** by either bus or train. To St. Petersburg, the bus is slower and cheaper (8-hr trip, 220–250 mk, less for students); the train is faster and more expensive (6-hr trip, about 300 mk, no student discount). Travelers to Russia need a visa. For train info, tel. 09/707-5700 or visit www.vr.fi/heo/english/heo.htm. For bus information in English, visit www.expressbus.com or www.matkahuolto.fi/ewww.

By boat to Stockholm: Silja and Viking lines sail between Helsinki and Stockholm nightly. (See the beginning of this chapter for details.)

By boat to Tallinn: Ferries and fast catamarans (summer only) travel the 80 kilometers between Helsinki and Tallinn many times a day. (See Tallinn chapter for details.)

By boat to St. Petersburg: In summer 1999, Kristina Cruises ran irregular visa-free cruises from Helsinki to St. Petersburg (2 days and 3 nights, sleep on the boat). Cost was about $300 per person in a double, but no independent free time ashore in St. Petersburg was allowed. You could only leave the ship with group excursions, for which you were required to pay extra (tel. 05/21144, www.kristinacruises.com).

Helsinki Ferry Terminals Guide: Helsinki has five ferry

terminals (*terminaali*); see map on page 163. The Olympia and Makasiini terminals are on the west (left) side of the main harbor. The Katajanokka and Kanava terminals are on the east (right) side of the main harbor. Most Silja boats use the Olympia terminal; most Viking boats use the Katajanokka terminal. The Kanava and Makasiini terminals are for fast catamarans to Tallinn. The Länsi terminal, in Helsinki's Western Harbor, is for large car ferries to Tallinn. To reach it, go to the bus station and take bus #15 from platform 46 to the end (runs every 15–30 min, 10-mk ticket, 15-min trip).

Airport: To get from downtown Helsinki to the airport, take the Finnair bus from the west side of the train station (25 mk), public bus #615 from platform 10 on the east side of the train station (15 mk, also stops at Hakaniemi), or the Yellow Line door-to-door shuttle service (70 mk for 1 person, 100 mk for 2, tel. 106464, www.airport-taxi.fi).

SIGHTS NEAR HELSINKI

Porvoo, the second-oldest town in Finland, has wooden architecture that dates from the Swedish colonial period. This coastal town can be reached from Helsinki by bus (1-hr trip) or by excursion boat from Market Square.

Turku, the historic old capital of Finland, is a two-hour bus or train ride from Helsinki. Overall, Turku is a pale shadow of Helsinki, and there is little reason to make a special trip. It does have a handicraft museum in a cluster of wooden houses (the only part of town to survive a devastating fire in the early 1800s), an old cathedral, and a market square. Viking and Silja boats sail from Turku to Stockholm every morning and evening (around 9:15 and 21:15; the cheap fare saves enough to pay for the trip from Helsinki to Turku, and the ferry companies can sometimes arrange discounted bus or train tickets).

Naantali, a cute, commercial, well-preserved medieval town with a quaint harbor, is an easy bus ride from Turku (4/hrly, 20-min trip). If you've seen or will see Sigtuna (near Stockholm), Naantali offers little. Porvoo may be for you.

ESTONIA

TALLINN

Estonia's history is like Finland's, with a few crucial exceptions that give Estonia a distinctly German and Russian accent. Both countries were colonized from the west in the 1200s; medieval Finland was settled by Swedes and Estonia by rich German merchants. Sweden ruled both Finland and Estonia in the 1500s and 1600s, later losing them both to Russia. Russia won Estonia in the 1700s, long before acquiring Finland in 1809. Russia had incorporated Estonia into its empire, but allowed Finland self-government. Both Finland and Estonia gained independence after World War I. Finland managed to preserve it through World War II, despite losing thousands of soldiers and a tenth of its territory. Estonia was swallowed up whole by the Soviet Union in 1944 and did not reemerge until 1991.

As a result, Estonia was much more influenced by Germany and Russia than was Finland. Though most Germans left Estonia during World War I, you can see the German influence in Tallinn's Hanseatic architecture and the manor houses of the countryside. The other legacy is that 30 percent of Estonia's population is now Russian. Most Estonian Russians' parents and grandparents were brought to Estonia in the 1950s and 1960s to work in now-defunct factories in Tallinn and the northeastern cities. Making Russians feel at home in Estonia, while at the same time building a distinctly Estonian culture and identity, has been one of independent Estonia's biggest challenges and will probably remain so.

With Soviet-era travel restrictions now almost 10 years in the past, Estonians are on the fast track to European Union membership and already think of themselves as part of the Nordic world. Language, history, religion, and dozens of daily plane flights and ferry departures connect Finns and Estonians. It's only 50 miles between Helsinki and Tallinn. Finns visit Tallinn to eat, drink, and shop more cheaply than at home. While some Estonians resent how Tallinn becomes a Finnish nightclub on summer weekends, most people on both sides are happy to have friendly new neighbors.

Helpful Hints

Expect few language problems with younger people, most of whom learned English at school. Older Estonians usually speak better Russian than English. Estonian is very similar to Finnish, and equally difficult. Two useful words to know are *tänan* (TAN-on, thank you) and *terviseks* (TEAR-vee-sex, cheers).

When in search of a bathroom in a restaurant, remember: A downward-pointing triangle means "men," an upward-pointing triangle means "women." (Think "missionary position.")

SAILING FROM STOCKHOLM TO TALLINN

Estline's ships leave Stockholm at 18:00 every evening, arriving in Tallinn at 10:00. The return trip leaves Tallinn at 19:00 and arrives in Stockholm at 9:00 (all times are local; Tallinn time is an hour ahead of Stockholm).

Deck passage costs about 275 Swedish kr ($40) one-way, 450 kr ($65) round-trip. Add about 75 kr ($10) for Thursday, Friday, and Saturday departures. Students and seniors get about 50 kr off each way. Cabins start at about 135 kr ($20) each way for a berth in a four-person room beneath the waterline. Breakfast is 55 kr and the *smørgåsbord* dinner is 150 kr (50 kr and 135 kr if you buy them with your ticket). As with the Helsinki ferries, if you go out and back on successive nights, special "cruise" prices include cabin and breakfast for 290 kr, little more than the cost of one-way deck passage (add 200 kr for Thu and Sat, 300 kr for Fri departures). In summer 1999, the cruise prices were also valid for nonsuccessive nights if you booked a hotel room in Tallinn through Estline—a good deal especially if you pick the less expensive hotel choices, like the Central and St. Barbara.

Depending on where you're leaving from, reserve by calling either the Stockholm reservations line at 46/8/667-0001 or the Estonian booking number at 372/631-8888. They prefer that you pick up your tickets at their downtown office (in Stockholm it's inside the train station), not at the port. Estline runs a special shuttle between gate 35 in Stockholm's Cityterminalen bus station and the Frihamnen harbor, where the ferry docks (15 kr, last departure 16:45). You can also take regular bus #41 (every 10–20 min, 14 kr, 25-min trip). In Tallinn, the ships dock at Terminal D.

For more info check out Estline's Web site at www.estline.ee /english.

Tallinn or Helsinki?

If you only have enough time to spend two nights east of Stockholm, should you visit Tallinn or Helsinki? If you're in it just for the round-trip ferry ride, go to Helsinki: it's a better party on board the newer and more luxurious ships. But if you want to spend time on shore, the quicker trip to Estonia means you get nine hours in Tallinn as opposed to only seven in Helsinki. Tallinn is less expensive than Helsinki, and has a medieval walled town center and better restaurants. Helsinki is more interesting for its 19th- and 20th-century architecture and its island scenery. If you have a little more time, base yourself in one city (Tallinn usually works out cheapest) and take a day trip or an overnight cruise to the other. Or take a triangle trip—Stockholm-Helsinki-Tallinn-Stockholm or vice versa. In fact, you can connect the triangle in three consecutive nights without ever sleeping on shore, since evening ferries between Helsinki and Tallinn let you stay on board overnight after the ship docks (see below).

SPEEDING BETWEEN HELSINKI AND TALLINN

From April to October, the fastest link between Helsinki and Tallinn is by catamaran or hydrofoil, which takes just an hour and a half. To keep things simple, I'll call all these fast ships "catamarans." The two most convenient catamaran terminals (Kanavaterminaali and Makasiiniterminaali) in Helsinki are just steps from Market Square and walking distance from the train station. Flip to the Helsinki chapter (Transportation Connections section) for a guide to Helsinki ferry terminals. Schedules change a lot from year to year, but in summer 1999 there were three catamaran companies with 18 daily departures from Helsinki. The first run left Helsinki at 7:30 and the last at 19:30. You can reserve a day or two in advance, but it's rarely necessary. Warning: Catamaran trips can be canceled in stormy weather.

Fares range from 150 mk to 200 mk one-way ($30–40); the cheaper fares tend to be on evening departures from Helsinki and morning departures from Tallinn. Round-trips start around 270 mk ($50), but there are special deals (as low as 175 mk) if you come back the same day. The helpful Tour Expert desk in the Helsinki TI sells tickets and has the most complete information on same-day-return deals. Though the Tallink catamarans look like the best deal, they leave from the less convenient Länsiterminaali. The bus ride out there takes time and adds 20 mk to the round-trip cost.

Big car ferries run year-round between Helsinki and Tallinn and normally take 3.5 hours. These trips are cheaper (70–120 mk one-way, minus student and senior discounts), less bumpy, and more fun, with great *smørgåsbord* buffets ($10–15 extra). I've never needed reservations. There are several trips a day, mostly leaving

Helsinki/Tallinn Connections

Company	Tallink	Linda Line	Nordic Jet Line	Silja	Eckerö Line
Type of ship	Ferries and catamarans	Catamarans	Catamarans	Ferries	Ferry (one daily)
Helsinki terminal	Länsi	Makasiini	Kanava	Olympia, Katajanokka	Länsi
Helsinki phone #	09/228-311	09/668-9700	09/681-770	0203/74552	09/228-8544
Tallinn terminal	Ferries: A Cats: D	Linnahall	C	D	B
Tallinn phone #	640-9808	641-2412	613-7000	631-8331	631-8606
Web site	www.tallink .fi/eng	www .lindaline.fi	www.eng .njl.fi	www .silja.fi	www .eckeroline.fi

from the Länsiterminaali in Helsinki's Western Harbor. This is convenient for drivers but requires foot passengers to use public transport: bus #15 from platform 46 at Helsinki's central bus station goes direct to Länsiterminaali every 15 to 30 minutes (10 mk ticket, 15-min trip). Some evening ferries let you sleep on the ship after docking at your destination.

For both ferries and catamarans, reserve tickets by visiting any travel agency, such as Tour Expert in the Helsinki TI; dropping by the town offices of one of the shipping companies (open business hours only); calling telephone reservations numbers (open a little longer) and picking your ticket up at the port; or going directly to the port (ticket offices are open whenever ferries run).

The ferry market between Helsinki and Tallinn changes every year, but the table below lists names, ship types, phone numbers, terminals, and Web sites for the main ferry operators in summer 1999. Visit the Web sites for current schedule information.

Arrival in Tallinn

By Boat: There are three different sections to the Tallinn passenger port: Terminals A/B/C (which are right next to each other), Terminal D (a 15-min walk east), and Linnahall (a 15-min walk west). See the Tallinn map for details. If you have no luggage, just walk into the center of town (20 min; see suggested walking tour below). With luggage, take a taxi (see taxi advice below). Buses will take you into town, too, but cost more than a taxi for groups of two or more. Trams #1 and #2 also stop close by the port area. Remember which terminal you arrived at so you don't miss your return boat.

By Plane: The airport is close to town; a taxi to the Old Town should cost between 45 kr and 50 kr, to Lilleküla 60 kr to 65 kr. An Express minibus circles between the airport and downtown hotels for 20 kr per ride, and public buses also run into town.

TALLINN

Tallinn is the best-preserved medieval city in Scandinavia. Its mostly intact city wall includes 29 watchtowers, each topped by a pointy red roof. Baroque and choral music ring out in its old Lutheran churches. Tallinn has more restaurants, more cafés, and more museums than any other city in this book. Yet it is much less expensive here than in Sweden or Finland.

Tallinn is busy cleaning up the mess left by the communist experiment. New shops, restaurants, and hotels are bursting out of old buildings. The city changes so fast it's hard for locals to keep up.

Tallinn is a quick ferry trip from Helsinki or an overnight from Stockholm. The sea approach to Tallinn and the walk up from the ferry port are a visual feast of walls, towers, and church spires. One of the best times to come is during the Old Town Days in early June.

The hill called Toompea is the core of old Tallinn. (Get the best view of it from near the train station.) Toompea was fortified by the Danes after they captured Tallinn in 1219. Medieval merchants and craftsmen lived in the Lower Town, beneath Toompea. Two steep, narrow streets—the "Long Leg" (Pikk jalg) and the "Short Leg" (Lühike jalg)—connect Toompea and the Lower Town. The Town Hall Square (Raekoja plats) in the center of the Lower Town is an important meeting point.

In the 19th and early 20th centuries, Tallinn expanded beyond its walls. Architects circled the Old Town, putting up broad streets of public buildings, low Scandinavian-style apartment buildings, and single-family wooden houses. After 1945, Soviet planners ringed this with stands of crumbling concrete high-rises where many of Tallinn's Russian immigrants settled.

Fairly small and modest, Tallinn doesn't knock your socks off, but it does deliver pleasing towers, museums, ramparts, facades, churches, and shops. It's a secure, stable detour for those who want to spice their Scandinavian travels with an ex-Soviet twist.

Planning Your Time

On a three-week tour of Scandinavia, Tallinn is worth a day. Start out with either the official walking tour (see "Tallinn Card," below) or my do-it-yourself walking tour. Check concert schedules if you'll be around for the evening. Buy a picnic or enjoy one of the restaurants in the Old Town for lunch. Pick a museum, a church, and a few shops to visit in the afternoon.

Tallinn

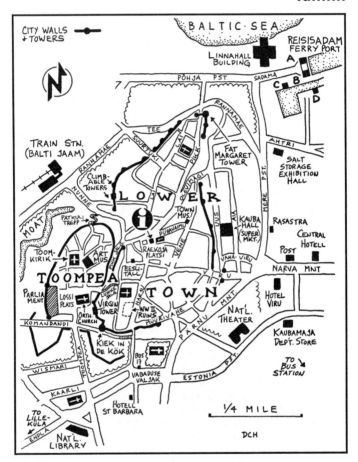

Orientation

Tourist Information: Tallinn's English-speaking TI has maps,
concert listings, booklets, phrase books, postcards, and free brochures (Mon–Fri 9:00–19:00, Sat–Sun 10:00–17:00, closes an hour
earlier off-season, on the main square, Raekoja plats 10, tel. 694-
6946, fax 694-6945, www.tallinn.ee/english).

Make sure to pick up a copy of *Tallinn in Your Pocket*, the
best city guidebook on Tallinn, which is on sale all over town for
16 kr. It has complete restaurant, hotel, and sights listings that go

far beyond what's listed in this book, plus a good map of the Old Town. You can look at the online version by going to www .inyourpocket.com.

The **Tallinn Card**, available at the TI, airport, and ports, gives you free use of public transport and entry to museums (24 hrs/195 kr, 48 hrs/270 kr, 72 hrs/325 kr, includes good info booklet). It also covers a 2.5-hour **bus and walking tour of Tallinn** that leaves from the Hotell Viru and the ferry port's Terminal A four times a day (tour costs 150 kr without the card). If you want to take the tour, the card will probably pay for itself, but you can also follow the do-it-yourself walking tour of Tallinn, below.

Laundry: Seebimull Pesumaja, a self-service and drop-off Laundromat, is at Liivalaia 7 (Mon–Fri 8:00–20:00, Sat 9:00–19:00, Sun 10:00–18:00, self-serve 48 kr per load, drop-off 69 kr, 1 block east of Pärnu maantee at corner of Liivalaia and Süda, take tram #3 or #4 to the Kosmos stop).

Internet Access: The National Library (Rahvusraamatukogu), at the corner of Endla and Tõnismägi, has a public computer room (40 kr/hr, buy a 5-kr library day card and get directions at the main doors, check your bags, open only Mon–Fri 12:00–19:00).

Telephones and Mail: The best way to call is with phone cards, sold in 30-kr, 50-kr, and 100-kr sizes around town and at the telephone office. These work in card phones all over town. International calls are still very expensive (7 kr per minute to Helsinki, 22 kr per minute to the United States). They are a little cheaper from the talk-first-pay-later booths at the Eesti Telefon office in the fortresslike building on Narva maantee across from Hotel Viru. The main post office is on the second floor of this same building (Mon–Fri 8:00–19:00, Sat 9:00–17:00).

Currency Exchange
14 Estonian kroons (kr) = about $1, 1 kroon = 100 senti
ATMs are everywhere and credit cards are widely accepted. Banks have the best exchange rates—usually about a 1.5 percent spread between buying and selling rates and a zero to 1 percent commission on traveler's checks. Uhispank, Hansapank, and Optiva Pank are the three main banks. Monex and the other small change offices at the ports and hotels have poor rates—avoid them except if you need to change a small amount for convenience on arrival. The American Express representative in the Old Town is good for lost traveler's checks but not for currency exchange (Mon–Fri 9:00–18:00, Sat 10:00–15:00, Suur-Karja 15, tel. 626-6213).

Getting around Tallinn
Taxis are cheap and handy in Tallinn. The largest and most reliable taxi company is Tulika Takso (white cars with a black and

yellow logo); the best way to summon them is to call 612-0000.
Tulika meters start around 20 kr and go up by 6 kr per kilometer.
Always make sure to take a marked, official taxi, even if that means
going to the second or third car in the taxi rank.

Tallinn has regular buses, trolley buses (with overhead wires),
and trams (on rails). Kiosks by bus stops sell tickets, which you
punch in the machines on board. Drivers also sell tickets at a small
markup. Some express and private buses (like the ones from the
port) cost extra. A 10-day card (*10-päeva-kaart*) gives you unlimited use of nonexpress public transport in Tallinn for only 70 kr.
The Tallinn Card also includes public transport (see "Tourist
Information," above).

Do-It-Yourself Walking Tour of Tallinn's Old Town

Start at any of the ferry terminals. Walk toward the center and enter
the Old Town through the archway by the Fat Margaret tower,
near the church with the tall tapering spire. This puts you on **Pikk
Street**, which for medieval merchants was the main drag leading
from the harbor up into town. You'll see many buildings in Tallinn
that were once warehouses for medieval goods shippers. The cranes
that stick out from the gables, and the line of doors down the center
of the facade, are leftovers from this. Notice how quiet it is. Few
people actually live in the Old Town, and Estonians (like Finns)
value silence. Where Pikk and Pühavaimu Streets merge, you'll
see the **Holy Ghost Church** (Pühavaimu kirik), a quintessentially
northern 13th-century church with a great old outdoor clock.
Inside, the hunched, whitewashed walls and wooden pews are
worth a look.

Continue up Pikk Street to the end, go underneath the tower
archway, and follow the steep Pikk jalg up to **Toompea**, the fortified hill where Tallinn was founded in the 13th century. At the top
of Pikk jalg, turn right and circle around Toompea. Make sure to
stop at the lookout points over the Lower Town, the port, and
Tallinn's residential neighborhoods. Inside the **Toomkirik** (the
tall white church with the dark spire), the shieldlike wooden wall
hangings are monuments to the rich burghers of Tallinn (free,
closed Mon). Walk by the Estonian parliament building on your
way back to the Russian Orthodox cathedral, a plump, out-of-
place, onion-domed edifice planted here in 1894. Look downhill
from the church and you'll see two towers. The square Virgin
Tower (Neitsitorn) houses a café; the round one is **Kiek in de
Kök**, my favorite museum in Tallinn.

Descending back to the Lower Town, make your way to **Raekoja plats**, the main town square. The town hall is occasionally open
for concerts. The big thermometer on its wall reads down to 40
below—for a reason. From the square, streets and minor sights fan

out in all directions. Most of Tallinn's good restaurants are nearby, though the ones in the square itself are not the best value. Finnish tour groups haunt the clothing, alcohol, and souvenir shops along Viru Street, just below Raekoja plats. If you want to climb more stairs, the Nunna, Sauna, and Kuldjalg towers are accessible through a door at the corner of Suur-Kloostri and Väike-Kloostri (7 kr, Tue–Fri 12:00–17:00, Sat–Sun 11:00–15:00, kind of scary—bring a flashlight).

Sights—Tallinn

Tallinn has dozens of small museums (complete listings in *Tallinn in Your Pocket*), most suitable only for specialized tastes. The first two below are my essentials:

▲▲**Kiek in de Kök**—This "Peek-in-the-Kitchen" tower was so named because one could supposedly spy on the Lower Town's residents from its heights. Now a fine museum, it mixes medieval cannons and charts left over from the Livonian wars (floors three through five) with modern photography exhibits (floors one, two, and six). There are good English captions. Make sure you see each floor—the stairways keep on going (7 kr, Tue–Fri 10:30–17:30, Sat–Sun 11:00–16:30).

▲▲**Tallinn Town Museum (Tallinna Linnamuuseum)**—This museum features Tallinn history from 1200 to the 1950s, and includes full English text. The museum is especially strong on the late 19th and early 20th century (5 kr, students-2.50 kr, Wed–Mon 10:30–17:30, closed Tue, Vene 17, at the corner of Pühavaimu).

▲**Rotermann Salt Storage Museum (Rotermanni Soolaladu)**—This strikingly renovated 19th-century warehouse is now used for temporary art and architectural exhibitions (15 kr, Wed–Sun 11:00–18:00, corner of Mere puiestee and Ahtri, near ferry port's Terminal D).

▲▲**Artwork, handicrafts, and shopping**—With so many Scandinavian tourists coming to Tallinn, the Old Town is full of trinkets, but it's possible to find quality stuff. **Diele Gallerii** sells the best postcards in town and displays work by Estonian artists (look for prints by Navitrolla; Vanaturu kael 3 just below Raekoja plats). The **Bogapott** ceramics store at Pikk jalg 9 is on the way up to Toompea. For jewelry by local artists, check out **A Galerii** at Hobusepea 8. For sweaters and woolens, go to the stalls under the wall on Müürivahe, near the corner of Viru. Wooden trivets and butter knives are a good value here. Sniff to find the ones made of sweet-smelling aromatic wood.

▲**Kadriorg**—This seaside park and summer residence was built by Peter the Great for Catherine after Russia took over Tallinn in 1710. The mansion is the home of the president of Estonia. The park, which runs down to the sea to the north, is the perfect spot for your picnic. Trams #1 and #3 go east from the center of

Tallinn to Kadriorg at the end of the line (where the tram makes a U-turn). It's an easy 15-minute ride out and back.

▲**Open-Air Museum (Vabaõhumuuseum)**—As in other northern European countries, Estonians salvaged farm buildings, windmills, and an old church from rural areas and transported them to a parklike setting along the shore west of Tallinn. It's a good picnic spot, too (21 kr, daily May–Oct 10:00–18:00, grounds stay open until 20:00, take bus #21 from the train station and ask the driver to let you know when to get off).

Music in Tallinn
Tallinn has a dense schedule of Baroque, Renaissance, and choral music performances, especially during the annual Old Town Days (every year in early June). Choral singing became a symbol of the struggle for Estonian independence after the first Estonian Song Festival in 1869 (which is still held every five years; next one in 2004). Even outside of festival times, it's a rare week in which there aren't a few performances in Tallinn's churches and concert halls, advertised on posters around town and listed in the weekly *Baltic Times* and in *Tallinn in Your Pocket*. Tickets are usually available at the door. Hortus Musicus is one of Estonia's best classical ensembles.

Estonia's three best modern choral composers and arrangers are Arvo Pärt, Veljo Tormis, and Erkki-Sven Tüür. Other Estonian groups have also put out a lot of good CDs. Though there are no bargains on music in Tallinn anymore, the record shop at Kuninga 4, around the corner from Raekoja plats, does have a good selection (Mon–Fri 10:00–18:00, Sat 10:00–17:00).

Sleeping in Tallinn
(14 kr = about $1)
Sleep Code: **S** = Single, **D** = Double/Twin, **T** = Triple, **Q** = Quad, **b** = bathroom, **CC** = Credit Card (Visa, MasterCard, Amex).

The best value and service is at hotels that are too small to take Finnish tour groups. Use a taxi to get to your hotel when you arrive, and then figure out how to use public transport later. On a quick trip, remember that the cheapest beds are on the ferries to Stockholm and Helsinki. If you're calling from the United States, dial 011-372, then the local number.

Sleeping in the Center
Olematu Rüütel is a quiet, out-of-the-way bar and restaurant on Toompea with three nice upstairs rooms: one twin with private bath, and two other twins that share a bath. These are the only affordable rooms in the Old Town. Call well in advance, especially in summer (Db-800 kr, D-600 kr, breakfast-35 kr, sauna-100 kr/hr, Kiriku põik 4a, 10130 Tallinn, tel. 631-3827 or 631-3872, fax 631-3826).

Hotell St. Barbara is expensive but tasteful and convenient, just two blocks from the Old Town in a nice building. Rates are lower when reserved as part of an Estline ferry package (53 rooms, Sb-1,200 kr, Db-1,400 kr, includes breakfast, CC:VMA, Roosikrantsi 2a, 10119 Tallinn, tel. 631-3991, fax 631-3992, www.finest.ee /StBarbara).

Central Hotell caters mostly to groups, but the location lives up to the name and the less expensive rooms on the blue side are comfortable (229 rooms, Sb-990 kr, Db-1,200 kr, includes breakfast, CC:VMA, a block beyond post office at Narva maantee 7, go through archway, 10117 Tallinn, tel. 633-9800, fax 633-9900, www.central.ee).

Sleeping in Lilleküla

Lilleküla is a quiet suburb of Tallinn built in the 1950s with a mixture of private houses and smaller Soviet-style apartment blocks. You'll get a clearer understanding of Estonian life by staying here, without losing comfort. A taxi from the ferry port should not cost more than 50 kr to 60 kr. To get to Lilleküla by bus from the center, go to Vabaduse väljak (see central Tallinn map) and board bus 17 or 17a from the stop across the square from the Palace Hotel (15-min ride, 5-kr ticket).

Hotell Nepi is a small but professionally run hotel with comfy public areas and big breakfasts (nine rooms, Sb-450 kr, Db-550 kr, breakfast-50 kr, Nepi 10, 11312 Tallinn, get off bus 17/17a at the Koolimaja stop, tel. 655-1665, fax 655-1664, e-mail: hotnepi@online.ee).

Valge Villa (White Villa) is a guest house run by Anne and Andres Vahtra and their family. They have bikes for rent (100–150 kr/day), a sauna (150 kr/hr), and a washing machine for guests (55 kr per load). Get off bus 17 or 17a at the Koolimaja stop. Five rooms have private facilities, while the other three share one big bathroom (eight rooms, S-400–450 kr, Sb-550–600 kr, D-610 kr, Db-700 kr, Tb-850–950 kr, includes breakfast, discounts for longer stays, CC:VM, Kännu 26/2, 13417 Tallinn, tel. & fax 654-2302, www.white-villa.ee).

At **Tihase B&B**, young English-speaking Ivo and Karin rent the double-bedded spare room in their home. Guests share the family bathroom. This is the loveliest guest room in Tallinn. There's a garden, a sauna house in the backyard, and a tabby cat. Get off bus 17 or 17a at the Hauka stop; it's two doors down the side street. It's a Scandinavian-style red wooden house with white trim (S-400 kr, D-500 kr, 100-kr less off-season, includes breakfast, Tihase 6a, tel. 655-2171, reserve on the Internet at www.tallinn.ee/tihase).

Sleeping in a Private Home

The **Rasastra** agency, run by English-speaking Urve Ansmann, coordinates a network of families around town who put up travelers in their spare rooms. Expect to be shown your room and mostly left alone by your host. Most rooms are a short bus or tram ride from the Old Town. Pickup at the ferry port can be arranged for an extra charge. Singles cost 150 kr to 235 kr and doubles 260 kr to 410 kr, depending on location. Breakfast (optional) costs 25 kr. The office is at Mere puiestee 4, near Hotel Viru and the post office; go up the stairs to the third floor (daily 10:00–18:00, tel. & fax 641-2291).

Sleeping in Hostels and Cheaper Hotels

The Barn (Hotell Küün), centrally located two blocks off the town square, is Tallinn's hostel. Everyone speaks English. There's space for 36 people in several big rooms with new blond-wood beds (dorm bed-195 kr, D-550 kr, showers down the hall, 10 percent off for hostel members or with own sheets, no breakfast, Väike-Karja 1, 10140 Tallinn, tel. 631-3252). The adjacent Erootika Bar looks like it's affiliated with the hostel, but it's not.

Eeslitall Guest House rents out upstairs rooms just a half block from the town square. The location is great, but only two showers serve nine very small rooms (S-450 kr, D-585 kr, breakfast-36 kr, look for Eeslitall Guest House sign and climb stairs to third floor at Dunkri 4, 10123 Tallinn, tel. 631-3755, fax 631-3210, e-mail: donkeys@netexpress.ee).

University dorms open up in summer for backpackers. Ask at the TI for details.

Eating in Tallinn

In contrast to Helsinki or Stockholm, restaurants in Tallinn are cheap, plentiful, and usually good. Visiting Scandinavians gorge themselves on inexpensive food. I watched two Finnish women's eyes bug out at the Maiasmokk pastry counter when they spotted decorated cakes on sale for only $4 or $5—a fraction of the price in Helsinki. They each bought three to take home on the ferry.

A few years ago it was hard to find authentic local cuisine, but now many places serve Estonian food. This typically means a warming northern mixture of meat, potatoes, root vegetables, mushrooms, bread, and soup. Pea soup is a local specialty. Estonia's Saku beer is good. Few restaurants have nonsmoking sections. Most accept credit cards.

At dinner and on weekends, Tallinn's best meal deals are in its Old Town pubs. This is where young Estonians eat out, so you can fill up (soup and a main dish plus bottled water) for about 75 kr ($5). I liked the potato pancakes (*torud*) stuffed with mushroom or shrimp at **Von Krahli Baar** (Rataskaevu 10/12, a block uphill from town square, near the well). **Kloostri Ait** has good soups, fine main dishes, a fireplace, mulled wine (*hõõgvein*), and, sometimes, live folk music (Vene 14, next to Dominican cloister). **Tehas 43**, at Pikk 43, also has a good kitchen. Check *Tallinn in Your Pocket* for the latest places to go. Go to the bar to look at the menu, order, and pay; then find a table and they'll bring your food out when it's ready.

A sit-down restaurant dinner costs about $10 to $15, but there are a few places worth the investment. **Vanaema Juures** (Grandma's Place) is a small cellar restaurant which serves homey, candlelit meals (like pork roast with sauerkraut and juniper berries). Entrées run 100 kr to 135 kr, and dinner reservations are strongly advised (Mon–Sat 12:00–22:00, Sun 12:00–18:00, Rataskaevu 10, tel. 631-3929). **Olde Hansa** is a kitsch but successful attempt at recreating medieval food before the arrival of the potato and tomato from the New World (those are turnips on your plate). It's just below the town square, and you can sit outdoors. The second-floor restaurant above the **Maiasmokk** café (at the corner of Pikk and Pühavaimu, a block from the town square) has nice views and a slightly refined, Victorian atmosphere (entrées 80–110 kr, daily 11:00–22:00).

On weekdays, many restaurants have good lunch buffets or daily specials. **Teater** at Lai 31 is a typical cellar restaurant with a rabbit warren of small rooms; ask them to translate their list of weekday lunch specials (closed Sun). **Elevant**, up the spiral staircase at Vene 5, has a lunch buffet spread of quasi-Indian food for 79 kr (Mon–Fri 12:00–15:00). Outside the Old Town behind Hotell Viru, **Tallinna Eesti Maja** (Tallinn Estonian House) has an all-you-can-eat lunch buffet of traditional Estonian food for 75 kr (Lauteri 1 by the corner of Rävala puiestee, and down the stairs).

For dessert or breakfast, the **Maiasmokk** café and pastry shop (founded in 1864) is the grande dame of Tallinn cafés. Point to what you want at the pastry counter, or sit down for breakfast or coffee on the other side of the shop. Everything's very cheap (Mon–Sat 8:00–19:00, Sun 10:00–18:00, Pikk 16, across from church with old clock). The **Creperie** at Müürivahe 23 is also good for dessert.

Both the downstairs, modern **Kompass** self-serve cafeteria and the upstairs **Primavera** Italian restaurant in Hotell Central are good values. Pizza lovers can visit **Pizza Americana** in the Old Town at Müürivahe 2 or Pikk 1/3.

The best supermarket in Tallinn is in **Tallinna Kaubamaja** (Tallinn Department Store) on Estonia puiestee, a block behind Hotell Viru. Enter around on the right side of the building (Mon–Fri 10:00–21:00, Sat 10:00–20:00, Sun 10:00–18:00). The smaller **Spar/Kaubahall** at Aia 7 is on the edge of the Old Town, near the twin Viru towers (daily 9:00–21:00).

Transportation Connections—Tallinn

If you're heading east or south from Tallinn, the bus is usually the best way to travel (to **Riga**, 7/day, 6-hr trip; to **Vilnius**, 2/day, 10-hr trip; to **St. Petersburg**, 3/day, 7-hr trip). To **Moscow**, the overnight train is the best (and only) option.

The **bus station** (Autobussijaam) is off Tartu maantee at

Lastekodu 46, too far from the center to walk. Take tram #2 or
#4 east from the city center to the "Bussijaam" stop, then turn the
corner to your right. For bus info call 642-2549 (the station) or
641-0100 (Eurolines, the biggest company). Most buses to and
from Riga and Vilnius also pick up and drop off at the ferry port's
Terminal A.

The Tallinn **train station** (Balti jaam) is a short walk (or ride
via tram #1 or #2) from the Old Town along Nunne tänav. Ticket
windows are upstairs. For train info call 615-6851.

For the latest bus and train schedules, consult www.ee/timetable
or *Tallinn in Your Pocket.*

Near Tallinn: Tartu and Islands

A good day trip from Tallinn is to **Tartu**, Estonia's university
town. Tartu has bluffs, ravines, a river, a ruined cathedral, and a
nice old town (built in a newer, more classical style than Tallinn).
Buses to Tartu leave roughly every 30 minutes from the Tallinn
bus station between 7:30 and 20:00, take 2.25 hours, and cost
75 kr one-way. If you have time for a one- or two-night trip out of
Tallinn and want to see the countryside, go to one of Estonia's big
islands—**Saaremaa** or **Hiiumaa**. Buses take you from Tallinn to
the coast at Virtsu, and then by ferry to Kuressaare, the largest
town on Saaremaa, in about five hours for 100 kr. The Tallinn TI
can give you advice on booking accommodations on the islands.

APPENDIX

Let's Talk Telephones

International Access Codes

When dialing direct, first dial the international access code of the country you're calling from. For the United States and Canada, it's 011. Virtually all European countries use "00" as their international access code; the only exceptions are Finland (990), Estonia (800), and Lithuania (810).

Country Codes

After you've dialed the international access code, dial the code of the country you're calling.

Austria—43	Finland—358	Norway—47
Belgium—32	France—33	Portugal—351
Britain—44	Germany—49	Spain—34
Canada—1	Greece—30	Sweden—46
Czech Repub.—420	Ireland—353	Switzerland—41
Denmark—45	Italy—39	United States—1
Estonia—372	Netherlands—31	

Calling-Card Operators

Country	AT&T	MCI	Sprint
Denmark	800 100 10	800 100 22	800 108 77
Estonia	800 800 1001	800 800 1122	————
Finland	9800 100 10	9800 102 80	9800 102 84
Norway	800 190 11	800 199 12	800 198 77
Sweden	020 795 611	020 795 922	020 799 011

Numbers and Stumblers

- Europeans write a few of their numbers differently than we do: 1 = 𝟙 , 4 = 𝟜 , 7= 𝟽. Learn the difference or miss your train.
- In Europe, dates appear as day/month/year, so Christmas is 25/12/00.
- Commas are decimal points and decimals commas. A dollar and a half is 1,50 and there are 5.280 feet in a mile.
- When pointing, use your whole hand, palm downward.
- When counting with fingers, start with your thumb. If you hold up your first finger to request one item, you'll get two.
- What we Americans call the second floor of a building is the first floor in Europe.
- Europeans keep the left "lane" open for passing on escalators and moving sidewalks. Keep to the right.

Public Transportation

You can tour Scandinavia efficiently and enjoyably by train and bus. And if you sleep on the comfortable Nordic trains, destinations not worth driving to on a short trip become feasible. Add your own Scandinavian highlights. Consider a swing through Finland's eastern lakes district or the scenic ride to Trondheim. I'd go overnight whenever possible on any ride six or more hours long.

The Norway chapter is heavy on fjord scenery (my kind of problem). Fjord country buses, boats, and trains connect, but not without one- to three-hour layovers. "Norway in a Nutshell" is an exception. The Flåm-to-Bergen boat is a great fjord finale.

Train, Bus, and Boat Connections

Pick up exact schedules as you travel, available free at any TI. Some lines make fewer runs or even close in the off-season.

Departures

Copenhagen to:	Daily	Hours
Amsterdam	2	11
Berlin via Gedser	2	9
Frankfurt/Rhine castles	4	10
Helsingør (ferry to Sweden)	40	.5
Hillerød (Frederiksborg)	40	.5
Louisiana (Helsingør train to Humlebæk)	40	.5
Odense	16	.5
Oslo	4	10
Roskilde	16	.5
Stockholm	6–8	8
Växjö via Alvesta	6	5

Stockholm to:		
Helsinki	2	14
Helsinki to Turku	7	2.5
Kalmar	6	8
	(1 night train)	
Oslo	3	7
Turku	2	10
Uppsala	30	1
Växjö to glassworks	TI tour or side trip by bus	
Växjö to Kalmar	9	1.5

Oslo to:		
Åndalsnes	3	6.5
Bergen	4	7–8
Lillehammer	12	2.5
Trondheim	3	7–8

Norway's Mountain and Fjord Country	Daily	Hours
Lillehammer to Åndalsnes	4	4
Åndalsnes over Trollstigvege to Geiranger Fjord	early each morning	4
Åndalsnes to Ålesund by bus (with each arriving train)	2	.5
Lillehammer to Lom (change at Otta)	3	4
Lom to Sogndal (bus departures 8:50 and 15:50, summer only)	2	4

Bergen to:		
Ålesund	1	10
Kristiansand	1 (bus)	12
Stavanger	3 (boat)	4

South Norway **Setesdal Valley, Hovden to:**		
Kristiansand	2	5

Kristiansand to:		
Hirtshals, Denmark (by ferry)	4	4
Oslo	6	4–5

Denmark		
Ærø to Copenhagen	5	5
Århus to Odense	16	2
Halsskov–Knudshoved	26	1
Hirtshals to Århus	16	2.5
Odense to Svendborg	16	1
Svendborg to Ærø (by ferry)	5	1

Metric Conversion (approximate)

1 inch = 25 millimeters	32 degrees F = 0 degrees C
1 foot = 0.3 meter	82 degrees F = about 28 degrees C
1 yard = 0.9 meter	1 ounce = 28 grams
1 mile = 1.6 kilometers	1 kilogram = 2.2 pounds
1 centimeter = 0.4 inch	1 quart = 0.95 liter
1 meter = 39.4 inches	1 square yard = 0.8 square meter
1 kilometer = .62 mile	1 acre = 0.4 hectare

Climate

*First line, average daily low temperature; second line, average daily
high; third line, days of no rain*

	J	F	M	A	M	J	J	A	S	O	N	D
Copenhagen,	29	28	31	37	44	51	55	54	49	42	35	32
DENMARK	36	36	41	50	61	67	72	69	63	53	43	38
	22	21	23	21	23	22	22	19	22	22	20	20
Helsinki,	17	15	22	31	41	49	58	55	46	37	30	22
FINLAND	27	26	32	43	55	63	71	66	57	45	37	31
	20	20	23	22	23	21	23	19	19	19	19	20
Oslo,	20	20	25	34	43	51	56	53	45	37	29	24
NORWAY	30	32	40	50	62	69	73	69	60	49	37	31
	23	21	24	23	24	22	21	20	22	21	21	21
Stockholm,	23	22	26	32	41	49	55	53	46	39	31	26
SWEDEN	31	31	37	45	57	65	70	66	58	48	38	33
	23	21	24	24	23	23	22	21	22	22	21	22

Faxing Your Hotel Reservation

Faxing is more accurate and cheaper than telephoning. Use this handy form for your fax (or find it online at www.ricksteves.com /reservation). Photocopy and fax away.

One-Page Fax

To: _____ @ _____
            hotel   *fax*

From: _____ @ _____
            name   *fax*

Today's date: ___ /_____ /___
            day *month* *year*

Dear Hotel _____,

Please make this reservation for me:

Name: _____

Total # of people: _____   # of rooms: _____   # of nights: _____

Arriving: ___ /_____ /___ My time of arrival (24-hr clock): _____
       day *month* *year* (I will telephone if I will be late)

Departing: ___ /_____ /___
       day *month* *year*

Room(s): Single___ Double___ Twin___ Triple___ Quad___

With: Toilet___ Shower___ Bath___ Sink only___

Special needs: View___ Quiet___ Cheapest Room___

Credit card: Visa___ MasterCard___ American Express___

Card #: _____

Expiration date:_____

Name on card: _____

You may charge me for the first night as a deposit. Please fax or mail me confirmation of my reservation, along with the type of room reserved, the price, and whether the price includes breakfast. Thank you.

_____
Signature

_____
Name

_____
Address

_____
City   *State*   *Zip Code*   *Country*

_____
E-mail Address

Road Scholar Feedback for
SCANDINAVIA 2000

We're all in the same travelers' school of hard knocks. Your feedback helps us improve this guidebook for future travelers. Please fill this out (or use the on-line version at www.ricksteves.com/feedback), include more info or any tips/favorite discoveries if you like, and send it to us. As thanks for your help, we'll send you our quarterly travel newsletter free for one year. Thanks! **Rick**

Of the recommended accommodations/restaurants used, which was:

Best _____

       Why? _____

Worst _____

       Why? _____

Of the sights/experiences/destinations recommended by this book, which was:

Most overrated _____

       Why? _____

Most underrated _____

       Why? _____

Best ways to improve this book:

_____

I'd like a free newsletter subscription:

_____ Yes   _____ No   _____ Already on list

_____
Name

_____
Address

_____
City, State, Zip

_____
E-mail Address

Please send to: ETBD, Box 2009, Edmonds, WA 98020

Jubilee 2000—Let's Celebrate the Millennium by Forgiving Third World Debt

Let's ring in the millennium by convincing our government to forgive the debt owed to us by the world's poorest countries. Imagine spending over half your income on interest payments alone. You and I are creditors, and poor countries owe us more than they can pay.

Jubilee 2000 is a worldwide movement of concerned people and groups—religious and secular—working to cancel the international debts of the poorest countries by the year 2000.

Debt ruins people: In the poorest countries, money needed for health care, education, and other vital services is diverted to interest payments.

Mozambique, with a per-capita income of $90 and a life expectancy of 40, spends over half its national income on interest. This poverty brings social unrest, civil war, and often costly humanitarian intervention by the United States. To chase export dollars, desperate countries ruin their environment. As deserts grow and rain forests shrink, the world suffers. Of course, the real suffering is among local people born long after some dictator borrowed (and squandered) that money. As interest is paid, entire populations go hungry.

Who owes what and why? Mozambique is one of 41 countries defined by the World Bank as "Heavily Indebted Poor Countries." In total, they owe $200 billion. Because these debts are unlikely to be paid, their market value is only a tenth of the face value (about $20 billion). The United States' share is under $2 billion.

How can debt be canceled? This debt is owed mostly to the United States, Japan, Germany, Britain, and France, either directly or through the World Bank. We can forgive the debt owed directly to us and pay the market value (usually 10 percent) of the debts owed to the World Bank. We have the resources. (Norway, another wealthy creditor nation, just unilaterally forgave its Third World debt.) All the United States needs is the political will . . . people power.

While many of these poor nations are now democratic, corruption is still a concern. A key to Jubilee 2000 is making certain that debt relief reduces poverty in a way that benefits ordinary people— women, farmers, children, and so on.

Let's celebrate the new millennium by giving poor countries a break. For the sake of peace, fragile young democracies, the environment, and countless real people, forgiving this debt is the right thing for us in the rich world to do.

Tell Washington, D.C.: If our government knows this is what we want, it can happen. Learn more, write letters, lobby legislators, or even start a local Jubilee 2000 campaign. For details, contact Jubilee 2000 (tel. 202/783-3566, www.j2000usa.org). For information on lobbying Congress on J2000, contact Bread for the World (tel. 800/82-BREAD, www.bread.org).

INDEX

Rick Steves' Postcards from Europe

25 Years of Travel Tales from America's
Favorite Guidebook Writer

1978   1998

TRAVEL GURU RICK STEVES has been exploring Europe through the Back Door for 25 years, sharing his tricks and discoveries in guidebooks and on TV. Now, in *Rick Steves' Postcards from Europe*, Rick shares stories—ranging from goofy to inspirational—of his favorite moments and his off-beat European friends.

Postcards takes you on the fantasy trip of a lifetime, and it gives you a close-up look at contemporary Europeans.

You'll meet Marie-Alice, the Parisian restaurateur who sniffs a whiff of moldy cheese and says, "It smells like zee feet of angels." In an Alpine village, meet Olle, the schoolteacher who lets Rick pet his edelweiss, and Walter, who schemes with Rick to create a fake Swiss tradition. In Italy, cruise with Piero through his "alternative Venice" and learn why all Venetian men are mama's boys.

Postcards also tracks Rick's passion for wandering—from his first "Europe-through-the-gutter" trips, through his rocky early tours, to his career as a travel writer and host of a public-television series.

These 240 pages of travel tales are told in that funny, down-to-earth style that makes Rick his Mom's favorite guidebook writer.

Rick Steves' Phrase Books

Unlike other phrase books and dictionaries on the market, my well-tested phrases and key words cover every situation a traveler is likely to encounter. With these books you'll laugh with your cabby, disarm street thieves with insults, and charm new European friends.

Each book in the series is 4" x 6", with maps.

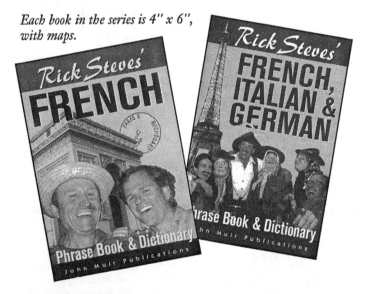

RICK STEVES' FRENCH PHRASE BOOK & DICTIONARY
U.S. $6.95/Canada $10.95

RICK STEVES' FRENCH, ITALIAN & GERMAN PHRASE BOOK & DICTIONARY
U.S. $8.95/Canada $13.95

RICK STEVES' GERMAN PHRASE BOOK & DICTIONARY
U.S. $6.95/Canada $10.95

RICK STEVES' ITALIAN PHRASE BOOK & DICTIONARY
U.S. $6.95/Canada $10.95

RICK STEVES' SPANISH & PORTUGUESE PHRASE BOOK & DICTIONARY
U.S. $8.95/Canada $13.95